PELICAN BOOKS

ROMAN CIVILIZATION

Dacre Balsdon was born in 1901 and educated at Exeter School, graduating in Literae Humaniores from Exeter College, Oxford, where he was a Stapledon Scholar. After two years' schoolteaching he was appointed tutor at Keble College, Oxford, and in 1927 he became a Fellow of Exeter College, Oxford. He is a D.Lit. of Oxford, President of the Society for the Promotion of Roman Studies, a council member of the British School at Rome, and a Fellow of the British Academy.

Dr Balsdon has published several novels as well as papers and reviews in specialist journals. He is also the author of *The Emperor Gaius* (1934, new edition 1965), *Oxford Life* (1957, new edition 1962), *Roman Women: their History and Habits* (1962), and *Julius Caesar and Rome* (1967).

ROMAN
CIVILIZATION

EDITED BY
J. P. V. D. BALSDON

PENGUIN BOOKS

Penguin Books Ltd, Harmondsworth, Middlesex, England
Penguin Books Inc., 7110 Ambassador Road, Baltimore, Maryland 21207, U.S.A.
Penguin Books Australia Ltd, Ringwood, Victoria, Australia

—

First published as *The Romans* by C. A. Watts 1965
Published in Penguin Books 1969

—

Copyright © C. A. Watts & Co. Ltd, 1965

—

Made and printed in Great Britain
by C. Nicholls & Company Ltd
Set in Linotype Juliana

CONTENTS

PREFACE

THIS book is a companion to *The Greek World*, published in Pelican Books in 1965. A comparison of the chapter headings of the two books illustrates the profound difference between the two peoples. While *The Greek World* was concerned in the main with the Greek achievement in art, literature and abstract thought, the largest chapters in the present book are devoted to Roman imperial administration, Roman law and Roman architecture and engineering.

That I have been singularly fortunate in persuading scholars of such great distinction to join in the writing of the book, is obvious; and I only regret that my own part in the book is far larger than I had intended. I had hoped that the chapter on Religion would be written by an expert on the subject, but to my great regret I was not sufficiently persuasive. I must, however, express my great debt to my friend Dr S. Weinstock for the generous help which he gave me when I found that I had to write the chapter myself. I had hoped that the chapter on Humour and Satire would be written by a foreign scholar but, because of an unanticipated misfortune, I had, in the space of a few days, to write it myself.

The content of a book is not unrelated to its length. Outside the fundamental subjects, of whose importance there can be no dispute, other editors in more than one case would have chosen different chapter subjects. Many would have included a chapter on the Roman army instead of leaving its story to be told in a number of separate chapters. A strong case could be made out for a chapter on Roman portrait sculpture and for another on the spread of the Latin language which, once spoken by only a handful of people in central Italy, was to become the first language of half the Roman Empire, largely understood, where it was not spoken, by the other half – and which is the foundation of more than one of the most beautiful of European languages. A chapter on the city of Rome would have been welcome. And many readers will regret that more space has not been given to Roman literature and Roman political thought.

Reluctantly as these omissions have been made, they are deliberate in a book which is designed to illustrate, against the background of their daily life, the practical and enduring achievement of a people whose original genius it was to build with skill and imagination, to spread civilization and enlightenment and to administer in the main with efficiency and justice.

Warm thanks are due to the owners of the copyright of translations which, most generously, we have been given permission to use. And, for myself, I cannot but express an editor's gratitude for a publisher's sympathetic understanding of his difficulties and dilemmas.

Exeter College, Oxford   J.P.V.D.B.
January 1965

CONTRIBUTORS

J. P. V. D. BALSDON, D.Lit., Hon. LL.D. Dalhousie, has been a Fellow of Exeter College, Oxford, since 1928. He is the author of *The Emperor Gaius (Caligula)* and of *Roman Women*.

P. A. BRUNT, M.A., Fellow of Oriel College, Oxford, since 1951, previously Lecturer in Ancient History in St Andrews University, has revised and edited Jowett's translation of Thucydides and has written a large number of important articles on Greek and Roman History.

M. L. CLARKE, M.A., has been Professor of Latin, University College of North Wales, since 1948 and was previously Reader in Latin and Greek at University College, London. His books include *Richard Porson*, *Greek Studies in England, 1700–1830*, *Rhetoric at Rome*, *The Roman Mind*, *Classical Education in Britain, 1500–1900* and *George Grote*.

M. W. FREDERIKSEN, M.A., who was educated at Sydney University and at Oxford, has been a Fellow of Worcester College, Oxford, since 1959. He was previously Junior Research Fellow of Corpus Christi College, Oxford. He has written articles on Roman topography for Pauly-Wissowa, *Real-Encyclopaedie der classischen Altertumswissenschaft*.

COLIN HARDIE, M.A., was Director of the British School at Rome from 1933 to 1936, and has been a Fellow of Magdalen College, Oxford, since 1936. He published *Vitae Vergilianae antiquae* in 1954.

A. H. M. JONES, M.A., F.B.A., F.S.A., Fellow of All Souls College, Oxford, from 1926–44 (excavating at Constantinople and Jerash in 1927–9 and Reader in Ancient History in the Egyptian University, Cairo, from 1929–34) was Professor of Ancient History

Contributors

at University College, London, from 1946–51 and has been Professor of Ancient History at Cambridge since 1951. He was President of the Society for the Promotion of Roman Studies from 1952 to 1955. Among his many distinguished books are *The Cities of the Eastern Roman Provinces*, *The Herods of Judaea*, *The Greek City from Alexander to Justinian* and *The Later Roman Empire*.

F. H. LAWSON, D.C.L., F.B.A., Hon. Doctor Louvain, Hon. Dr Jur. Frankfurt, Hon. LL.D. Glasgow, was Professor of Comparative Law at Oxford from 1948–63. Among his many important books are *Cases in Constitutional Law*, *Negligence in the Civil Law*, *The Rational Strength of English Law*, *An Introduction to the Law of Property*.

A. H. MCDONALD, M.A., Ph.D., previously Professor of Classics in Sydney University, has since 1951 been a Fellow of Clare College, Cambridge. The author of numerous articles in classical periodicals, he has been occupied for several years in the collation of manuscripts of Livy as Editor of the Oxford Classical Text of Livy, now in process of publication.

SIR IAN RICHMOND, Hon. LL.D. Edinburgh, Hon. Litt.D. Leeds, Hon. D.Lit. Belfast, Hon. D.Lit. Manchester, Director of the Society of Antiquaries, F.S.A. Scotland, F.B.A., a past President of the Society for the Promotion of Roman Studies, is Professor of the Archaeology of the Roman Empire at Oxford. He was Director of the British School at Rome from 1930–2 and Professor of Roman-British Archaeology in the University of Durham from 1950 to 1956. Apart from reports on his numerous and important excavations, particularly in Britain and in Scotland, he has published *City Wall of Ancient Rome* and *Roman Britain*.

A. N. SHERWIN-WHITE, M.A., F.B.A., Fellow of St John's College, Oxford, since 1936, has published a number of books including *Roman Citizenship*, *Roman Law and Roman Society in the New Testament* and *A Historical Commentary on the Letters of Pliny the Younger*.

DATES

Roman Civilization

Dates

I

EARLY ROME: HISTORY AND LEGEND

J. P. V. D. Balsdon

MORE than one Greek, writing in mainland Greece, had mentioned Rome by name in his book, from as early as 400 B.C.; but those books have not survived, and in Rome itself no history of early Rome was written and published until just before 200 B.C.

The past which confronted Rome's first historians was very empty of reliable historical facts, and very full of picturesque legend. The 'facts', preserved by priests in writing and in short obituaries placed under the death masks of distinguished ancestors in the houses of leading Roman families, were arid as well as scarce, names of magistrates (who were also in most cases generals), with a bare achievement to their credit. But there was also folk and family memory, alive particularly in religious tradition and in stories of individual and national prowess and heroism.

The great wars of the third century, first against Pyrrhus and then against the Carthaginians, were well enough remembered. Familiar too by tradition, however much distorted, were the outlines of the 'Struggle of the Orders', the fight of the underprivileged plebeians under their leading families through the fifth century and the fourth to improve their social and political status, to abolish the vested interests of the patricians and to secure equality with them. Half way through the fifth century there had been the Decemviri and the publication of the Twelve Tables, which were for years to come the foundation of all Roman law. Two signal events of the early fourth century, the capture and destruction of the Etruscan capital Veii, ten miles from Rome, and only six years later the pillage, arson and near-destruction of Rome herself by Gallic invaders from the north were firmly stamped in the tradition – and, a century or more earlier, the expulsion of the last of the Kings, Tarquinius Superbus, and the conversion of the Roman constitution to a Republic, with two annually elected consuls as the chief magistrates, and the Senate (which survived from the period of the Kings) as their advisory council. L. Junius Brutus was the hero of this revolution, himself one of the first two consuls, the man whom later M. Brutus, Caesar's murderer, was to claim as an ancestor.

Before that there were, in the tradition, two centuries and a half of monarchical government, during which King Numa gave Rome its established religion and Servius Tullius a city rampart and a popular assembly (of the people marshalled as for war in their centuries); and there the historian's task finished. He had got back to the start of everything, the foundation of Rome by Romulus and Remus, the twins whom in infancy a she-wolf had suckled.

There was, however, another legend, very difficult to fit into this story, that the Romans were Trojans, descendants of Aeneas, who had fled from Troy at its fall (more than three centuries before the time of Romulus) with his father Anchises on his back, with the palladium and with Ascanius his son, the story which in due course Virgil was to embellish. Aeneas was the son of Venus; so the goddess Venus was the Romans' ancestress.

In the course of time the historians were to supply dates for some of these events – 753 or thereabouts for the foundation of Rome, 509 for the expulsion of the last King and the establishment of the Republic.

Rome, lying on the east bank of the river Tiber, was from the start a Latin city. West of the river and also through Praeneste (Palestrina) into Campania in the south were the powerful Etruscans, different in culture and in language. Early Rome has been rightly described as 'an enclave in an Etruscan empire'. Two of the last Roman Kings, Tarquinius Priscus and Tarquinius Superbus, were certainly Etruscans. In the moment when the last Tarquin was expelled – against the legendary background of the outrage of Lucretia by his son – Rome freed herself from Etruscan domination, though she retained, particularly in the observance of the auspices, much of its culture which she had absorbed.

Modern archaeology, together with scholarly study of the information preserved by Roman antiquarians of the late Republic and early Empire, variously amplifies, confirms and corrects the legendary account of early Rome. There were separate settlements on the various hills of Rome, the largest on the Esquiline and on the Palatine, the most defensible hill of all, where eighth-century post holes of the first simple dwellings have been discovered. The 'city' came into being when the settlements amalgamated in a single community whose business and civic centre was to be in the valley between the Palatine and the Esquiline, marsh land which would require draining, eventually by the Cloaca Maxima, whose exit into the Tiber is still visible today.

The communities on the Palatine and the Esquiline were the first to amalgamate, and then those on the Caelian (Monte Celio). At a later stage the Capitol (the Campidoglio) was included in the city, where Juppiter's great temple was built by the last Tarquin.

This expansion and amalgamation (its early stages remembered in the annual December festival of the Septimontium) evidently took place under the Kings. Though one archaeologist of great distinction considers the available evidence to prove that Rome was founded in 575 B.C. and that the rule of the Kings lasted from then to 450 B.C., it is more commonly held that the foundation of the city (the first amalgamation of communities) took place about the date which the later Romans themselves accepted, around 753 B.C., and that the monarchy was deposed and the Republic established, again as the Romans thought, about 509.

Much of the 'Servian wall' is still to be seen in Rome. The remains may be dated about 378 B.C. and are evidence of reconstruction after the sack of Rome by the Gauls in 390 B.C. Of the fire itself, when the invaders burnt the city, large traces have been found on the Palatine and in the Comitium at the west end of the Forum, above the sixth-century 'black stone', the legendary sepulchre of Romulus; and the tourist today, descending below the ground, can see under the black stone how a small pyramid with an archaic inscription was defaced by the Gauls more than two thousand years ago.

2

PRE-REVOLUTIONARY ROME

A. H. McDonald

IN 189 B.C. Antiochus the Great, whose Seleucid empire recalled the glory of Alexander's conquests, with Hannibal at his side, was defeated by Scipio Africanus in Asia Minor. He saluted the triumph of Rome: 'The king's envoys,' says Polybius, 'urged the Romans to use their victory magnanimously, since Fortune had granted them world dominion.' It was a historic moment, touched with personal drama. For Roman power now controlled the Mediterranean from west to east, while Scipio had won a second bout with his old Carthaginian adversary. Rome's success closed a period of seventy-five years' strategic expansion, during which she had compelled Fortune to take her part.

From 264 to 241 B.C. Rome fought the First Punic War to expel Carthaginian influence from Sicily and the western waters of Italy. When Carthage regained strength through her control of Spain, and Hannibal took command, Rome intervened again in 218 B.C. to fight the Second Punic War: sixteen years of endurance, and in 202 Scipio Africanus won the war. In the darkest hour Philip V of Macedon had supported Hannibal. The First Macedonian War was only an episode, but it showed the importance of Greece on Italy's eastern approaches. In 200 B.C. Rome undertook the Second Macedonian War to confine Philip to his kingdom. In 196 Flamininus declared 'the freedom of Greece', which meant in effect that no major eastern power would be allowed to occupy the country as a threat to Italy. Antiochus challenged this policy; Rome made war again, and by 189 B.C. Scipio Africanus had put an end to his claims. The course of events shows how Roman policy developed: the growth of militarism confirmed her methods, and the strength of Italy made them irresistible.

Conquest, however, is only a political half-way post. Long warfare causes social tensions, victory may have economic consequences. An expanding field of administrative responsibility is as much a temptation to exploit as a challenge to good government. The military virtues do not necessarily suit the demands of peaceful development; for militarism engenders not only its rigid conventions but a corrupting sense of power, which hinders the play of policy at home as well as abroad. The year 189 B.C. also marks in Rome the beginning of troubles that in fifty years would subvert politics and lead to a centry of revolution.

Our subject is the strength and weakness of the Roman tradition at its testing point in the second century B.C. Let us first go back to 280 B.C. and stand with Pyrrhus on the battlefield of Heraclea. One of the great Hellenistic soldiers, he had come to defend the Greek cities of southern Italy against the advancing power of Rome. When he saw the legions, 'The order of these barbarians,' he said, according to Plutarch, 'is not barbarous.' His impression was right. Though he defeated the Romans in the field, he was not able to win the war. Behind the Roman discipline there stood the loyal manpower of central Italy, and we have to consider Rome's politics as well as her military technique.

The rule of the Etruscan Kings had taught the Romans a double lesson about their position on the Tiber: if they were weak, they would be controlled by others; if they used their strength, they could extend their influence. When they established the Republic, they inherited a foreign policy. In the fifth century B.C. they consolidated the State and defended their territory, until they removed the last Etruscan threat of Veii. The sack of Rome by Gauls in 390 B.C. checked their resurgence, but during the fourth century they improved their military system. To support this policy they made constitutional reforms that concentrated the energies of the entire citizen body, the plebs as well as the ruling patrician class. Then they co-operated with the Latin League in measures for common protection, until by 338 they were able to combine the whole Latin region under their leadership. Some Latin cities they received into full citizenship;

with the others they made treaties that left them with local autonomy but granted the private rights of citizenship, as far as they
wished to use them, and in return prescribed a levy of troops for
the Roman army. These arrangements evidently suited the life
of Latium. Rome also extended her relations beyond Latium,
partly with states that were already well established, partly with
communities that lacked local government, by granting them
the private rights of citizenship.

Constitutionally this was a liberal policy: in practice it was a
flexible way of meeting the social conditions of central Italy.
Rome herself was a Latin state – some of her leaders traced their
descent from Latin immigrant families – and the Latins enjoyed
a common culture. Where we find easy political relations we may
assume that the local nobles were in sympathy with Rome and
the Roman nobles were ready to trust them. In general, too, the
political arrangements reflected the economic conditions of the
time. As Etruscan influence receded, the communities of central
Italy lived their own local life, and in normal times Rome could
afford to respect their autonomy. If there were a threat to their
general security – if, for example, the Gauls made a serious in-
cursion from the north – the Latin allies would gladly lend military support to the capable leadership of Rome: once the danger
passed, they knew that they could return to their own affairs.
Under these conditions Rome's policy was practical and fair,
and she gained a reinforcement of first-class manpower.

But let us not mistake the spirit of Roman policy. The liberal
conditions we have outlined were dictated at Rome's discretion.
Her leaders assumed the patron's privilege of requiring simple
loyalty from their allies. Where they could not impose reliable
co-operation, they crushed all opposition: alongside the Latin
treaties we have to set the Samnite Wars in the south. In the late
fourth century B.C. Rome's growing connexions with Campania
were threatened by the warlike Samnite tribes, whose way of life
gave little hope that they would accept any Roman arrangement.
From 328 to 290 the legions campaigned in the mountains of
Samnium, far from secure bases and exposed – as they found at
the Caudine Forks – to ambush and destruction. They subdued

the Samnites ruthlessly, wasting their land with fire and sword: the peace they established was a solitude.

During those stern wars Rome strengthened her military system; we may trust Pyrrhus' observation of the army. Her leaders also enlarged their strategic view. Small colonies of Roman citizens were placed as garrisons on the coast of Roman territory; larger settlements with Latin rights, established at key points in central Italy, were designed for municipal development, so that they should not only control but help in binding together the diverse communities of the region. Meanwhile the needs of central direction encouraged the technical improvement of Roman administration, in the time of Appius Claudius the censor, about 300 B.C.

After Pyrrhus had retired in 275 and the Greeks of southern Italy made their submission, the Romans could safely resume the system of treaties, now adapted to looser relations with states which had different traditions and more distant regional interests. They reserved the power to direct policy in matters of general security; for the rest they considered the particular circumstances. Some Italian allies they received into equal terms; on others, it would seem, they imposed an explicit recognition of their hegemony; but to all they allowed the rights of local autonomy. The arrangements were suited to encourage or induce cooperation by the leaders of the communities. Then, after the First Punic War, when Sicily became a province, its new charter included the grant of local rights to some Greek cities in order to claim their loyalty within the setting of provincial government. In this way Rome built up an Italian confederation to support her power and adapted her policy further to the control of overseas territories.

Yet Roman policy, we must repeat, was a two-edged blade. The Romans allowed freedom where they could expect support, they destroyed opposition if they thought it might threaten them. Such a policy fitted the conditions of Italy before the Mediterranean conquests: it reflected a hard practical genius in the art of controlling men. But the balance of judgement could be disturbed by the impact of new conditions, all the more for the far-reaching consequences of success. We must now look at the human factors, in the men – or rather the families – who established the Roman tradition of government.

In the early Republic the patrician nobles held the political initiative. The families had wealth and prestige, and strong influence in their own locality. In particular, they exercised 'patronage' over free citizens who had attached themselves by ties of 'clientship': the patron granted general protection, while the client returned social and political support. The relationship was one of trust and mutual obligation, and it persisted in Rome even when the civic administration was fully developed, helping to maintain the influence of the leading families. While the nobles devoted themselves to politics and war, as a public duty which also served the family honour, their clients stood by to reinforce their dignity. Personal relations thus became part of political thought. When the plebs set up their own assembly (the Concilium Plebis) in 471 B.C., their tribunes, annually elected officers, defended the rights of individual citizens as if they were the people's patrons. The rising plebeian families also accepted the attachment of poorer citizens, and when – during the critical period of the fourth century B.C. – they won the right to share in the nigh offices of state, they used their clients to extend their influence. As social conditions remained constant, the great families – patrician and plebeian – established the use of clientship among their political conventions. This development led to the paradox of the Lex Hortensia in 287 B.C. by which resolutions of the Concilium Plebis were binding on the whole Roman people. It put the mark of equality on the relations of patricians and plebs, and the Concilium Plebis assumed the character of a popular assembly: constitutionally the climax of a democratic process. In practice the ruling families of Rome combined to form a new patrician–plebeian nobility, which based its status upon the holding of office, in particular, the consulship. They applied the patron's authority to their political dealings both at home and with their allies.

Rome's expansion in Italy did not disturb the setting of aristocratic leadership. The nobles remained good landowners and responsible politicians. They organized their connexions with other families so as to secure their position, through suitable marriages and, where necessary, by the adoption of sons, and play their part in public life from one generation to another; their education and training were directed to these ends. Such is the conduct of artistocratic government in normal times. Where urgent problems arose, however, they used independent judgement, settling their differences of opinion, in order to achieve a common policy, and there was scope for outstanding individuals to make their mark, especially in military commands. While the family ambitions for civic dignity coloured the background of politics, Rome would not have won an empire if her leaders had failed in their patriotic duty. Above all, the pressure of external danger enforced the unity of the people. The Romans later admitted that the efforts of victory changed their standards of public morality.

During the third century B.C. we may note the growth of the administrative system through which the nobles exercised their leadership. They encouraged and regulated the progress of technical skill in engineering, roadmaking, town planning and public building, developments that would increase their strength. Rome now spoke for Italy, and the Greek states recognized her importance in the Western world; in 273 B.C. Ptolemaic Egypt opened political relations. About 269 Rome struck her first silver and established a bimetallic currency of silver and bronze, initially to meet the conditions in southern Italy. The First Punic War took the legions to Sicily and forced Rome into naval activity: one does not build, man, equip and supply fleets without an efficient shore establishment. In the Second Punic War Hannibal set a major problem of handling manpower and supporting military operations: there were Roman armies in Spain, Sicily and Greece, as well as in Italy – not to forget the ships at sea – before the war was over. Then the campaigns in Spain, Cisalpine Gaul and the east added to Rome's experience in the technique of war and confirmed her militaristic methods.

Of course we should not oversimplify our description. The noble families had to reckon with the people at times of intense agitation. Popular support made Flaminius consul in 217 B.C., but he died at Lake Trasimene; in the following year it put Terentius Varro in command at Cannae, the darkest of all Roman defeats. Thereafter Fabius Cunctator restored the nobles' control of strategy, until Scipio Africanus brought his genius into the counter-offensive against Carthage. Popular feeling again sent Scipio against Antiochus, once Hannibal re-entered the field; but the nobles did not let him enjoy the glory of his success. For the long period of widespread warfare had strengthened the executive side of Roman government, not only in the consulship but through the Senate. Constitutionally an advisory body, the Senate had assumed many of the functions of direct administration, in terms of policy, appointments, and finance. It became a war council, using the experience of its members and devoting its full attention to the conduct of affairs, where a popular assembly was incapable of acting expeditiously or with successful judgement. Within the Senate the nobles made an inner circle: their influence dominated the Senate's deliberations, while their strongest men handled the practical affairs of state. How far would their judgement and good faith stand the rest of imperial responsibility?

The new features of Roman life after the Mediterranean expansion are well known. It is usual to list them: the influx of wealth and investment in land, the importation of overseas grain, the supply of cheap slave labour, thus the spread of *latifundia* as estates supplying the cities, and the decline of the peasantry; the rise of a commercial and industrial class along with an urban proletariat; all of which led to the corruption of public life, weakness in the military system, and social unrest, leading to a revolutionary situation. The list is correct enough: the Romans themselves drew it up and emphasized the part of luxury in lowering the standards of traditional morality. But it is not enough to generalize in this way about seventy years of fundamental economic and social change such as most developing countries have had to experience. We have sufficient evidence from Polybius and Livy to attempt a closer analysis of the trends in Rome and Italy as well as the effect of Roman policy upon the Mediterranean.

The second Punic War had displaced large numbers of the Italian population, especially in the south, and brought about strategic changes of economic activity, which strengthened the urban life of central Italy. Rome's military levies kept the young men on service, while the growth of war industries brought others into the cities; footloose veterans were as likely to take urban work as return to farming. Rome itself was the chief centre of production, and the Etruscan cities contributed to the supply of military equipment; after Hannibal's withdrawal Campania made an economic recovery. Overseas campaigning throughout the Mediterranean continued the demand for army material. We have to appreciate the general effect of this development; for the basic industries promoted the growth of the other trades and business occupations that support city life, and the increasing urban population provided a larger market for varied agricultural produce. Rome, for example, had to undertake more building and improve the city's water supply; the main trades required metals, leather, and wool; the workmen and their families needed grain, oil, and wine, which had to come cheaply and conveniently. The city had already begun to import grain in bulk, largely from Sicily; this would expand the port of Ostia and its shipping. The other food supplies could be provided locally, if agriculture adapted itself to the market needs. Such production, however, was not the work of peasant farming but of specialized agriculture with resources of capital, whether it established olive groves and vineyards or developed the pastoral side. This kind of farming, long practised in Etruria and southern Italy, was now encouraged by the urban growth of Latium and Campania. The influx of wealth and slave labour had yet to take economic effect; but we can already discern the economic pattern which would soon allow the profitable investment of Roman capital in land.*

Meanwhile the city of Rome had become a focus of commercial activity. In 193 B.C., since Roman money-lenders were using Latin agents in order to escape the Roman restriction on rates of interest, transactions of this kind were brought under Roman

*See further, p. 171f.

law. At the same time Latins were moving into the city, where they could find work and acquire citizenship by residence, and the Latin states had difficulty in raising their quota of troops. In 193 B.C. the consul agreed to take a proportion of the eligible men; but in 187, as the drift went on, Rome agreed with the Latin authorities to repatriate Latins who had migrated since 204. The implications of this situation seem clear enough : that is, social conditions in Latium were changing and the treaty relations were obsolete, while both the Roman and the Latin leaders hoped to save the old order. In Campania the Capuans, who had lost their citizenship after joining Hannibal, were re-enrolled at Rome, as a step towards citizenship again, while three munici-palities with private Roman rights were granted the full rights of citizenship; soon the ancient Greek foundation of Cumae would use Latin as its official language. All this is evidence for the closer social organization of central Italy.

In southern Italy, where Hannibal's occupation and the Roman measures of recovery had disrupted the life of the country, it was left to local enterprise to restore normal conditions. Here the Greek cities, as they recovered, and the rural gentry took the lead. When Rome let out her public land again, the local land-owners leased it in order to farm it in conjunction with their own estates, and they increased their stock in the confidence that they would have security of tenure. Their grandsons would be horrified when the Gracchan agrarian legislation took this land from them.*

In 187 B.C. the legions were back from the east and the long period of imperial expansion came to an end. There was still need for military levies in operations that established two provinces in Spain and brought Cisalpine Saul and Sardinia under control, and the legions would return to Greece to destroy the ancient kingdom of Macedon in 171–168 B.C. Even then armies were kept standing in provinces, especially in Spain, where their pre-sence would maintain order; the old militia system was not well suited to these overseas demands. Above all, the changes in Rome

*See pp. 41f.

and Italy raised difficulties which the Roman leaders, aristocratic in spirit and militaristic in their experience, were slow to understand, and their position enabled them to resist the pressure of circumstances. The Italian nobles, too, preferred a policy that would not threaten their local influence – as long as Rome did not sacrifice their interests.

The Roman government repaid its citizens twenty-five and a half imposts of taxation which the wars had made necessary, and it was able to embark upon a programme of public expenditure, especially in the crowded cities. We learn of an abundance of money on the Roman market in 186 B.C.; it would include the profit which generals, officers and soldiers had made in the eastern wars. From this time it is fair to assume that capital played a decisive part in expanding the Roman economy along the lines it was already following. The contractors enlarged their operations; the senatorial class invested their wealth in the only secure field of business available to them, viz., in agriculture, but it was the new agriculture that served the needs of the urban markets. Soon the supply of slave labour became relevant; for the enslavement of 80,000 Sardinians in 176 and the enslavement of 150,000 Epirotes in 167 B.C. – even if they did not all come to Italy – exercised a strong economic effect, especially on the growth of large country estates.*

Meanwhile the soldiers who had fought in Greece, under conditions that encouraged plunder and licence, brought back habits of Eastern luxury, more often than not to the cities, and the Roman moralists from Cato onwards would trace the decline of Roman conduct from this period. But we shall look rather to the state of Italy itself, influenced by the shift of population and the spread of Greek culture from the south. In 186 B.C. the Senate believed that the worship of Dionysus, with its orgiastic rites, had become a threat to public morality, and it decided to regulate the practice of the cult throughout Italy. Livy describes the harsh measures of repression and his account is confirmed by a copy of the decree which the consuls transmitted to the Italian allies,

*See further, p. 174.

advising them how to act in their own locality. The Roman policy
had portentous features. The Senate, in effect, was determined
to control social behaviour, but it could only do so by treating
misbehaviour as politically subversive, that is, as a 'conspiracy'
against the State; then the consuls could take emergency measures, almost in terms of martial law. Only on this basis, too,
could the Senate at all properly issue a strong instruction to the
allied authorities. But was the principle itself a proper one? The
definition of what constituted 'conspiracy' and 'emergency' had
hitherto covered conditions that posed a direct threat of violence
to the State. How could this include the excesses of a degenerate
cult? Only by extending the definition of 'subversion' far beyond its original scope; for the Dionysiac devotees were hardly
capable of overthrowing Rome. There is no more dangerous
weapon in the hands of any government than the power to in-
tensify police action by arbitrary reinterpretation of the law;
this is how dictatorships make a first parade of legality. Sixty
years later the Senate would turn this weapon against its Gracchan opponents: we have here the germ of the 'ultimate decree',
the decree for 'the defence of the State', which brought the
element of force into the internal politics of Rome. For the moment the Senate aimed merely at using its authority to overcome
the obstacles of earlier practice in Rome and Italy in order to
meet the new circumstances.

The policy was strengthened by the severe censorship of Cato
and Valerius Flaccus in 184–183 B.C. The Roman censors not only
held the census of the people and let out the contracts for public
work: they also kept the roll of the Senate and the list of the
equestrian class, where they had the right to apply moral as well
as financial standards of qualification. Cato and Flaccus spent
large sums on building and public projects, and they used their
office to discipline the senatorial class and control business
methods. Although the Senate as a body maintained its political
integrity, the young nobles were tempted by the new opportunities to exploit wealth and buy influence. The list of Cato's
prosecutions shows how strictly he scrutinized the conduct of
officials. In 181 B.C. the consuls carried the first law against

electoral bribery and in 180 the Lex Villia Annalis regulated the legal age of candidacy for the offices of State; for the ruling nobles were as conscientious as Cato. The censors of 179–178, Aemilius Lepidus and Fulvius Nobilior, if less drastic, were equally constructive during their term of office. The climax of this policy appears in 179, with a reform of the Comitia Centuriata, the assembly of the Roman people for regular State business, which changed the arrangement of voting and drew up the tribal lists of voters according to birth, family status, and financial circumstances. Its purpose is plain : it increased the voting power of the urban *bourgeoisie* of free citizens and freedmen with sons, so as to gain their support for the policy of the Senate.

So far, so good – but political measures could not stem the course of events. The industrial activity of Rome still drew Latin workmen into the city, while the loss of manpower left the Latin authorities unable to raise their military levies. An arrangement to allow Latins to migrate to Rome providing they left a son at home had been easily outwitted, and the position became critical – at least from the standpoint of the Roman and Latin authorities. In 177 B.C. the Senate decided to repatriate the recent immigrants and the next censors enforced the measure. We need not speak of Roman discrimination against the Latins : the truth is rather that the leaders on both sides wanted to preserve their existing form of relationship. The urban drift seems to have been general in Latium and Campania. In 177 B.C. Sempronius Gracchus' subjugation of Sardinia loosed a flood of cheap slave labour on the Italian market, and when in 174 the Senate reversed its liberal policy towards freedmen, we may assume that it felt doubts about the future character of the slave population.

The Third Macedonian War (171–168 B.C.) brought the underlying discontents to the surface. Though the Senate was determined to crush Macedon, the army was less ready to endure what turned out to be a tedious course of campaigning. Generals oppressed their Greek allies, soldiers sank into slackness and insubordination, and when Rome called on her most experienced general, Aemilius Paullus, he had first to silence criticism at home and then restore discipline in the field before he was able to win the war. The Senate made a brutal and unsatisfactory settlement when it divided the Macedonian kingdom into four helpless republics and undermined the power of its allies Pergamum and Rhodes, whose influence was necessary to the life of the Aegean world. This was the policy of men who had lost the foresight of their fathers, sacrificing the element of goodwill that had served even the most strategic calculations in the past. At home the business (equestrian) class gained popular support against the censors of 169–168, such distinguished men as Sempronius Gracchus and C. Claudius Pulcher. Victory and the profits of war gave relief and the nobles felt secure again, but the balance of Roman affairs, under less pressure than Rome had borne a generation earlier, had betrayed its instability. And in 167 B.C. the Epirote slaves came on the market.

Among his many works Cato wrote a small book *On Agriculture*, and he was not a man to write to no purpose. He describes how to farm for profit under the conditions that now existed in Latium and Campania. For small estates he recommends the production of grapes, vegetables and olives rather than grain : a vineyard of sixty acres with sixteen slaves, an olive grove of 160 acres with thirteen slaves and contract labour at the height of the season, not to forget grazing on leased public land. His account shows the practical countryman, but – for all his praise of life on the land – not an old-fashioned landowner with his free peasants. He has in mind the city markets for wine and oil, vegetables and meat, leather and wool. This is the new farming which flourished on capital and slave labour by the mid century, and Cato was writing to advise his fellow senators about investment in agriculture. What then of the peasant farmers? Large numbers moved to the cities to find work. What of the military system, which rested upon property holders, not upon an urban proletariat? Here was the rub, as we have already seen. And the old relations of client loyalty? If these persisted after the peasants reached Rome, they had become artificial, and it was a short step to paying for political support on the streets. We see slaves comprising the rural working class, even on the small estates. And in Etruria, southern Italy and Sicily, where great estates had long been in fashion, the influx of slaves allowed chain-gang methods with their accompaniment of brutality and savage resentment, which would issue in the slave wars of the latter part of the century.

After the Third Macedonian War the Greek historian Polybius came to Rome, a hostage for the Achaean League but a man whose knowledge and experience won him a favoured place in the circle of the Scipionic family. His history of Rome's conquest of the Mediterranean has first-class authority, and his analysis of the sources of Roman strength reflects the impression he had gained during the middle years of the century. Following orthodox Greek theory Polybius believed that political conditions could be defined in constitutional terms: in any state the elements of monarchy, aristocracy and democracy, if they had absolute power, tended to degenerate in turn – one into another – and the only way to delay the process was to mix the elements in government. Rome, argues Polybius, had achieved a balance of the monarchic consulship, the aristocratic Senate, the democratic assembly of the people, each element with its strength and weakness against the others, as he illustrates in concrete detail. He gives a vivid impression of a state uneasily balanced on contending forces, and we may draw our own picture.

Rome – in modern terms – had 'representative' but not 'responsible' government; we have to think of the American constitution, which borrowed Roman ideas, rather than of British parliamentary practice. On the executive side the consuls were elected but, once elected, they exercised the power of their *imperium* of office, limited only by law. Lift the legal restrictions by emergency decree and the consuls were the masters of Rome, for the length of the emergency. The Senate was in origin an advisory body, but the exigencies of major warfare had given it administrative functions that made it a political force – with privileges, let us say, of initiative, advice and consent. In the mid-second century, as the nobles had effective control of both consulship and Senate, they could impose their will on the State. The assemblies of the people meeting in their centuries or tribes as well as the Concilium Plebis after 287 B.C. were the legislative bodies, normally deciding upon matters that were proposed to them by their presiding officials after discussion in the Senate. We have considered the part of the consuls: the tribunes of the plebs also came into account, for they had gained wide powers of initiating as well as vetoing legislative business. By the second century B.C., it is often said, the tribunes were merely political agents of the Senate. The truth is rather that many were members of the nobility and that the political situation induced their co-operation; but if conditions should change, for instance in the levying of troops, so as to inflict hardship on individuals, they would not hesitate to use their primary right of intervention. The position, as Polybius saw, was one of balance – a balance that rested upon political conventions. What then if the conditions favourable to these conventions should change? The rights and powers that now functioned together would break apart in conflict. Consuls and tribunes presiding over their assemblies could take the political initiative; then the Senate, using friendly magistrates, might apply its discretionary powers; the people, once they tasted power, would no longer acquiesce in aristocratic leadership. These were the possibilities if the nobles should fail to govern successfully.

Let us look again at the Roman nobility, as they receive their friends and clients, supported by the presence of their ancestors' busts and the records of traditional distinction which they felt a duty to maintain. Their attitude had become more exclusive. The code was laid down: it only had to be fulfilled in action. There was a consistency in ambition and, we may assume, normally a continuity of ideas, while disputes belonged to the struggle for personal distinction; it is always worth studying a noble of this period against his family background. The examination of individual careers, with their political alliances, by the technique of 'prosopography' has thrown light upon the nature of their government. This is not to suggest that the nobles reacted mechanically to critical problems. Often family alignments are related to dominating figures. The great families which almost monopolized high office preferred to impose a regular career on their members, yet they did not hesitate to support the right man, e.g.,

Scipio Aemilianus, repeatedly in urgent commands. Their only proviso was that he should stay faithful to the code. Nor were these men culturally narrow: they knew Greek literature and their historians were beginning to show Rome to the Hellenistic world. But their political conventions were fixed. Bad magistrates could offset the work of the good and damage the authority of the whole order, and even the best did not see far enough, where differences of class and condition inhibited their thought. The Stoic philosopher Panaetius endeavoured to give the Romans an ethical conception of power and responsibility, and many found that Stoicism made new sense of their inherited standards. But social conditions were changing too fast, the old habits too slowly, to allow time for political development.

The situation in the middle of the second century B.C. is obscure; but it seems that economic progress continued in Rome, where the treasury still had ample reserves in 157; and we see the signs of Campanian prosperity in Pompeii. Italians went into trade in the east – as one can see at Delos – or moved north into the Po valley. The business class must have resented increasingly the pressure of senatorial control and they could appeal to popular support. The nobles applied their old methods: they prevented philosophers and rhetoricians from influencing the younger generation; in 154 the brilliant Diogenes, Critolaus and Carneades were not allowed to parade their learning when they visited Rome.

But towards 150 B.C. events took charge of Roman policy. The Spanish tribes had accepted a settlement at the hands of Sempronius Gracchus,* but they would not tolerate misgovernment by the smaller men who succeeded him. In 154 B.C. the Lusitanians revolted and fought until 138, when they lost their leader Viriathus. In 153 the Celtiberians joined them and fought till 151, then again from 143 to 133, when Scipio Aemilianus finally crushed their resistance at Numantia. We need not follow the course of the Spanish wars, but we should ask some questions. Had there been injustice that called for remedy? In 149 the Lex

---

*Consul in 177 B.C. and father of the famous tribunes.

Calpurnia would establish a court to handle cases of corrupt provincial administration. If Marcellus could negotiate a settlement in 151, why did the Senate not follow Gracchus' method of combining diplomacy with force? And how far had it calculated the cost in manpower of campaigns in central Spain? For although Roman military organization in the field was now professional, the levy of citizens for service was old-fashioned, and the reserve of qualified men was reduced. Overseas wars could not appeal to patriotism, as the wars against Carthage had done. Even if a citizen were liable for service during sixteen years, there must be a limit to any period of continuous campaigning. And if a man had served a period, how soon should he be recalled to the legions simply because he was an experienced soldier?

The Senate stood too firmly on the principle that it would accept no peace save a dictated one. The Roman people refused to be sacrificed to this policy in Spain. In the levy for 151 B.C. the tribunes of the plebs intervened to secure exemptions and ended by arresting the consuls, while the young nobles were reluctant to serve as officers. Lot was introduced to forestall discrimination at the expense of veterans, but Fabius in 145 and Pompeius in 140 had to be content with raw recruits. By this time the situation was out of hand, and in 138 tribunes would again intervene in a levy to arrest the consuls. However, it was the generals who disgraced the name of Rome. Lucullus and Galba treacherously violated the rules of war, Caepio and Pompeius arbitrarily repudiated treaties, and finally Mancinus made a humiliating surrender. A far cry from the resistance to Hannibal – but then we have tried to show that this was another age.

Meanwhile the Senate added to the black record. Conditions in Macedonia allowed the revolt of Andriscus, which was crushed in the Third Macedonian War (149–148 B.C.) Neglect in Greece encouraged the Achaean League to defy Rome, and in 146 Mummius destroyed Corinth. In North Africa trouble between Carthage and the expanding power of Numidia brought Roman intervention in the Third Punic War (149–146), and Scipio Aemilianus destroyed Carthage. The nobles, it is true, had differed about this policy, when Cato won the day, but the end of

Carthage is marked by Roman bad faith. It is hard to find rational grounds for the death penalty on Corinth and Carthage, two great civilized cities. The Romans applied their old Samnite policy of annihilating opposition where it hindered their will – a brutal method, since they need not now seriously fear any threat to themselves. A policy with an irrational element in it? If this is so, it is because the Senate could hardly handle the combination of military problems that suddenly arose at this time. But these were problems that need not have become critical, had the nobles learnt the lessons of imperial responsibility. The Spanish tribes exacted the penalty. Above all, Rome would suffer at home, as Italian conditions degenerated and a slave war (135–132) broke out in Sicily, even before Tiberius Gracchus entered on his tribuneship.

The discontent in Rome about the military levies was only a symptom of the deep social unsettlement. The spread of large estates drove men off the land into the cities, where previously they had been attracted by the opportunities. The allied communities felt less secure in their relations with Rome, and arrogant Roman magistrates were less careful about respecting their local rights. In Rome the stringency of war conditions reduced the amenities of urban life, with its cheap corn and games, and the largess of wealthy patrons; the spoil from Corinth and Carthage afforded only temporary relief. And all the time unwilling citizens from the country were drafted into the army, while unhappy veterans returned to the cities with the violence and indiscipline of their soldiering. More seriously for Roman policy the nobles and the Senate had lost the authority of success. The situation called for reform, as far as Rome's leaders could envisage it. Their minds turned first to the regeneration of their manpower, for it was the yeoman class that had been the source of their strength.

The dominant figure of this period is Scipio Aemilianus, the son of Aemilius Paullus, adopted into the Scipionic family. Cultured but conservative he had the military ability which the times demanded and he won distinction in the Spanish war; it was he who destroyed Carthage. In Italy he set himself to preserve the confederate relations between Rome and her allies. His associate Laelius proposed a measure of close land settlement to restore the manpower that was necessary to the military system by resuming the free disposal of public land. When the proposal was withdrawn, we may believe that Scipio feared the disturbing effect that it would have upon Italian landholding, both Roman and allied, and its political consequences. The influence of Roman patrons upon domestic politics is shown by the attempts to limit it, through laws to introduce secret ballot for elections in 139 B.C. and for the law courts in 137, so as to leave clients free to vote as they wished.

The Scipionic group, with their liberal tradition, were not the only nobles to face the problems of Roman policy. Appius Claudius, censor in 136, with a circle of able supporters, rivalled Scipio Aemilianus in the field of domestic politics. Tiberius Gracchus was his son-in-law, and he supported Tiberius' agrarian reforms with less feeling for Italian susceptibilities than Scipio had shown. We need not enter into details, for the main point is clear. The leading Roman nobles had realized that the change in economic conditions in Italy was threatening the social basis of the military organization upon which they depended, and they still hoped to restore something like the old order. Yet the situation had become too complex for traditional thinking. Given time, could the Scipios and the Claudii have led Rome out of her impasse? Perhaps so in Italy, through painful negotiation with the allied authorities. Less likely in Rome, where the nobles were more firmly set against the equestrian class. But this is historical speculation: they were not given the time.

The traditions of the Roman ruling class were too strong, the social changes in Rome and Italy too deep; the very success of imperial expansion had intensified its own problems. Fifteen years would define the internal questions; it would be fifty years before Italy forced a decision upon Rome; and, as for the provinces, a century would elapse before the issues of power and responsibility were resolved.

BIBLIOGRAPHY

The books listed in this bibliography are relevant to Chapters I and II.

FOR GENERAL BACKGROUND

Heichelheim, F. M. and Yeo, C. A., *History of the Roman People*, Prentice-Hall, 1962.

Rostovtzeff, M., *Rome* (paperback edition), Oxford University Press, 1928.

Scullard, H. H., *History of the Roman World, 753–146 B.C.*, 2nd ed., Methuen, 1951.

ON ROME, ITALY AND THE MEDITERRANEAN

Bloch, Raymond, *The Etruscans* (1958); *The Origins of Rome* (1960), Ancient Peoples and Places Series, Thames & Hudson.

Woodhead, A. G., *The Greeks in the West*, Ancient Peoples and Places Series, Thames & Hudson, 1962.

Harden, Donald, *The Phoenicians*, Ancient Peoples and Places Series, Thames & Hudson, 1962.

FOR ARCHAEOLOGICAL EVIDENCE IN ITALY

MacKendrick, P., *The Mute Stones Speak*, Methuen, 1962.

FOR THE SECOND CENTURY B.C.

Adcock, F. E., *Roman Political Ideas and Practice*, University of Michigan Press, 1959.

Badian, E., *Foreign Clientelae*, Oxford University Press, 1958.

Hill, H., *The Roman Middle Class*, Blackwell, 1952.

Scullard, H. H., *Roman Politics, 220–150 B.C.*, Oxford University Press, 1951.

Sherwin-White, A. N., *The Roman Citizenship*, Oxford University Press, 1939.

Smith, R. E., *The Failure of the Roman Republic*, Cambridge University Press, 1955.

Syme, R., *The Roman Revolution* (paperback edition), Oxford University Press, 1961.

Consult *Cambridge Ancient History*, Vol. VIII, and *Oxford Classical Dictionary*.

3

THE REVOLUTION
AND THE END OF FREEDOM

J. P. V. D. Balsdon

UNDER the aristocracy, which itself developed in a liberal fashion from patrician to patrician–plebeian 'nobility', the Romans had grown, in the Mediterranean world, into being by 146 B.C. the only 'world power'. From the battle of Actium in 31 B.C., under the government of a single man, first a masked and later an overt autocracy, they succeeded in governing a vast and flourishing empire. The period between 146 and 31 B.C. was at once the most exciting and the most disastrous period of their history. In it they reduced Spain to order, they conquered Gaul (France) and brought the whole of Asia Minor, Syria, Cyrene and Cyprus into their empire; yet the administration of provincial governors was frequently corrupt and at home the period was one of recurrent civil war and public disorder. In the years between 133 and 82 seven consuls, one praetor and four tribunes of the plebs, while in office, were murdered or died fighting other Romans in Italy. Yet no period of Roman history produced men of greater public distinction: Tiberius Gracchus and his younger brother Gaius, Marius, Sulla, Pompey, Julius Caesar and Antony – to say nothing of Cicero, the younger Cato and Cato's nephew Brutus. A biography by Plutarch survives for each of them – and, indeed of Sertorius, Lucullus and Crassus also. And the final thirteen years of conflict when, after Caesar's murder, Antony was pitted against Caesar's great-nephew Octavian (the later Emperor Augustus) are splendidly imagined in Shakespeare's *Antony and Cleopatra*.

The limited number of great families who determined government policy in senatorial debate and who, through their pledged supporters (*clientes*) in the public assemblies, had carried legislation and controlled elections to the great offices of state

39

(praetorship and consulship), were in this period to be known, in their conservatism, as the *Optimates*. Unwilling or unable to adapt themselves to the need for change, they were on the defensive against attack from three different quarters: from young politicians (*Populares*) of their own social class – most of them highly enlightened – who, as tribunes of the plebs, confronted problems that they thought urgent by legislation which, without consulting the Senate, they introduced (as they were entitled to do) directly to the plebeian assembly; from men outside politics with Empire-wide business interests, the *Equites*, who constituted an increasingly strong pressure group; and from generals (proconsuls) who, with their armies, could coerce the government, and whom the government could not coerce. There was no adequate police force in Rome and, under the constitution, troops could not be employed to restore order within the city. There were other grave problems: the growing discontent of the Latin and other Italian allies of Rome who, by the terms of their treaties with Rome, provided troops to share in Rome's conquests, but received no advantage from those conquests; the growing unpopularity among Romans of conscription for military service, now that this might involve absence from home for years on end and, apart from this, the shortage of available Romans among the propertied classes which were liable for conscription; and the presence of large gangs of discontented slaves all over the Italian countryside.

This is a period in which great personal fortunes were quickly made, whether corruptly or not, by senatorial generals and provincial governors (proconsuls) and by Equites; so there was a new standard of living, aped disastrously by those who had not the means. Hence the power of the great money-lenders (like Crassus) and the lawlessness of the impoverished (men like Catiline). With increasing cosmopolitanism and, in particular, Roman penetration of the Hellenistic world, a new culture developed and a new morality, relaxed and cynical, which conflicted with the close-knit moral integrity and religious piety of Roman tradition. In the city of Rome itself the proletariat grew as the countryside emptied. Consisting of hard-working men as well as of idlers, it was despised and, because of its votes in the assemblies (for it was, to all intents and purposes, the sovereign people of Rome) indulged, by the politicians; it expected its price – subsidized food and extravagant public games. In the country towns of Italy, a more old-fashioned Roman survived, who was still a countryman, fond of the soil and anxious to make his living from it.

Tribune of the plebs in 133 B.C., Tiberius Gracchus, son of a most distinguished family, brother-in-law of Scipio Aemilianus, and himself a Scipio on his mother's side, was the first of the reformers, inspired by an inborn integrity and an education in Greek philosophy. He had the simple idea that, if the State reclaimed from the great cattle and sheep ranchers, rich Romans and Latins alike, State domains (*ager publicus*) on which they or their ancestors had encroached, the land so reclaimed could be divided out in small-holdings, to increase the number of propertied Romans, agriculturalists who might be expected to have sons – and traditionally the sons of countrymen made the best soldiers. As the demands of military service had already driven smallholders off the land (and so assisted the spread of the great ranches), the success of Gracchus' proposal was uncertain. But his public behaviour was more important than the reform which he proposed. For, when his opponents secured a tribune to veto the proposal, Tiberius drove a horse and cart through the Roman constitution by persuading the plebs to dismiss the tribune from office. Tiberius' agrarian bill was passed, and a commission appointed to give it effect. When the Senate refused to vote a sum for the commission's expenses (the voting of supplies being traditionally a senatorial function), Tiberius defied the constitution a second time, carrying a resolution in the plebeian assembly to meet the commission's expenses from the treasure of King Attalus III of Pergamum, who had just died, leaving his kingdom to Rome. He then further defied tradition – the law in this matter was not clear – by seeking re-election to the tribunate for the following year. The elections broke down in rioting and disorder. Wild rumours circulated and, when the consul refused to act,

Scipio Nasica, ex-consul and high priest, led a band of excited senators into the fray. Tiberius was clubbed to death and in the following year, secure in victory, the Senate appointed the two consuls as a commission to try Tiberius' supporters, a number of whom it condemned to death. Scipio Aemilianus returned and triumphed, a war hero; for his capture of Numantia in the year of Tiberius' tribunate meant that, after twenty years of Roman bungling and incompetence, Spain was pacified and its rebellions at an end. Scipio made no secret of his opinion that Tiberius' murder was justified, and he curtailed the operations of the Land Commission by inducing the Senate to transfer to one of the consuls the adjudication of disputes in cases where public land was reclaimed from Latins or allies.

If Tiberius Gracchus was an inspired fanatic, his brother Gaius, tribune in 123 B.C. and again (without any question raised) in 122, was a resourceful and imaginative politician. He too took his measures directly to the assembly of the plebs. Determined to avenge his brother's death, he reintroduced Tiberius' agrarian bill, on the strength of which considerable numbers of men had already been settled on reclaimed public land, and he proposed further the dispatch of overseas colonies. He legislated not only to prevent a recurrence of the consular commission of 132 B.C. (on the ground that the people alone could constitutionally condemn a Roman to death), but also to punish those who had taken part in its activities. Since all corn sold in Rome came from overseas (Sardinia, Sicily and Africa) and, because of speculators and because of the suspension of shipping in the winter months, was frequently exorbitantly expensive, he inaugurated a system that was to last for centuries, by which the government shipped corn directly after the harvest, when it was cheap, stored it in vast granaries at Rome and families domiciled in Rome were entitled to draw a monthly corn ration at a regular and remarkably low price throughout the year. (Not until the end of the Republic was it given free.)

Next, the reduction of the Senate's privileges. For the future they were to select the consuls' provinces before the consuls were elected, to prevent favouritism and victimizing. And senators (chiefly ex-magistrates) impeached for corrupt administration were no longer to be tried by their peers. Instead the juries in the extortion court were to be selected from rich men who were not in politics (Equites). Also he introduced a system, which afterwards spread to other provinces, by which, in the manner of the public contracts, the collection of taxes in the new rich province of Asia, the bequest of Attalus, was to be sold in Rome for five-year periods, to the highest bidder from among syndicates of business men (the *publicani*). The corn tax in Sicily was already collected in this way, but the auction took place annually in the province, at Syracuse; the system was one to which the Romans were driven by the fact that they had no civil service. Its extension, particularly to Asia, had pernicious consequences. Private companies, working for a profit, have not the integrity of public servants; and henceforth provincial governors were confronted with the alternatives of conniving at equestrian injustice (with, of course, a share in its profits) or, if they checked it, facing trial themselves at Rome on a trumped-up charge, before an equestrian jury whose sympathy was estranged by the very fact of their integrity. This was a result of his legislation that, however unimaginatively, Gaius Gracchus certainly did not foresee.

His bravest display of statesmanship was in the proposal that the Latins should be given Roman citizenship and the other allies of Rome in Italy be raised to the status of Latins. The proposal had been mooted unsuccessfully a few years earlier by his friend Fulvius Flaccus when consul, and Flaccus now, against all precedent, held the tribunate after being consul, to support the proposal. The bill was opposed both by Roman aristocrats, who feared that an influx of new voters would disturb the control which they exercised through their clients over the elections, and by the Roman proletariat, which had no wish to share its own lucrative privileges. Even the beneficiaries of the measure were suspicious: rich Latins and allies because their tenure of public land would fall for adjudication by the Gracchan land commission, poorer men because they feared conscription as Roman citizens, and would rather be given simple *provocatio* (the right of appeal against summary punishment of Roman magistrates), which, indeed, is what Fulvius had offered. The Senate, adroit in political manoeuvre, put forward a tribune of its own, M. Livius Drusus, to outbid Gracchus by making more palatable proposals (including, in the case of the allies, *provocatio*) – proposals which, once the crisis was over, they did not intend to implement. Their manoeuvre succeeded. Gracchus was not elected tribune for 121. Instead, in 121, a tribune moved the cancellation of the whole of his legislation. Disorder prevailed, and a public servant was murdered. Gracchus, Flaccus and their supporters seized the Aventine. The Senate met and passed a novel resolution, afterwards called 'the last decree', *senatus consultum ultimum*, empowering the consuls to take whatever measures they thought necessary for the restoration of law and order. Authority moved in to the attack. Flaccus, his two sons, Gracchus, and thousands of their supporters were killed before order was restored. In the following year Opimius, consul of 121, was charged with killing citizens in disregard of a citizen's right of appeal to the people, and was acquitted. The 'last decree', it seemed, was a stroke of genius the Senate had discovered a way of ridding itself of trouble-makers. It was even possible after a short interval to abolish the Gracchan land commission and to stop any further allocation of public land.

For the next quarter of a century nothing more was heard of the Italian problem. Interest switched to the provinces: to Numidia on the border of Africa, where Jugurtha dispossessed his two fellow rulers and in 112 B.C. killed a number of Roman businessmen resident in Cirta, and to Transcipline Gaul (Provence), a province since 121 B.C., which was invaded by a vast emigration of Cimbri and Teutones from central Europe. Whether or not Jugurtha's numerous epigrams about the readiness of leading Romans to take bribes are authentic, they have point. Both wars exhibited corruption and inefficiency in the field and were indeed the last serious wars in which the Romans sent out a fresh consul each year to command the army. At home there were commissions of inquiry; indeed in 109 four ex-consuls, one of them Opimius, were condemned for bribery and misconduct in the fight against Jugurtha, and in 103 treason (*maiestas*) was defined as an indictable offence. It was to have a long history. Under the aristocrat Q. Metellus Numidicus, consul in 109, success in Africa was at last in view, when he was superseded by C. Marius of Arpinum, a 'new man', consul in 107. With L. Sulla on his staff, Marius captured Jugurtha and ended the war in Africa in 105. He was at once transferred to the war in Gaul, elected consul continuously (contrary to constitutional precedent) from 104 to 100, and defeated the Teutones at Aix-en-Provence (Aquae Sextiae) in 102 and, with Q. Catulus, consul of 102, the Cimbri in Italy a year later.

The military genius of Marius (who, like Jugurtha, had served on Scipio's staff at Numantia) is no more to be disputed than is the fact that he was uncultured, spiteful, cruel and impolitic. In 107, before he took the field, he had altered the whole basis of military service and, doubtless without appreciating the fact, the whole balance of forces in politics as well. For, instead of calling up men from the five property classes of the censor's lists, he invited volunteers even from the unpropertied (the *proletarii*). These were to be the soldiers of Rome's future armies, men who signed on for a war and expected a gratuity, normally in land, on their discharge. For this, during the remainder of the Republic's history, they would depend on their general, to whom they were to offer, before and after their discharge, the kind of political support which an aristocrat was accustomed to receive from the clients of his family and its friends.

Marius' African legions were settled in North Africa when the war was over. In 100 B.C. the tribune L. Appuleius Saturninus moved bills to settle other veterans on land taken from the Cimbri in Gaul, and to dispatch colonies to Sicily, Achaea and Macedonia. The Optimates, hostile always to land allotments, opposed the Gallic bill, and Metellus Numidicus, who refused to take the oath to observe it, was forced into exile. The elections followed, with Saturninus standing again for the tribunate and his associate, the praetor Glaucia, for the consulship. A rival candidate to Glaucia was murdered, and the events of 121 B.C. were re-enacted – turbulent rioting and the Senate's retort, the 'last decree'. Marius, as consul, was forced to act against

Saturninus and Glaucia who, in part at least of their legislation, had worked in his interest. They were arrested on the Capitol and locked in the Senate House. There – but not by Marius' act – they were murdered. The Senate seems to have ruled that Saturninus' legislation was passed unconstitutionally; so it was not put into operation. The veterans may have received money for the purchase of land.

This in 100 B.C. In 91 history came to life again in the person of an imaginative young aristocrat, the tribune M. Livius Drusus, a very different man from his father, who was the Senate's catspaw against Gaius Gracchus. His sister's blood was to descend by her first marriage to Marcus Brutus, her grandson, and by her second marriage to the younger Cato, her son. Drusus proposed the foundation of coloniese voted by his father but never dispatched. He sought to strengthen the Senate against the Equites, but to do this by a compromise, drafting three hundred Equites into the Senate, to double its size, and then replacing Equites by senators on the juries of the extortion court, reform of which seemed urgent after the condemnation in the previous year of an administrator in Asia whose only crime was his integrity. More important, Drusus proposed the extension of the full franchise to Rome's Italian allies, among whose leaders he had personal friends. Suspicions were easily roused against these proposals which the conservative aristocracy particularly disliked. Drusus' measures were rescinded on technical grounds and his own sudden death raised suspicion of murder. Events now moved with disastrous speed. The Italians, whose ambitions had been frustrated for thirty-five years and who were particularly incensed by a tactless ruling of the consuls of 95 B.C., broke, in the south and east of the peninsula, into open revolt. The Marsi and Samnites took the lead. Corfinium was their capital, seat of a government which copied the Roman. The Roman government itself acted quickly. Each of the consuls of 90 B.C. took the field with an army, Marius serving as subordinate commander, and, to arrest the spread of the revolt, citizenship was offered (two years too late) to states which did not join the insurgents. By 89 the back of the revolt (the Social War) was broken and Roman citizenship conceded to all Italians as far north as the river Po.

The settlement was timely, for in 88 Mithridates, King of Pontus, whose activities had caused alarm for some years, invaded the province of Asia and 80,000 Romans, business men for the most part, were murdered. The province of Asia – and therefore the conduct of the war – had already been allotted to the consul L. Cornelius Sulla, a moneyless libertine with strongly conservative inclinations, member of a noble but recently undistinguished family. He had a good military record, both under Marius in Africa and in the Social War. In this crisis the tribune P. Sulpicius Rufus, an aristocrat and friend of Livius Drusus, proposed, against a mean Optimate move to nullify the voting power of the newly enfranchised Italians by enrolling them in only a small number of Roman tribes, that they should be distributed among all the tribes; and, with the strong support of the business men, that Marius (now close on seventy years old) should replace Sulla as commander in the war against Mithridates. After scenes of disorder in the city, Sulla joined his army in Campania and, to the horror of his officers, marched on Rome and took military possession of the city. Sulpicius was killed. Marius, declared an exile, escaped to Africa. After passing measures to establish firm senatorial control of government, Sulla crossed with his army to Greece. In Italy his fellow consul was murdered by his troops and in the following year L. Cornelius Cinna, discharged from his consulship and even deprived of citizenship, then copied the example of Sulla and captured Rome by arms, with the help of Marius, who was recalled and became consul with him – for the seventh time – in 86. Their political opponents, men of great distinction like M. Antonius (grandfather of Mark Antony) and Q. Catulus, who had commanded with Marius against the Cimbri, were murdered. After which, mercifully, Marius died. For four years the Populares (with Cinna as consul for four years running, until his army killed him) controlled the government, but were unable to supersede Sulla in his military command because armies, thanks to Marius, were now personal armies, and Sulla's troops were not prepared, in their own interest, to desert their general.

Meanwhile Sulla defeated an army of Mithridates in Greece (capturing Athens by siege and acquiring, by whatever means, the manuscripts of Aristotle) and made peace with him. He returned to Italy in 83 B.C. and by the end of 82 had captured Rome and defeated the government's forces (killing Marius' son, their last commander). He was unconstitutionally nominated to an unconstitutional office, to be 'Dictator for the revision of the constitution. A hideous massacre of his opponents followed; their property was sold by auction, one of the profiteers in this traffic being M. Licinius Crassus, by whose avarice even Sulla was shocked; Crassus' father and brother had been Marius' victims in early 86. A young man, only twenty-four years old in 82, who raised his own army on behalf of Sulla and whom Sulla employed to recover Sicily and Africa from their Marian governors, was Cn. Pompeius. Another officer who served under Sulla in the east, and won his trust to a unique degree, was L. Lucullus.

Sulla was statesman enough to accept the division of the new citizens among all the thirty-five tribes. He established his soldiers in colonies, largely on confiscated land – at Pompeii, for instance, and at Fiesole (Faesulae). He increased the number of permanent criminal courts – one of the new courts being concerned with treason, which was now carefully defined to cover any act of insubordination on the part of a proconsul. Senators once again were to be jurymen. He doubled the size of the Senate, and made recruitment to it automatic, through the annual election of quaestors, whose number was raised to twenty. These measures showed admirable statesmanship. He gave the Senate a stranglehold on government, in particular by emasculating the tribunate, leaving it with no independent function except the primitive right of intervening, in answer to appeal, to save a plebeian's life. He took the name of Felix, to mark the favour of the gods, which he had enjoyed; and then in 79, like the enigma which he had always been, he resigned the dictatorship, returned to the raffish private life from which he had emerged and a year later he died.

The revived senatorial government had a life of ten years. It failed partly because, after the successive massacres of the eighties, there were no elder statesmen to guide its deliberations and partly because, given the history of the tribunate as a 'popular' office, it was impossible to suppress it, as Sulla had tried to do. Aemilius Lepidus, consul in 78 B.C., father of the later Triumvir, defied the government, and so did Q. Sertorius, a Marian officer who, with his supporters, set up a rival government in Spain. Pompey was appointed with special (proconsular) powers to deal with both insurgents. He returned, after victory in Spain, to suppress the last of the slaves, who had joined in the alarming revolt of Spartacus, against whom Crassus had been fighting. At the end of 71 B.C. he celebrated his second triumph, though he was not yet a senator; and was elected consul with Crassus for 70, with a programme to rescind the most offensive of Sulla's reforms. The powers of the tribunes were fully restored and, after the scandalous revelations in the trial of Verres for extortion as governor of Sicily, the Senate lost its exclusive control of the permanent courts; juries for the future were to be partly senators and partly Equites.

Pompey was already Pompey the Great (Pompeius Magnus), so called, probably, because he was thought to look like Alexander. His career – a succession of outstanding military successes achieved before he entered the Senate – was without precedent, and the Optimates already regarded him with apprehension. Crassus, nine years his senior, had, since Sulla's time, been intensely jealous of his success.

For the remainder of the Republic the issues on which there was division in politics were no longer deep questions of principle, as with the Gracchi and the younger Drusus they had been. The severe republicanism of Cato, the pleadings for orderly and balanced government made by Cicero in his speeches and writings and the idealism of M. Brutus were not the determining forces of history. Instead events moved in the direction to which Marius' reforms and Sulla's career had pointed: towards the conflict of great army commanders and the personal rule of the ultimate victor. The restored power of the tribunes was chiefly exercised in the interest of the great generals. Since voting took place still in Rome, the votes of the newly enfranchised Italians counted for little, and it was not until the Empire that leading Italians found their way into the Roman governing class.

In 74 B.C. King Nicomedes of Bithynia had died. His kingdom, which he bequeathed to Rome, was at once invaded by Mithridates. Once again there was war in the east, and Lucullus was sent out in command. Though successful at first, he could not finish the war off and, when discipline in his army broke down, he was replaced as commander by a consul of 67 B.C.; and in this same year Pompey was given a special commission with very wide powers for three years to deal with piracy, which had been rampant in the Mediterranean for the past forty years, to the detriment of Roman business interests, except those of the slave-dealers. Both these proposals came from a tribune Gabinius and were carried in the popular assembly. Pompey concluded his task in a mere three months; with typical efficiency he divided the Mediterranean into areas, and organized a 'sweep' of each by his subordinates. In 66, by another tribunician bill, he was given command in the war against Mithridates. By 63 Mithridates was dead and the war was won. The Empire was enlarged by two new provinces, Bithynia-Pontus and Syria, and the territory of Cilicia was greatly increased.

Optimate politicians, whose political authority suffered severely from the failure of Lucullus, opposed both Pompey's commands, harking back to the outmoded practice by which the command in foreign wars was held by one or other of the consuls of the year. Defeated in this, they took a risk, and a successful risk, in supporting for the consulship of 63 a 'new man', a native of Arpinum (like Marius), and a man whose career to date had been that of a Popularis; for M. Tullius Cicero had as a young man spoken in the courts, however tactfully, against Sulla; he had prosecuted Verres in 70 and he had supported the proposal to give Pompey the command against Mithridates. They backed him because of rumours that Catiline, who might have expected their support, was plotting revolution. They were right; and by the autumn of 63 Cicero had unmasked a plot by which the city of Rome was to be seized by a *coup d'état*, while in the north an army of Sulla's now penniless veterans at Fiesole took the field.

On 21 October the 'last decree' was passed; Catiline left Rome for the north and incriminating evidence was secured against five of his associates in Rome, one of them a praetor. The men were arrested and, two days later, on 5 December, the Senate voted against the proposal of the praetor-elect, Julius Caesar, that they should be imprisoned, and in favour of Cato's motion that they should be put to death. They were executed on Cicero's instruction that night. The Populares had never recognized the validity of the 'last decree' which, and not the Senate's vote, was Cicero's authority for executing Roman citizens without trial and, though at the time he had the fullest support of every section of Roman society, the legality of his act was very soon a matter of hot dispute; for it could reasonably be claimed that, with the arrest of the conspirators, the crisis in Rome, and with it the emergency power of the consul, were at an end. Hastily raised armies commanded, among others, by Cicero's consular colleague, defeated Catiline and his army at Pistoia in January 62.

At the end of 62, a year of considerable disturbance in Rome, Pompey landed with his army at Brindisi. Despite hysterical Optimate fears that, like Sulla, he would march with it on Rome, he dismissed his troops on landing, and entered Rome in triumph the following year. A display of political ineptitude followed. Cato opposed a concession to the Asiatic tax farmers for which Crassus, as their patron, asked. Pompey arrogantly refused to agree to the Senate's discussing his eastern settlement; and the Senate countered by refusing to ratify that settlement or to make allotments to his troops. Caesar, as adroit in politics as in all else, secured election to the consulship of 59 B.C. with the support of Pompey's and Crassus' backers as well as his own, on the understanding that Pompey's acts should be ratified, Crassus' request met, and he himself should be given a great military command in the north, where the presence of Ariovistus and large numbers of his German followers on the border of Transalpine Gaul and the threat of a large migration of Helvetii from Lake Geneva to the west recalled the menace of the Cimbri and Teutones fifty years earlier. The measures were passed : an agrarian bill in the interest of Pompey's veterans, in circumstances of

violence and disorder, in which Caesar's Optimate colleague
Bibulus was insulted and injured; and the other measures in disregard of a religious veto which Bibulus interposed. This resolution – indeed, illegality – was as typical of Caesar as it was
untypical of Pompey; its shadow lay over the politics of the remainder of the fifties. The political association of the Three, so
far from being a temporary convenience, had now, in the interest of all of them, to be maintained. Pompey, moreover, was
married in 59 to Caesar's daughter Julia. At the same time Optimate politicians hoped to dissociate Pompey from Caesar by suggesting that the legislation of 59 should be repealed on the ground
of illegality, but that those measures which were in Pompey's
interest (but not the rest) should be re-enacted with full legality.

As tribune in 58 B.C. Publius Clodius, who represented Caesar's
interest in Rome, and who for three year had been a personal
enemy of Cicero, raised the question of the execution of Catiline's associates, moving a bill that anyone who had executed
a Roman citizen without trial should be exiled. Without waiting for a summons, Cicero retired into exile across the Adriatic.
He was recalled in August 57, partly because of the general
offensiveness and lawlessness of Clodius' behaviour, but also
because the tribune T. Annius Milo, a supporter of Cicero, had
challenged Clodius and beaten him at his own game, by organizing an even better gang of terrorists. Pompey, who lived
in morbid fear of assassination by Clodius' gangsters, disregarded
Cicero's plight in 58, but co-operated in his recall. The Senate gave
him, on Cicero's motion, a five-year commission, with a staff and
troops, to organize the corn supply of Rome. With Cicero back,
the hopes of driving a wedge between Caesar and Pompey increased. But once again Caesar was on the alert. He met Crassus
and Pompey at Luca in 56; they agreed that Caesar's five-year
command in Gaul should be extended for a further five years;
that Pompey should be given the government of Spain for five
years, and Crassus the government of Syria for the same period.
Pompey and Crassus were to be consuls in 55.

In the north, taking frequent risks and trusting always in his
fortune, Caesar thundered on from success to success. Ariovistus

and the Helvetii were disposed of in 58. The whole of Gaul seemed to be mastered in the following two years. From 55 to 53 he was twice for short periods in Britain and twice across the Rhine in Germany. But already there were signs of trouble, and in 52 a full-scale rebellion broke out, under the inspired leadership of Vercingetorix. By the capture of Alesia and the surrender of Vercingetorix at the end of 52 the back of the revolt was broken. Meanwhile Crassus had perished at Carrhae in 53, in an inept attempt to invade Parthia, and Pompey's personal bond with Caesar was cut when Julia died in 54.

In 54 and 53 intrigue, bribery and street fighting produced something like anarchy in Rome; in neither year could the elections take place. Pompey stayed outside the city because of his military command, but did not leave Italy for Spain. The Optimates feared Caesar's return; yet, in view of his past, were reluctant to make an ally of Pompey. Pompey himself was as enigmatic and maladroit as, in politics, he always had been. Catastrophe came in January 52, when Milo and his gang killed Clodius at Bovillae, south of Rome, and Clodius' supporters carried his corpse into the Senate house and, for its cremation, burnt the Senate house down. The 'last decree' was passed, and Pompey appointed sole consul. He acted for once with resolution in politics, packing the court with troops, to ensure that Milo was condemned for Clodius' murder.

The final crisis which precipitated civil war arose over a formal matter: whether Caesar, intending to be consul again in 48 should, contrary to custom, be excused attendance at the elections in 49. For he was afraid that, if he surrendered his command and entered the city for the elections, he would be debarred from candidature through prosecution for his illegalities as consul. The issue seemed solved when, by a bill of the ten tribunes, passed with Pompey's backing, leave was given in 52; but the next year the Optimates showed that they did not intend to honour the undertaking. Caesar replied, through a subservient tribune, by vetoing all provincial appointments, so that he could not be superseded in Gaul. Had Pompey showed willingness, negotiation was possible. Instead he accepted a melodramatic commission from the consuls of 50 to save the State. The 'last decree' was passed. Antony and another tribune were warned on 7 January 49. They fled to Caesar who, with this as his feeble pretext, then invaded Italy. Pompey took a correct military decision, to evacuate Italy with the government and its troops (who were no match for Caesar's trained legions) from Brindisi, and to build up resistance across the Adriatic which, without a fleet, Caesar could not immediately cross.

While transport was assembling, Caesar, acting with almost superhuman speed, marched to Spain and defeated Pompey's armies there; he returned and crossed the Adriatic late in the year, and defeated Pompey at Pharsalus in Thessaly in 48. He followed him to Egypt (where Pompey was murdered), captured Alexandria, became Cleopatra's lover, left her there as queen, defeated Mithridates' son Pharnaces (who had taken advantage of the civil war to extend his territory at Rome's expense) at Zela in 47, the reconstituted republican army at Thapsus in North Africa in 46, and Pompey's sons at Munda in Spain in 45. He visited Rome only for short intervals between campaigns, leaving its administration to consuls and prefects, who were his nominees, and to his Master of the Horse; for at Rome he was proclaimed Dictator in 48, given the dictatorship for ten years after Thapsus and, at the end, made perpetual dictator. The cowed and subservient Senate, reinforced to a total strength of nine hundred by his own nominees, voted him honours indiscriminately, human and divine, as if he was a Hellenistic king. He returned to Rome in October 45, intending to leave in March 44 for an eastern campaign to avenge the defeat of Crassus at Carrhae; and the five months before he was murdered on the Ides of March 44 were the only substantial period of his residence in Rome since 59. A number of healthy administrative reforms had been made under his authority : land allotments for his veterans, on land bought in the open market; a reasonable settlement of the chronic problem of money-lenders and debtors; an adjustment of the calendar (whose benefits we enjoy today). He was an autocrat such as Rome had not seen since the Republic was established. His behaviour towards the Senate was frequently offensive and, in view of the honours which he accepted (a statue in the temple of Quirinus, for instance) it was easy to forget the honours which he refused (the crown which Antony offered him at the Lupercalia in 44) and also the fact that his 'clemency' was anything but an idle boast, for, unlike Marius and Sulla, he was never vindictive, and there were no proscriptions of his opponents. Indeed, as Cicero and Brutus, his murderer, had good cause to know, he was anxious, like few men in history, to pardon those who had fought against him. Whether, in defiance of the whole of Roman tradition, he contemplated a continuance of undisguised authoritarian government, even to the extent of accepting divine honours such as had been lavished on Hellenistic kings, or on the other hand regarded the constitutional problem as one which could be shelved until his return from the east, is a question which can never be solved. Certainly there was nothing at all to suggest that he intended to restore republican government; and this was why Brutus, in a conspiracy of sixty persons, killed him, under Pompey's statue at a meeting of the Senate, three days before he was due to leave for the east.

So far from receiving public acclamation, his murderers were from the start in danger of their lives. When the Senate met on 17 March, they were granted an amnesty. Antony, who had been joint consul with Caesar in 44, with Lepidus, Caesar's Master of the Horse, controlled the situation. So far from Caesar's memory being damned, his acts were confirmed, and Antony was given authority to pronounce on their genuineness. The creaking machinery of republicanism started to work again; and Cicero, who had not been brought into the conspiracy, was ready to play the part of elder statesman. In April from Caesar's camp across the Adriatic arrived a youth of eighteen, Caesar's great-nephew Octavian, who was Caesar's heir and adopted son by his will.

To Antony, already discharging the functions of Caesar's heir and squandering the treasure which he had left, Octavian's arrival was anything but welcome. The Optimates, therefore, who was already frightened of Antony's pretensions, opened their arms to Octavian, without facing the fact that he could never be reconciled to Caesar's murderers. To Brutus and Cassius this was very evident; they were out of Rome, and in the summer they left for the east, where Brutus took possession of Macedonia and Cassius of Syria. In June, through a bill of the people, Antony secured Cisalpine Gaul, with four of Caesar's legions. In October, behaving as treasonably as Catiline, Octavian raised a private army, from Caesar's veterans in Campania, with the addition of two legions who deserted Antony. So powerful, with Caesar's soldiers, was the magnetism of Caesar's name. The senators, Cicero in particular, were deceived by Octavian's youth into thinking that he could be used, and then dispensed with. Among the credulous masses his prestige was enhanced by the unanticipated appearance of a comet at games held in Caesar's honour in July, visible evidence (it was thought) of Caesar's godhead.

Antony went north to his province, pursued by Cicero's strident Philippic orations; but Cicero failed to induce the Senate to declare him a public enemy. However, the consuls of 43, with Octavian as a commissioned subordinate, went north, with Octavian's army, to evict Antony from his province, and in April he was defeated, but escaped over the Alps, and won over the republican armies, one of them commanded by Lepidus, in Gaul and Spain. Octavian was now prepared to drop the mask. Both consuls having died, he marched with his army on Rome, and demanded the consulship. He then met Antony and Lepidus at Bologna (Bononia) and they formed the Triumvirate, a dictatorship of three men, subsequently legalized at Rome, to last for five years. The Triumvirate was inaugurated by proscriptions as vile as Sulla's. Cicero, whom Octavian had so easily deceived, was one of the first victims.

The elimination of the tyrannicides at Philippi in Macedonia in 42 was the Trumvirs' next successful operation. Lepidus was overshadowed by his colleagues and in the end discounted. The threat of a breach between Octavian and Antony was averted at Brindisi in 40 (when Antony, recently widowed, married Octavian's sister Octavia) and again in 37, when the Triumvirate was renewed for five years at Tarentum. Antony was in the east, increasingly embroiled with Cleopatra (whom in 37 he married); his invasion of Parthia in 36 was a disastrous failure. Octavian in Italy had been confronted after Philippi with great difficulty in the settlement of discharged soldiers on the land, and even had to fight Antony's wife Fulvia and his brother, who made capital out of the soldiers' grievances; and in Rome itself there was great discontent because of the interruption of the corn supply through the piracy of Pompey's surviving son, Sextus Pompeius whom, after an attempted reconciliation in 39, M. Agrippa defeated in the naval battle of Naulochus in 36. After this a virulent war of propaganda developed. Octavian made capital of Antony's desertion of Octavia and suggested that, with Cleopatra as his queen, he planned to turn the Roman Empire into a revived Hellenistic monarchy, with its capital in Egypt. Antony and Cleopatra claimed that her son Caesarion was Caesar's son by birth, not merely (like Octavian) by adoption. In 32 both consuls and many senators left Rome for the east to join Antony, but were shocked on arrival to find how strong a hold Cleopatra had over him. In Italy and the western provinces a carefully contrived oath of allegiance was taken, with some show of spontaneity, to Octavian, and war was declared on Cleopatra. She and Antony were defeated at Actium in north-west Greece in 31, and escaped to Egypt, followed by Octavian. There in 30 they committed suicide, Antony before Octavian's arrival, Cleopatra after.

BIBLIOGRAPHY

Smith, R. E., *The Failure of the Roman Republic*, Cambridge University Press, 1955. In outlook and sympathy in disagreement with the account given in this chapter.

Scullard, H. H., *From the Gracchi to Nero*, Methuen, 1959.

Syme, Ronald, *The Roman Revolution*, Oxford University Press, 1939.

Taylor, Lily Ross, *Party Politics in the Age of Caesar*, University of California Press, 1949.

The last three books are available in paperback editions.

4

THE LAST CRISIS:
THE ROMAN EMPIRE TO ITS DECLINE

A. H. M. Jones

BY his victory over Antony at Actium (31 B.C.) Imperator Caesar, as Julius Caesar's great-nephew and heir then called himself, became the sole ruler of the Roman Empire. Being, however, a man of singular political tact, he soon realized that he would not long remain so unless he did something to placate the strong republican sentiment of the Roman aristocracy and the Italian middle class. In 28 B.C. he with his fellow consul Agrippa, having obtained censorial powers, revised the roll of the Senate, purging it of many unworthy members enrolled by Caesar and the triumvirs and reducing it to the establishment of six hundred which Sulla had fixed. Having thus restored the Senate to its republican shape, the young Caesar on 1 January 27 B.C. solemnly renounced all his extraordinary powers and restored the Republic. The Senate in gratitude voted him the name of Augustus, by which he was henceforth known and which all his successors bore, and begged him not to desert the Republic, pressing powers upon him; but he consented only to receive for ten years a huge province comprising most of the unsettled areas which required military force to subdue or protect them – Spain (except for the peaceful province of Baetica in the south), Gaul, Syria and Egypt. Such a grant of a large province for a term of years had many precedents in the commands given to Pompey, Caesar and Crassus. It was exceptional only in that, being so much larger, it gave Augustus command of nearly all the armed forces of the Republic.

Henceforth the normal machinery of the Republic functioned again. The people elected the annual magistrates; the magistrates resumed their proper powers and functions; proconsuls went out each year to govern the provinces which were not included in

Augustus' special command. Augustus might normally have been expected when his consulship expired to go and govern his provinces as proconsul, but he continued to stand for the consulate and was re-elected year after year – he had been consul continuously since 31 B.C. This situation caused mounting dissatisfaction amongst the Roman aristocracy, who found their chances of achieving the consulate halved, and amongst the Italian upper and middle classes generally; for it was quite contrary to republican law and tradition that the consulship should be repeated save at long intervals, and the only precedent was Marius, an equivocal figure. In 23 B.C. dissatisfaction came to a head in a conspiracy headed by his fellow consul of that year and Augustus saw that he must make a further concession to republican sentiment. In the middle of the year he resigned the consulship, never to hold it again save on two special occasions. In compensation he was given a *maius imperium* over all other proconsuls and the tribunician power, the rights of a tribune of the plebs. This power does not seem to have been of much practical importance, and was perhaps mainly intended to symbolize the popular support which he enjoyed and to reassure the common people that he would protect their liberties. In the following year he left Rome and spent the next three years in various parts of his great province. The Roman people did not take kindly to his withdrawal, repeatedly offering him the dictatorship or a perpetual consulship and electing him consul although he was not a candidate. The Senate was in a humbled mood when Augustus eventually returned in 19 B.C., and if they did not formally bestow consular powers upon him, allowed him to assume and exercise them. At any rate from 19 B.C. Augustus raised and maintained troops and exercised capital jurisdiction in Rome and Italy, just like a consul, and exercised the ancient consular prerogative of appointing a prefect of the city of Rome during his absence.

The constitutional structure of the principate was virtually complete and underwent very little subsequent change. In 12 B.C. Augustus was elected to the religious office of *Pontifex Maximus*, which all his successors held until Gratian and Theodosius dropped it as being pagan. But this honour did not add to his powers. Augustus had his province renewed for successive terms of ten or five years, but his successor Tiberius and all subsequent Emperors received all their powers for life. Augustus seems to have received censorial powers on two or three occasions, and Claudius and Vespasian held the office of censor, while Domitian declared himself perpetual censor. Subsequent Emperors exercised certain censorial functions, notably that of adding new members to the Senate and enrolling the members of the equestrian order, without any specific grant of powers.

The power of the Emperor grew, but it grew in the main imperceptibly, as precedents hardened into custom, and as more and more functions and provinces passed into his hands. Augustus as a gesture in 23 B.C. handed back to the Senate two pacified provinces, southern Gaul (Narbonensis) and Cyprus, but apart from this the number of public provinces never grew and was at times reduced, while all newly conquered territories, and annexed client kingdoms went to swell the Emperor's share. By the end of Augustus' reign only one legion, that stationed in Africa, was not under his command; when Gaius was Emperor, he took this legion over.

While Augustus possessed very wide constitutional powers, which gave him the necessary authority to command the army, govern his own provinces, and intervene elsewhere when he thought it desirable, he preferred in the last case to use his *auctoritas*. This was the respect paid, according to republican tradition, to senior statesmen who had held the consulship and distinguished themselves in war and in the conduct of public affairs. Augustus possessed these qualifications in a unique degree – under the Republic there had been 'first men in the state' (*principes civitatis*); he was *the* princeps and was commonly so called unofficially – and his opinions, whether delivered in a senatorial debate or addressed to individual magistrates, thus acquired exceptional weight. He had little need to propose resolutions to the Senate or laws to the people, since the consuls normally acted on his suggestion, nor did he need to exercise his *maius imperium*, since proconsuls accepted his advice. The accumulated *auctoritas* of the Emperors grew and hardened into customary powers. It seems to have been in this way that the Emperor's support of certain candidates for magistrates became a formal power of recommendation (*commendatio*) whereby he nominated them.

Besides his constitutional powers and his *auctoritas* other more imponderable elements contributed to the imperial supremacy. In the year 32 B.C. the young Caesar, preparing for his final struggle with Antony, had organized a 'spontaneous' oath of personal loyalty to himself by all the inhabitants of Italy and the western provinces which he then controlled. A similar oath to himself and to his family was administered later to the eastern provinces and to new provinces as they were annexed. This oath was taken by all the inhabitants of the Empire to Tiberius and subsequent Emperors on their accession, and had by the later years of the first century become an annual event. To the ordinary provincial and to the common people of Italy, and above all to the army, this personal oath of loyalty probably meant more than all the constitutional powers of the Emperor.

Finally the Hellenized inhabitants of the eastern provinces, who had in the recent past worshipped their kings, eagerly deified Augustus as soon as he became master of the Roman world. Remembering the resentment that Caesar's seeming acceptance of divine honours had caused amongst the Italian upper class, Augustus dealt warily with the worship offered to him. Since his adoptive father had been officially deified posthumously, he built him a temple and was proud to call himself 'son of the divine (Julius)', but he countenanced no worship of himself by Roman citizens. In the provinces he organized an official cult, conducted by a council of the cities of each province, but insisted that Rome be coupled with his name. This cult of Rome and Augustus was eagerly taken up by all the eastern provinces and Augustus seems to have appreciated its value in expressing and stimulating some kind of imperial loyalty; for he introduced it into Gaul and some other western provinces, where there seems to have been no spontaneous demand for it.*

*See further, pp. 189f.

Augustus was himself officially deified after his death, and so were his successors, except for those whose conduct had outraged the Senate. With a few aberrant exceptions, such as Gaius and Domitian, living Emperors did not officially demand worship from the Roman State until the latter part of the third century.

The Emperor was all things to all men. To senators and the Italian upper classes he was the *princeps*, the great general and statesman who commanded the armed forces of the Republic and guided its councils by his *auctoritas*. To the soldiers he was their *imperator*, and it was perhaps to emphasize this aspect of his position that the young Caesar, even before he became Augustus, adopted Imperator as his first name (*praenomen*); it was not used by his immediate successors but became a regular part of the imperial nomenclature from Nero onwards. To the ordinary people, both in Italy and the provinces, he was the leader to whom they swore allegiance. And to most provincials, especially to those of the Greek East, he was king and god.

The succession proved an intractable problem which was never quite satisfactorily solved. Popular sentiment in the army and the provinces and the lower classes generally favoured the hereditary principle. Augustus himself had fought his way to power as the adopted son of Caesar, and such was the prestige of that name that later Emperors from Claudius onwards, who had no claim to it by descent or adoption, nevertheless assumed it and it eventually became an imperial title. But constitutionally the powers which made up the imperial office were granted by the Senate and people to an individual for life, and the principate thus theoretically ceased to exist every time the Emperor died. There was moreover among senators a certain hostility to the hereditary principle. The Empire, they felt, should not pass like private property to a dead Emperor's son, who was not necessarily the best qualified to rule. The *princeps* should be the best man in the state, in other words a senior and distinguished senator, approved if not chosen by the Senate as a whole.

Augustus evidently considered that the stability of the Empire required that he should somehow bequeath his position to an heir of his name and family. Unfortunately he had no son, and his daughter's sons, whom he adopted as his own and raised to high positions early in life, both died young. He had to fall back upon his stepson, Tiberius, whom he adopted when he was already middle-aged and made his colleague in the imperial powers. Tiberius succeeded both as Augustus' son, and thus heir to the loyalty of the army and people, and as already vested with most of the powers of the imperial office.

Augustus not only achieved a final solution of the constitutional problem. He greatly extended the bounds of the Empire and he reorganized the army and the administration on lines which were to endure for three centuries. Militarily his greatest achievement was the establishment of the northern frontier. Pompey had completed the conquest of Asia Minor and annexed Syria; Caesar had reduced Gaul. But between these areas the land immediately north of Italy and the whole Balkan peninsula except for the coastal strip of Dalmatia and Macedonia and Greece were unsubdued. By the reduction of the Alpine tribes and of Pannonia and Moesia Augustus advanced the frontier to the Danube. He also fought many campaigns to conquer the German tribes up to the Elbe, but after a severe defeat in A.D. 9 he abandoned this project and fixed the frontiers on the Rhine and the Danube.

He finally converted the Roman army into a standing professional force. Of the vast forces under his command after Actium he retained twenty-five legions, which became permanent units – some continued to exist down to the sixth century. The legionaries were mainly obtained by voluntary recruitment and were signed on for a regular period, at first sixteen, later twenty years. The problem of their bounties on discharge, which the Republic had left unsolved and which had given rise to recurrent political crises, he solved in A.D. 6 by the establishment of a special military treasury, which bought land for allotments to discharged soldiers or paid them cash bonuses. This new treasury was mainly fed by a new tax on Roman citizens, the five per cent tax on inheritances. Augustus also converted the hitherto casual levies raised from the provincials into regular and permanent units of infantry (*cohortes*) and cavalry (*alae*). Finally he established at Rome itself a permanent force, the praetorian cohorts, commanded by an equestrian officer, the praetorian prefect.

The public provinces continued to be governed by proconsuls (ex-praetors and ex-consuls) as under the Republic. His own provinces Augustus placed under *legati* of consular or praetorian rank, whom he himself chose and who served for such periods as he determined, normally for several years. Consulars were employed in the more important provinces whose garrisons comprised several legions, praetorians in provinces which were ungarrisoned or had one legion only. The only important exception to this rule was Egypt, which was too rich in corn and money and strategically too well protected by its deserts to be entrusted to a senator, a possible rival. It was governed by a prefect of equestrian rank, who was by a special law given the powers of a proconsul. A few small and unruly provinces, such as the Alpine districts, were ruled by military governors of equestrian rank also called prefects. To manage his financial interests in the provinces Augustus employed what were technically private agents, *procuratores*, usually of equestrian rank but sometimes freedmen. These procurators in the public provinces were responsible only for the Emperor's extensive private estates, but in the imperial provinces they collected the taxes and paid the troops.

In the taxation of the Empire Augustus completed a reform begun by Caesar, abolishing the tithe system and substituting a tribute, consisting of a poll tax (*tributum capitis*) and a land tax (*tributum soli*). For the equitable assessment of these taxes a series of censuses were conducted throughout the provinces. The *publicani*, who had been the curse of the provinces under the Republic, were thus eliminated from the direct taxes, which were collected by the cities, and left only with the customs and the new inheritance tax.

Augustus also introduced many reforms into the administration of Rome itself, hitherto mismanaged by annual magistrates. For some departments, such as the aqueducts, he established permanent boards of senators (*curatores*); others such as the corn supply and the fire service he eventually took over himself and administered through equestrian prefects. For the maintenance of law and order he revived the obsolete office of prefect of the city. This officer was a senior senator, appointed by the Emperor, at first only temporarily during his absences from the capital but later permanently, and he had at his disposal a body of Roman troops, the urban cohorts.

Tiberius was an able and experienced general and a conscientious administrator, but he lacked Augustus' vast prestige, and he was a sour and unsociable character, utterly deficient in his predecessor's political tact. He was soon at odds with the Senate and died hated by the aristocracy. He had made no provision for a successor but the Senate promptly voted the imperial powers to the only surviving adult Julius Caesar, Tiberius' young great-nephew Gaius (commonly called Caligula). Gaius proved utterly irresponsible, if he did not actually become mentally unbalanced; and he was murdered after a four years' reign (A.D. 37–41). The Senate at first thought of restoring the Republic or at least of choosing an Emperor from amongst themselves, but the praetorians were determined that some member of the imperial family should succeed and they proclaimed Claudius, Tiberius' nephew and Gaius' uncle, who had been considered a backward boy and had hitherto played no part in public life; he had not even been adopted into the Julian family. Claudius accepted the nomination, giving a donative to the praetorians, and the Senate had perforce to vote him the imperial powers. Though lacking in dignity and tact and, it would seem, too much influenced by his wives and freedmen, Claudius (41–54) proved quite a shrewd and hard-working ruler. To give himself military prestige he undertook in 43 the conquest of Britain, a task which took several generations to complete. He was liberal in granting citizenship to provincials, notably by enfranchising members of the auxiliary units on completion of their twenty-five years' service. He seems also to have enlarged and reorganized the secretarial and financial staffs of the Emperor. Little is known of them prior to Claudius' reign, but Augustus and Tiberius had apparently employed their own slaves and freedmen to manage their immense official correspondence and the intricate accounts both of their huge private fortunes and of the public money which they handled. Under

Claudius a number of departments appear, headed by freedmen in charge of finance (*a rationibus*), correspondence (*ab epistulis*) and petitions (*a libellis*). These freedmen under Claudius achieved great power and were unwisely given public honours; they were not unnaturally hated by the senators, who were obliged to seek their good offices, and involved Claudius in great unpopularity.

Claudius was eventually poisoned by his wife Agrippina, who had prepared the way for the succession of her young son Nero (54–68). He had already received the proconsular *imperium* and was duly acclaimed by the praetorians and voted the rest of the imperial powers by the Senate. The government was at first carried on by his tutor, Seneca, and his praetorian prefect, Burrus, but when he threw off their control he proved utterly irresponsible. His only interests were in music and literature and he flagrantly neglected his public duties. Conspiracies were formed against him by senators and he subjected the Senate to a reign of terror. Eventually Galba, the governor of Spain, revolted and Nero committed suicide.

Up till now the loyalty of the troops had been to the family of Caesar, and as long as the Emperors could claim, even by the most tenuous link of adoption, to be Caesar's heirs, the army knew whom to obey. Now they were at sea, and not unnaturally ambitious men, particularly if they were in command of armies, exploited their bewilderment. The result was a round of civil wars. Otho, when Galba, whom he had backed, failed to adopt him as his heir, promoted a mutiny of the praetorians, who lynched Galba and proclaimed Otho. Next Vitellius, governor of Lower Germany, exploited the jealousy which the German legions felt for the pampered praetorians and was proclaimed Emperor by them. He captured Rome, but shortly afterwards Vespasian, commander of the forces engaged in the Jewish war, was proclaimed by the eastern legions. The Danube legions also rallied to him and conquered Rome for him.

Vespasian (69–79) was a man of humble origins, an experienced general and a man of great practical sense and financial ability. He restored the finances of the Empire, which had been shaken by Nero's extravagances and the civil wars, considerably increasing the rate of taxation in many provinces. He was determined to found a dynasty, and despite much opposition from the Senate carried the day, conferring the proconsular and tribunician powers on his son Titus. Titus died after two years' reign (79–81) and was succeeded by his brother Domitian. Domitian was a firm and able administrator but autocratic and suspicious. Relations between him and the Senate became increasingly embittered and eventually he was murdered.

The conspirators had ready a candidate for the throne who would be acceptable to the Senate, Nerva, a respectable senator of good if not very ancient ancestry, a distinguished lawyer, over sixty years of age, in fact a safe man. His reception by the army was more dubious, but the praetorian prefects, who were in the plot, managed to get the praetorian guard to proclaim him. About a year later the guard mutinied, demanding the punishment of Domitian's murderers, but Nerva saved himself by adopting as his son and heir one of the great army commanders, Trajan. Nerva died a year later. Trajan (98–117) was above all things a military man. Of his conquests Dacia, annexed in 106, was profitable, since it contained important gold mines, but its exposed strategic position eventually rendered it untenable; it was abandoned by Aurelian (270–5). In 113 Trajan opened his campaigns against Parthia and annexed Armenia and Mesopotamia. But the newly conquered provinces soon revolted, and at the same time a widespread rebellion broke out among the Jews of the eastern provinces. As he was returning to the west the Emperor died in Cilicia and it was announced that he had on his deathbed adopted Hadrian as his son.

Whether the official story was true or not, Hadrian was elected emperor without opposition. He promptly abandoned Trajan's eastern conquests, and spent the rest of his reign in consolidating and fortifying the frontiers of the Empire. Hadrian was a man of literary, artistic and antiquarian tastes, but with these graces he combined great administrative, legal and financial abilities and a high devotion to his imperial duties. He spent most of his reign in prolonged tours of the provinces in which he combined the business of inspection with the pleasure of sightseeing. Shortly before his death he adopted and associated with himself in the imperial office Antoninus Pius, whose reign (138–61) was uneventful, and he in his turn was succeeded by Marcus Aurelius (161–80), whom he had adopted in deference to Hadrian's wish. Marcus associated with himself as joint Augustus with equal powers his brother by adoption, Lucius, but the latter lived only eight more years, dying in 169. Marcus Aurelius was a deeply religious man, an adherent of the Stoic school of philosophy, and has left behind in his *Meditations* a vivid record of his spiritual life. He was a conscientious and devoted Emperor and he had to contend with many troubles. On his accession he was faced with a Parthian war. It was brought to a triumphant conclusion in 166, but the returning troops brought back with them a great plague which ravaged all the provinces of the Empire. At the same time the northern barbarians, who had long been quiescent, burst over the Danube and even invaded Italy. For the rest of his reign Marcus was constantly occupied with wars against the Germans and Sarmatians on the Danube front.

Since Nerva the problem of the succession had been solved by a compromise. The Emperor selected his successor and adopted him as his son; the Senate conferred upon him the imperial powers. Senators could accept this procedure, since in theory at any rate it embodied the Stoic theory that the best man should rule; the Emperor was presumed to be the best man and so was the man of his choice. In practice the Emperors so chosen cooperated with the Senate and were respectful of its dignity. For the army on the other hand the dynastic principle was maintained. Each Emperor was the son of his predecessor, and Marcus could claim four deified ancestors. The maintenance of the system depended, however, on the lucky chance of the Emperor's having no son, and unluckily Marcus Aurelius had a son, Commodus. He could hardly avoid nominating him his successor and advanced him to the rank of Augustus in 176, when he was only fifteen.

On Marcus' death in 180 Commodus, defying his senatorial advisers, made peace on not wholly satisfactory terms with the Germans and returned to Rome. His relations with the Senate were thus from the first strained and he proved to be an utterly irresponsible youth whose only interest was in gladiators and who left the government to favourites. He nevertheless lasted for twelve years, until he was murdered in 192. The conspirators again had ready a candidate acceptable to the Senate, Pertinax, an aged senator of humble birth but of long military and administrative experience. But once again the hereditary succession had been broken and the armies were restless. Pertinax was a severe disciplinarian and alienated the praetorian guard, who mutinied and lynched him and were then induced by vast donatives to acclaim a very wealthy senator, Didius Julianus. The commanders of the provincial armies were not inclined to acquiesce in this choice, nor were their troops. Septimus Severus, governor of upper Pannonia, was acclaimed by the armies of the Danube and the Rhine and, declaring himself the avenger of Pertinax and champion of the Senate, he marched on Rome and captured it, disbanded the praetorians and replaced them by men from his own armies. Meanwhile the eastern armies acclaimed the governor of Syria, Pescennius Niger. In the civil war which followed Severus was successful. He stayed two years in the east and on his return was faced with another pretender, Clodius Albinus, the governor of Britain, whom he defeated next spring. Discovering that Clodius Albinus had received help from many senators, he changed his policy towards the Senate. Many senators were executed, and their confiscated estates went to a new financial department, the *res privata* of the Emperor. At the same time Severus declared himself not only the son of Marcus Aurelius but the brother of Commodus, thereby bidding for the dynastic loyalty of the armies, whose goodwill he further conciliated by liberal donatives and a rise in pay and by authorizing them to contract legal marriages while serving.

Like Vespasian, Severus was determined to found a dynasty, and raised his elder son Caracalla to the rank of Augustus in 198, and his younger son Geta in 209. On their father's death in 211 the two brothers soon quarrelled and in the next year Caracalla murdered Geta. Caracalla is chiefly famous for the constitution which granted the Roman citizenship to all free inhabitants of the Roman Empire. This apparently liberal measure, which gave equality of status to all free persons and brought them all under Roman law, was, it would appear, a financial device, for it also made all the inhabitants of the Empire liable to the inheritance tax, now raised to ten per cent. For Caracalla was in great financial straits, having once again raised army pay. Detested by the Senate, he lasted only six years, being murdered in 217 by his praetorian prefect, Macrinus, whom the army of the east, unaware that he was responsible for Caracalla's death, proclaimed Emperor. But once again dynastic sentiment prevailed and the army deserted Macrinus for a young man who was high priest of the god Elagabalus at Emesa, a grandson of Severus' wife's sister and, it was alleged, the illegitimate son of Caracalla. Elagabalus, as he is commonly called, was a sexual pervert who flaunted his vices, and a devotee of his god, a meteoric stone which he carried to Rome and installed on the Palatine. After four years (218–22) his vagaries became so intolerable that his grandmother arranged for his assassination and for the accession of another of her grandsons, his cousin Alexander Severus. Alexander enjoyed a longer reign (222–35). He was personally inoffensive and he enjoyed the hereditary prestige of the Severi, and his grandmother and mother who ruled in his name took pains to placate the Senate by appointing a regency council of sixteen senators during his minority. Eventually, however, his military incapacity provoked one of his generals, Maximinus, to seize the throne.

Three years later the Senate gave a surprising demonstration of its latent strength. It gave its official blessing to the revolt of Gordian, proconsul of Africa, and his son Gordian II, and when they were promptly killed by the legate of Numidia, elected two Emperors, Balbinus and Pupienus, rallied the provincial governors and organized the defence of Italy against Maximinus. Aquileia held out for the Senate and Maximinus' besieging army was reduced to starvation and eventually killed their Emperor and submitted to those of the Senate.

The influence which the Senate continued to wield for so long in the government of the Empire is rather a mysterious phenomenon. As a corporation it exercised no real power, merely registering the enactments of the Emperor. It was moreover a timorous body, easily cowed into submission; yet few Emperors who defied it died in their beds. The Senate retained some measure of that prestige which the republican Senate had enjoyed; it formed public opinion among the upper classes as it has shaped our historical tradition. From its members moreover were drawn the governors of the provinces, and, what was more important, the commanders of the legions and the armies. An Emperor who outraged the Senate had cause to mistrust the loyalty of his generals.

The Senate maintained to a remarkable degree its traditional tone. It no longer expected to govern the Empire, but it expected the Emperor to treat it with courtesy and respect and to heed the advice of its more eminent members. It was a co-optative body, since it was, from the accession of Tiberius, the Senate which elected the twenty quaestors who were added to it each year. It was also to some extent an hereditary body, since sons of senators had the legal right to stand for the quaestorship. But as the senatorial aristocracy failed to reproduce itself and senatorial families tended to die out, there was a considerable influx of outsiders in order to keep numbers up, and this influx was controlled by the Emperor, whose permission was required for an outsider to stand for the quaestorship; the Emperor could also enrol older men directly into the Senate, giving them appropriate seniority. New men thus entered the Senate from an ever-widening area, first from the cities of Italy, then from the most Romanized provinces, Gallia Narbonensis, Spain, then Africa; a few members were also enrolled from the Greek-speaking provinces. The Senate thus came to be more and more representative of the Empire as a whole, though the east was grossly under-represented. It might have been expected that the Senate would have become more subservient to the Emperor, as it came to consist more and more of imperial nominees and their descendants. But in point of fact it retained its traditional tone. The new-comers were for the most part drawn from the same social class as the old members, the richer landed proprietors, and had the same educational and cultural background. Introduced as young men of twenty-five into the Senate, they not unnaturally adopted the traditional attitude of the venerable assembly.

From the end of the first century an equestrian civil service began to take shape. Augustus had employed men of equestrian rank, often ex-officers of the army, as his procurators in the provinces, as prefects of some minor provinces, and for a few posts of major importance, the prefectures of the fire brigade and the corn supply at Rome, the prefecture of the praetorian guard and the prefecture of Egypt. Gradually new posts were created, and from the time of Domitian the posts of *a rationibus, ab epistulis* and *a libellis,* hitherto entrusted to imperial freedmen, were filled by men of equestrian rank. A regular service was thus formed, which gradually expanded under the Antonine and Severan Emperors. A man normally began his career with three officer posts in the army, but civilians were also admitted, especially lawyers who had held the office of counsel for the treasury. The procuratorships were graded in four salary classes, which received 60,000, 100,000, 200,000 and 300,000 sesterces a year, and one or two posts were normally held in each class.

The equestrian service was neither hereditary nor aristocratic. Its members were selected and promoted by the Emperor, and the only qualifications for entry were free birth and a fairly modest fortune – 400,000 sesterces. Its members were more trusted by the Emperor than were senators, and it was for this reason that Augustus defied constitutional precedent in appointing equestrian officers to govern Egypt and to command the praetorians, his own bodyguard. It is significant that when Marcus Aurelius, whose relations with the Senate were friendly, stationed legions in Raetia and Noricum, he substituted senatorial legates for the previous equestrian procurators, but that Severus, when he annexed Mesopotamia, put it and its two legions under an equestrian prefect.

After the death of Alexander Severus, the last of the Severan house, in 235 no Emperor reigned long enough to establish a dynasty, and for the next fifty years there was a riot of military pronunciamentos. There were no less than twenty-two Emperors who were acknowledged as legitimate, and countless usurpers who ruled parts of the Empire for longer or shorter periods. There were constant civil wars and scarcely an Emperor died in his bed. At the same time the external enemies of the Empire became more aggressive. In the east the feeble Parthian dynasty of the Arsacids was in 226 overthrown by the vigorous Sassanids, who restored Zoroastrianism and revived Persian national sentiment. As successors of the Achaemenid dynasty they laid claim to Egypt and the Asiatic provinces of Rome, and at times asserted their claims by war. In Europe there were profound disturbances amongst German tribes hitherto unknown to the Romans, such as the Goths and Vandals, who had been trekking southward from their homes on the Baltic and now appeared on the Danube and invaded the Balkans and Asia Minor. On the Rhine the old enemies of Rome, pushed on from the rear, became more aggressive, grouping themselves in two great confederations, the Franks and the Alamans.

Eventually a series of soldier-emperors, of whom the most notable were Aurelian (270-5) and Probus (276-82), were able to restore the unity of the Empire and to beat back the invaders; the old frontiers were restored save that the Agri Decumates between the head waters of the Rhine and the Danube and the outlying province of Dacia north of the lower Danube had to be abandoned. The Empire was, however, terribly exhausted by the civil wars and invasions of the past forty years. The population, greatly reduced by the great plague which had swept the Empire under Marcus Aurelius (165-6), failed to recover, checked by recurrences of the plague and the slaughter and famines consequent on the constant wars. The finances of the Empire were moreover utterly disorganized. The Severan Emperors, in order to find money for the increase of army pay which they granted, had begun to debase the silver currency. By the third quarter of the third century the silver coins had become copper pieces washed in silver and issues of gold had virtually ceased. There was a vast inflation; by the end of the third century prices had risen to two hundred times the second-century level. This proved disastrous for the inflexible financial system of the Empire, where the principal taxes were fixed money payments. Somehow the government had to feed and clothe the troops, and it fell back on making requisitions (*indictiones*) of foodstuffs and clothing and whatever else it required and supplying the troops in kind.

During this period the tension between the Emperors and the Senate came to a head. Gallienus, who is represented in the senatorial tradition as a worthless idler, but who nevertheless managed to reign for fifteen years (253–68), excluded senators from all military commands and employed only equestrian generals and officers.

It was also during this period that the Roman government made its first systematic attempts to stamp out Christianity. Nero had attributed the blame for the great fire of Rome to the Chrisians in order to divert suspicion from himself, and Christianity had probably been a prohibited religion from that date; under Trajan at any rate the mere profession of Christianity was punished by death. But no attempt was made to enforce this rule systematically. Trajan even forbade Pliny, governor of Bithynia, to hunt down Christians; he was to try them only when denounced in regular form by informers. Moreover Christians who abandoned their faith and sacrificed to the gods were to be pardoned. Christians, however, were very unpopular. It was commonly believed that they sacrificed infants and indulged in sexual orgies, but the main charge against them was that they were atheists and by insulting the gods provoked their wrath against the Empire. Whenever there was a famine or an earthquake it was put down to divine anger against the Christians, and the cry was raised, 'The Christians to the lions!'

There were thus a number of sporadic persecutions, due mainly to popular agitation, in the late first, second and early third centuries. But as the Christians grew in numbers and the disasters of the Empire increased the imperial government appears to have come to the conclusion that the popular view was justified. Decius in A.D. 250 issued an edict that all the inhabitants of the Empire should sacrifice to the gods and obtain certificates that they had done so. Many Christians lapsed, but a minority were tortured and executed for their recusancy. Decius died next year and the persecution was halted, but in 257 Valerian renewed the attack on different lines. Senators and others in the imperial service were ordered to renounce their faith, and the bishops and clergy were arrested and exiled, and some were eventually executed. Churches were confiscated and religious meetings banned. But Valerian was soon captured by the Persians, and his son Gallienus granted to the Church a toleration which lasted for forty years and he even restored to it its buildings and graveyards.

Diocletian (284–305) set the Empire upon its feet again. During his twenty-one years' reign he gave it peace from civil wars, cleared up its surviving internal disorders, reinforced its frontier defences and thoroughly reorganized its administration and finances. His success was partly due to his policy of devolution of authority. In 286 he appointed a colleague, Maximian, to rule the west while he himself governed the east, and in 293 he appointed two Caesars, Emperors of subordinate grade, Constantius to assist Maximian, and Galerius to assist himself. With an Emperor on the spot in all quarters of the Empire usurpation was made much more difficult and civil wars precluded so long as all members of the imperial college agreed, and this Diocletian secured by his dominant personality.

Diocletian enormously strengthened the army, probably doubling its numbers, and greatly increasing the proportion of cavalry. He tried to create a sound gold and silver currency, but in this he failed, since he lacked the necessary bullion and had to strike increasing quantities of silver-washed copper coins. He tried to check the rise in prices by his famous edict in 301, but the inflation continued despite ruthless attempts to enforce the law. The Emperor did, however, organize the requisitions in kind, hitherto irregular (*indictiones extraordinariae*) into a system whereby all levies were annually estimated in one *indictio* and more or less equitably assessed on units of land (*iuga*) and heads of the population (*capita*); to establish these a series of censuses was held throughout the Empire. Annual conscription was required to fill the ranks of the enlarged army and the preparation of the indiction demanded complicated calculations and the collection of the increased levies was an exacting tax. Diocletian greatly strengthened the administrative service, doubling the number of provinces, and organizing the whole Empire into twelve groups of provinces, styled dioceses.

At the end of his reign Diocletian initiated what proved to be the last great persecution of the Christians. Though a religious man he was tolerant of these atheists for more than twelve years and was only provoked to action when Christian soldiers, by making the sign of the cross, prevented the taking of the omens at a public sacrifice when he himself was celebrating. He at once dismissed all the Christians from the army and the civil service, and some years later, urged on by his Caesar Galerius, closed the churches, burnt the scriptures, arrested the clergy, and finally ordered a general sacrifice to the gods.

In 305 Diocletian and Maximian abdicated and the two Caesars succeeded. As soon as Diocletian's dominating personality was removed usurpations and civil wars broke out again, until Constantine, the son of Constantius, proclaimed Emperor at York in 306, first conquered in 312 Maxentius who ruled Rome, and in 324 by the defeat of Licinius, the Emperor of the eastern parts, made himself the sole ruler of the Empire. Before he embarked upon his war against Maxentius Constantine witnessed a rare meteorological phenomenon, a cross of light radiating from the sun. This he interpreted as a sign that the God of the Cross, whom he at first identified with the sun, promised him victory, and before the decisive battle of the Milvian Bridge he ordered his soldiers to paint the monogram of Christ on their shields. His victory over Maxentius convinced him of the might of the Christian God, and he forthwith showered privileges on his Church. He also at once found himself involved in ecclesiastical controversies. He was told that in Africa besides the true Christians, the Catholics, there were others who had broken away from them, the Donatists, and that such quarrels were deeply displeasing to God. Fearing that if he were to tolerate such a situation 'the Highest Divinity may perhaps be moved to wrath not only against the human race but against myself, to whose care He has by His celestial will committed the government of all earthly things', he summoned councils of bishops at Rome and at Arles to settle the quarrel, and when the dissidents appealed to him, himself gave judgement. All his efforts were in vain; he was driven to persecute the Donatists and, when persecution failed, to leave them to the judgement of God. When he conquered the eastern parts he found that there too a controversy was raging between Alexander, bishop of Alexandria and Arius, one of his priests. To settle this controversy, which divided all the Greek-speaking churches, he summoned an ecumenical council at Nicaea in 325.

Constantine also increased and reorganized the army. Under Diocletian the troops were still mostly distributed, as they had been ever since Augustus' day, along the frontiers. Constantine somewhat reduced the strength of the frontier forces, but created a new mobile army, the *comitatus*, which could be moved to any part of the frontier which was specially menaced. It was henceforth the *comitatus* which increasingly bore the main burden of defence. By confiscating the treasures of the pagan temples Constantine acquired sufficient bullion to launch a sound gold and silver currency. The bulk of taxation continued to be levied in kind until the end of the fourth century, but by the fifth century most taxes had been commuted into gold, and the Empire once again possessed a money economy. Constantine's gold coin, the *solidus*, maintained its weight and purity until the eleventh century.

Shortly after his defeat of Licinius, Constantine refounded Byzantium, where he had won his final victory, as Constantinople. Since he founded the new city 'at God's command' to celebrate the victory which God had given him over his pagan rival, Constantinople was a Christian city and was provided with a group of splendid churches. From its foundation it was styled the New Rome and became the normal residence of the eastern Emperors, but it was not until the reign of Constantine's son Constantius II that it acquired its own magistrates and senate and prefect of the city.

Constantine divided the Empire between his three sons. The last survivor of the three, Constantius II (337–61), reunited the Empire under his own rule, and towards the end of his reign appointed his nephew Julian Caesar of Gaul. In 361 Julian was proclaimed Augustus by his troops, but before the armies of the rival Emperors met Constantius died and Julian became sole Emperor. Though brought up as a Christian he was a devoted worshipper of the pagan gods, and as soon as he came to the throne he reopened the temples which Constantine had closed, restored their endowments and withdrew the imperial subsidies paid to the Church. But eighteen months later he was killed in battle against the Persians and the generals elected as his successor Jovian, a Christian, and on Jovian's death another Christian, Valentinian, who appointed his brother Valens as his colleague to govern the east, while he himself undertook the defence of the west.

The economic burden of supporting the enlarged army was a heavy strain on the resources of the Empire, but the increasing pressure of the barbarians on the Rhine and Danube frontiers was successfully held. Now a new menace appeared. The Huns, advancing from the east across the south Russian plains, struck terror into the Ostrogoths and Visigoths, and the latter begged to be given refuge within the Empire. Valens acceded to their request, but it proved impossible to feed the horde of immigrants, and the Visigoths, who were joined by the Ostrogoths, turned to plunder. In 378 a great battle was fought at Adrianople, where Valens was killed and his army destroyed. Theodosius, Valens' successor, was only able to retrieve the situation by allowing the Visigoths to settle in Thrace as allies, bound to supply troops to assist the Roman forces.

From now on the pressure of the German tribes, pushed against the Roman frontier by the Huns, proved too strong to resist. Under Theodosius' son Honorius (395–423) Italy was invaded by vast hordes of Germans under Radagaesus, and no sooner was he defeated than Alaric led his Visigoths into Italy and captured and sacked Rome in 410. Meanwhile in 406–7 the Vandals, Alans, Sueves and Burgundians swept over the Rhine into Gaul and Spain, and in 429 the Vandals crossed the straits of Gibraltar and occupied Africa. The Western Empire kept up the struggle until in 476 the German mercenaries in Roman service mutinied and proclaimed their leader Odoacer king of Italy.

The main pressure of the barbarian onslaught was directed to the west. In the east the Emperors who reigned at Constantinople, though the Balkans were often overrun and ravaged by the Huns and other barbarian tribes, were able to hold the line of the Bosphorus, and Asia Minor, Syria and Egypt remained at peace. The economic strain was heavy, but the eastern provinces were richer and more populous and could better support the burden. At length the Emperor Justinian (527–65) felt strong enough to attempt the reconquest of the west. The Vandals were quickly overcome and Africa restored to the Empire. The Ostrogoths proved tougher foes, but at length they too were conquered and Italy was recovered. Southern Spain was conquered from the Visigoths.

It was Justinian's ambition not only to recover the lost provinces of the west, but to suppress the last remnants of paganism, to stamp out heresy and schism in the Church, and to reform the law. His most permanent achievement was his great codification of Roman law.

BIBLIOGRAPHY

Bury, J. B., *History of the later Roman Empire from the death of Theodosius I to the death of Justinian* (available as a paperback), New York, 1957.

Gibbon, Edward, *Decline and Fall of the Roman Empire*. Remains one of the most readable books of all time. An abridged version is available in the Pelican library.

Jones, A. H. M., *The Later Roman Empire*, 284–602, Blackwell, 1964.

Parker, H. M. D. (rev. B. H. Warmington, 1958) *A History of the Roman World from 138 to 337 A.D.*, Methuen.

Rostovtzeff, M. (rev. P. M. Fraser, 1957), *Social and Economic History of the Roman Empire*, Oxford University Press.

Scullard, H. H., *From the Gracchi to Nero*, Methuen, 1962.

5

ROMAN IMPERIALISM

A. N. *Sherwin-White*

THE Roman Empire by the end of the great wars of conquest in
A.D. 14 stretched from the Saharan verges to the northern rivers
Rhine and Danube, and from the Euphrates and the mountains of
eastern Turkey in the Orient to the Atlantic coasts of France,
Spain and Morocco in the west. In the next century the Emperors
sought political prestige through carefully selected border warfare, and the Empire increased only by the annexation of Britain
and the addition of the mountain zone of Romania, ancient
Dacia beyond the middle Danube. It was a period of small local
wars and general peace. So the Emperors and their officials came
to be concerned with the problems of peace and administration.

The area of the Empire was immense and contained many
peoples, languages and forms of civilization. There were Celts
and pre-Celts throughout Europe, Semites speaking Aramaic, a
precursor of Arabic, in the Syrian area, while in north Africa
Egyptian, Numidian or Berber and Phoenician were in use. The
Romans dismissed these languages and the accompanying cultures as 'barbarian'. For them Greek and Latin language and
civilization were supreme, and these under the Roman peace
spread through the barbarian world. The Roman Empire was a
land of two cultures, summarized by the phrase 'our two languages'. Hellenic civilization had spread into the eastern lands
from Greece in the period before the Roman conquest. Under
Roman rule this Hellenism intensified its hold on the area of
modern Turkey, Syria and Egypt. Previously it had been the
civilization of the great towns and cities, and most regions retained their native cultures outside the large civic centres. But
under the Empire Hellenism won its way into the small towns
and even the villages. The Romans encouraged the foundation of

Greek townships and helped the spread of Greek education and Greek institutions in the east.

In the West Rome championed her own culture. In the Celtic lands of Europe and in North Africa from Tunisia to the Atlantic coast of Morocco the Latin civilization of Italy had no serious rival. The iron-age Celts, Iberians, Moors and Numidians showed artistic abilities of varying intensity in the manufacture of small objects in iron, pottery and precious metals, and their societies had tribal structures of their own, but these had never fused into a coherent and complex civilization. The spoken word had never precipitated a written literature. Folk usage had not developed into a legal system. The Romans introduced the iron-age barbarians of the west to a civilization which combined sophisticated literature, philosophy and a developed legal science, with all the material comforts of a well-organized urban society. The effect on the barbarian world was overwhelming. Celts, Iberians and Africans alike embraced the new attractions so far as their wealth and productivity permitted. The final result was the Romanization of the western and northern provinces.

Colonization and Romanization

In the first fifty years of the Empire there is little sign that the Romans actively propagated their civilization among the conquered peoples. It was rather a by-product of the material exploitation and military control of their Empire, of colonization and of the army system. Large numbers of veteran soldiers, who at this time were all Roman citizens from Italy, were given land in the provinces on discharge and grouped together in organized communities called 'colonies'. The settlers built a township in the centre of their lands on the lines of an Italian municipality, with annually elected magistrates or mayors, a town assembly for elections, and a town council. They lived according to Roman civil law, spoke Latin and learned Latin and Greek literature in their schools. They built Roman theatres and public baths, circuses and amphitheatres for Roman games and shows, and appointed a secular priesthood for the cult of Roman gods. These colonies played a great part in spreading Roman civilization among barbarian tribal communities which surrounded them. By the middle of the first century A.D. they were being settled at key points with this intention. Tacitus says that a colony was founded at Camulodunum (Colchester) in Britain in A.D. 50, 'in order to introduce the subject peoples to the practices of civilization'. The Emperor Trajan in A.D. 100 settled a great colony at Timgad among the recently stabilized nomadic tribesmen of southern Algeria with the same idea. Its ruins still dominate the region.

There was also much unofficial migration of land-hungry peasants, traders and business men, with retinues of followers, from Italy to the coastlands of the western Mediterranean. These settled in informal groups within barbarian townships and organized associations for the management of their own affairs. Such a *conventus* was a city within a city, and when it increased in size and prosperity it would be given the official status and organization of a Roman borough *inside* the native township. A double community of this kind in North Africa made a joint dedication to the Roman Emperor Augustus in the name of 'the Romans and the Numidians' with the latter name inscribed in smaller letters. The impact of these settlements on the native population, side by side with whom they lived without any material separation of walls or quarters, using the same streets and markets, was intense. Populations and customs mixed, and the sequel usually was the grant of Roman status to the natives themselves, who were till then technically foreigners living under their own Celtic, African or Iberian customs. Finally the two communities of immigrant and native-born Roman citizens might be merged into a single Roman borough.

The tendency of the native peoples to imitate the more complex Roman civilization was voluntary. Long before they acquired the Roman citizenship they were apt to take the initiative by adopting Roman names or Latinizing their barbarian names into odd dog-Latin forms. The Phoenician 'Muttumbal son of Auchusor' starts calling himself Muttumbalius Auchusorius. They also adopt Latin language and Latin technical terms for use in their own civic affairs. The son of a Celtic local magistrate or *vergobret* may hold the same office as his father, but use the Latin term *duovir* or *praetor* for it long before his tribe has secured official Roman status. The Greek traveller Strabo observed this evolution with surprise about A.D. 14. He wrote about the people of southern Gaul (Provence) and southern Spain: 'They have changed their ways and altogether gone over to the Roman fashion. They wear togas and even speak Latin and have changed the pattern of their laws.' Half a century later the Roman administrator Pliny the Elder wrote in his *Natural History* that the peoples of Provence in their way of life and standard of living and agricultural technique – which was the chief economic activity – were more like Italians than provincials.

Eventually the Roman government set about encouraging these tendencies. Agricola, governor of Britain from A.D. 77 to 83, on a 'whistle stop' tour of the chief centres urged the tribal leaders to build townships on the Roman model with market squares and modern houses, promising material assistance. This meant that the Roman governor would provide military personnel and lay out the townships with walls and streets, while the natives were left to develop the residential quarters and civic buildings. Thus Thugga, modern Dougga, in central Tunisia was a collection of primitive houses and shrines around a market until about A.D. 160, when a group of wealthy landowners tore down the old shacks and built a splendid group of temples, theatres and public buildings in the contemporary Italian style.

Local Government

The provincial municipalities were the basic units of the Roman Empire, which was a vast experiment in local self-government. Every province was divided into a number of communities which varied in type and civilization from region to region, but were each responsible for the detailed administration of their area. Jurisdiction over property rights and crimes was left, below a certain magnitude or value, in such cases as might come to a county or police court in Great Britain, in the hands of local magistrates. Civic services – maintenance of roads and markets, town walls, drainage, water supply and police, the care of cults, temples and festivals, public entertainments in the theatre, circus or amphitheatre – all these were managed by a group of four to six yearly elected magistrates acting with the advice of a local council of ex-magistrates who remained aldermen for life. The most elaborate pattern of local government is found in the cities of Italy and the western provinces which possessed the Roman citizenship, and in the Greek cities of the eastern provinces. But in large areas the native communities long retained their original institutions and customs, which the Romans never sought to alter against the will of the inhabitants. In essence these conformed to the basic pattern of elected magistrates and councils, and performed the same basic functions, even if the magistrate was a hereditary tribal chief with feudal rights and a queer foreign title, and the council only a moot of village elders.

The Roman Empire depended greatly on the support of the social class that provided the municipal magistrates and councillors. Their loyalty enabled the Romans to control the greater part of the Empire with minimal forces or none, and to govern them without a bureaucracy. This class, called 'curial' from *curia*, a council-chamber, mostly consisted of landowning *bourgeoisie* of moderate wealth. The Romans favoured it at the expense of the working peasantry and city craftsmen, who were excluded from any serious share in local government except for voting at the annual election of magistrates. Even in the East, where the Greek city councils had once been fairly democratic bodies selected annually by lot from all the local citizens, the Romans introduced or encouraged their own system of wealth qualifications and life membership for councillors. Curial status tended to become hereditary as sons succeeded fathers in the same positions, and the old families tried to exclude outsiders from gaining power. The younger Pliny once observed to Trajan: 'In Bithynia they would rather elect the sons of the respectable classes than common folk to the councils.' These 'respectable classes' in the second century A.D. began to take the place of the ordinary Roman citizen as the most privileged class. By the third century, when the Roman citizenship had become universal and hence devalued, they ranked in privilege next to Roman knights and senators. The Empire tended thus to harden the class structure of society, though the Roman army by its promotion system still gave the capable commoner a chance of rising above his social origins.*

The Provincial Councils

The Romans made one addition to local life. This was the provincial council. Each major community in a province, such as the sixty-four cantons of Gaul, elected two or three deputies who met at the provincial capital under an elected chairman. The original function of these councils was to hold the ceremonies of the imperial cult, the official worship of the Emperor and of the spirit of Rome. Hence the chairman was called the Priest of Rome and Augustus. This device exploited the political ambitions of the native aristocracies in the interests of loyalty to Rome. The priesthood was the highest dignity open to a provincial subject, and was eagerly sought. The delegates also ranked high, and had special titles in some provinces, such as Asiarchs or rulers of Asia. The imperial cult was celebrated with great pomp on occasions such as the Emperor's birthday and accession day, and at the New Year,† with beast-fights, gladiators and chariot races. As provincial capitals in the West were Roman cities of great magnificence, such as Lugdunum (Lyons) in Gaul or Roman Carthage near Tunis in Africa, these festivals introduced the leading men from every quarter of the province to the material splendours, pleasures and comforts of Roman civilization. The councils also served to promote the unification of provinces. Northern Gaul was divided administratively into three Roman provinces, Lugdunensis, Belgica and Aquitania, but the delegates of its sixty-four cantons met annually in a single body at Lyons, and had every opportunity to unite in matters of common interest, and even to plot together against the Roman government if they wished.

These councils were not intended to act as regular local par-

*On the structure of town life *see further*, pp. 162–7.
† On the imperial cult *see* pp. 189f.

liaments, but they gained a foothold in the administration of their own provinces. They were allowed to send deputations to the central government at Rome, if they had complaints against their provincial governors. By taking advantage of the Roman law of extortion they secured the privilege of debating the conduct of departing governors. If they were dissatisfied, they could institute a prosecution at Rome, or else they could pass a vote of thanks which virtually prevented any other party from starting a prosecution. So a genuine, though limited, political life developed inside the provincial councils, especially in those provinces which had annual governors, and hence a chance of action every year. Provincial grandees whose interests had been harmed by a governor would instigate a prosecution as soon as he left the province. A Spaniard who had been sent into exile by a proconsul of the Spanish province of Baetica is found later leading a deputation that successfully secured the proconsul's condemnation at Rome, and hence his ruin.

The men who became delegates and presidents of the provincial councils were the cream of the curial class. Through the councils they came to know Roman governors and senators, and with their help were able to secure the entry to Roman public life and the senatorial class for themselves.

The Governors at Work

The detail of daily administration fell to the tribal and municipal magistrates. What did the Roman governors do? In the peaceful provinces, which had no external frontiers bordered by wild peoples, they were concerned with the general control of public order and with the more serious jurisdiction. For they were vested with absolute authority over the persons of provincials.

All great crimes, such as murder, forgery, brigandage, rape, adultery, incendiarism, for which the penalties were hard labour, exile or death, came to their courts. So too all great law suits between private persons involving large sums of money and questions of personal status, which were frequent in the complex social system, all disputes between cities, tribes, and townships over boundaries markets and festivals, or about the interpretation of the local laws, came to the governor's tribunal.

There was no regular mechanism by which the central government at Rome could control or check or even receive routine information about the governors of non-military provinces. But the governors might submit problems to the Senate or the Emperor at Rome, and the provincials were free to send deputations to Rome about their difficulties. This was not a regular process of appeal, because the Senate or the Emperor would not lightly reverse the decisions of the governor, but it was a means of checking any excessive arbitrariness in his actions. Normally, a governor would follow the 'precedents of his predecessors', but nothing required him to do so since precedent was not held so binding in Roman as it is in modern times. Only the decision of the central government could bind successive governors. So if new problems and new circumstances arose, the provincials liked to secure a ruling from Rome.

How Rome regarded local affairs can be seen from the replies of the Emperor Trajan to the problems put to him by the governor of Bithynia, Plinius Secundus, known as the Younger Pliny, in about A.D. 110. Pliny was keen to establish general rules for the whole province. But he was normally instructed to follow the usage of the local community, though this might differ from city to city. Still less uniformity existed between different provinces.

The Emperor was prepared to impose uniformity only where Roman security was involved. For example, he was suspicious of private clubs and associations of a professional or trade character, which were common throughout the working population. So Pliny was instructed to abolish them throughout his province. To his surprise he was not allowed to exempt from this order a fire-brigade in the capital city, which was frequently devastated by fires, because it took the form of a trade club. This veto was applied later to the whole of the eastern provinces, and fire-fighting measures in the great cities were limited to the use of household brigades and domestic equipment, such as buckets and stirrup-pumps. The veto shows the suspicion which the government felt for the proletarians of the eastern cities. Yet in Italy and the west it was normal for the towns to have several fire-brigades of the type forbidden in the East.

Diversity was thus the rule in the usages and institutions of local life throughout the provinces. The famous Roman civil law was uniform, but it was a legal system that applied only to transactions between Roman citizens.

Until the early third century A.D. these were only a minority, though a large minority, of the provincial populations. In any provincial community there would be two systems of private law at work, the local and the Roman. Naturally the local law, like everything else in provincial life, tended to become Romanized. When matters came to court before Roman governors, these mostly interpreted law according to their own notions. But over great areas of the Empire change was slow and discouraged by the central government.

In all the reports of Pliny and the replies of Trajan the advantage of the provincials is put first, except in the rare instances where this conflicts with security. Governor and Emperor do not always see eye to eye on particular questions, but they agree about the principle. When Pliny suggested that a military guard should be posted at a route-centre called Juliopolis, to check the abuses which officials and soldiers travelling on the highways inflicted on the local citizens, by demands for lodging, supplies and transport, Trajan refused, because it would establish an expensive precedent, but he laid down rules for the control of such abuses. His instructions reveal a weakness of the Roman Empire that is not often noticed: 'Arrest any soldiers who misbehave, and if their crimes are serious report them to their regimental commanders, or to me if they are on their way to Rome.' How did this work? There were no officers of the governor stationed at Juliopolis. Trajan did not expect that Pliny would supervise the matter directly, but that the city magistrates or the injured parties would take the initiative in bringing charges to the attention of the governor, who alone had the power to deal with them. Less scrupulous governors than Pliny often winked at offenders of this type, who were themselves officials. Complaints about highway abuses were continuous. Earlier the Emperor Claudius in A.D. 46

declared that though he had taken the strictest measures to prevent abuses the 'wickedness of men', by which he meant the collusion of officials, frustrated all his efforts.

Throughout the Roman Empire the righting of wrongs, and the whole enforcement of laws and regulations, depended upon the initiative of private individuals and local authorities, according to the circumstances. The personnel of the central government was spread very thin, and there were no State or imperial prosecutors. Hence if the interested parties were frightened of taking action there would be no redress. Conversely, laws and regulations of the central government were only enforced when local opinion or particular interests were in their favour; and it was possible for illicit practitioners to elude an official ban unless public opinion was against them.

A convict might even evade a sentence of exile or hard labour if his private enemies did not denounce him. Pliny reports the case of an offender who coolly resumed his ordinary life after he had first been banished and then offered a retrial. The Emperor angrily instructed that the man was to be sent in chains to Rome: 'It is not enough to restore the sentence which he eluded by his wanton disobedience.'

This disobedience was a serious matter for the governors, because outside the military provinces they generally lacked adequate forces to impose their will throughout their province if the municipal authorities did not co-operate. Few of the peaceful provinces had more than a Roman cohort of 500 men, stationed at the capital city, under the orders of the governor, and some had none at all. In the four Gallic provinces, which covered most of modern France, there was only a single cohort, stationed at Lyons. The great army which occupied the Rhine lands was not under the governors of the four Gauls, and could not enter their provinces, except to deal with a serious rebellion.

Complaints against Officials

The law of extortion was the principal means by which the Romans tried to protect their subjects against the misbehaviour of their own agents. Trials were held in Rome, and the law never worked very satisfactorily, though its history shows remarkable anxiety over a long period to maintain justice. More governors were acquitted than were condemned, largely because they were tried by courts of senators, who were apt to regard such activities as a perquisite of their class, and hence to impose the lowest penalties or none. But even the lightest sentence meant the loss of official status, and hence the ruin of a governor's career. The senators felt the pressure of the law, and resented the influence of provincial magnates who could decide in their council whether a governor was to be prosecuted or not. A proconsul of Bithynia once complained that his prosecution was an act of revenge by influential provincials who had found him too strict for their liking.

The law itself was limited in scope to crimes that involved the taking of money or property from provincial subjects. Its severest penalty, of perpetual exile, was for extortion with violence. It was difficult to prosecute a governor for crimes of violence that did not involve extortion. Since the governors mostly had very few troops to enforce their decisions it was essential that their authority should not be lightly challenged. But provincials were protected against extreme use of arbitrary power by the Roman custom that punishment should be inflicted on subjects only after formal trial in due course of law, by the governor sitting on his tribunal and taking the advice of a court of assessors. Arbitrary executions were held to be justifiable only in times of rebellion and public rioting. Otherwise the central government at Rome might construe the action of the governor as a form of treason against the State. But this was not an easy form of redress for the provincials to secure. When a proconsul of Asia in A.D. 9 executed 300 men in a single day, and strolled among the corpses exclaiming 'What a royal deed', the Roman Senate construed the extortion law to cover such an extreme act of violence. But these forms of redress applied only to exceptional abuses.

The extortion law was concerned with the rights of men of property, the magnates of the province, who sat on the provincial councils, and who had the leisure and means to make the journey to Rome, and to meet the costs of a prosecution which involved paying the expenses of the witnesses on this long undertaking. The only redress available to the ordinary man, the peasantry and day labourers, lay in the submission of a written petition to the Emperor himself. This too involved difficulty and expense in dispatching the petition to Rome, unless a friendly official allowed them the use of the imperial postal service. Such petitions were quite frequent. Invariably the Emperor does his best to redress wrongs and to prevent abuses. But the weakness persisted throughout the heyday of the Empire. The central government was too dependent on the honesty and good will of its individual officers, and the means to enforce its will from afar were not adequate. These petitions reveal the remarkable accessibility of the Roman Emperor to the complaints of small communities and little men. The tenants of a great imperial estate in a remote corner of North Africa complain :

The Agent has sent soldiers into our farms and ordered us to be seized, harassed and enchained, and some, though they are Roman citizens, to be beaten with rods and clubs. So we wretched men are compelled to supplicate your Divine Providence, venerable Emperor. Do not allow the Agents to increase our dues and obligations. . . . Come to our aid, for we are needy peasants, supporting life by the work of our hands, and we cannot stand up to the Agent who gives substantial bribes to the Procurator.

This petition reached the Emperor Commodus at Rome in A.D. 180–3. He ordered that the abuses were to cease, and the petitioners set up his reply, carved in stone, in a public place, to make sure.

The Administrative Service

Historians are apt to speak of the Roman civil service and the Roman bureaucracy. But the only bureaucracy was in the offices of the imperial secretariat at Rome, which managed the paper work through which the Emperors communicated with the governors and army commanders and administered the taxes and military forces. Roman provincial government was direct and unbureaucratic. There were no hordes of minor officials and no specialized departmental offices for this or that activity. Government was personal, and the officials were very few in number. The chief governor was called either proconsul, if he was a senator appointed by the Senate, or legate of Augustus if he was a senator appointed by the Emperor, or procurator if he was one of the so-called Roman knights (Equites), who ranked below the senators, in charge of a small imperial province. The governors never had more than three assistant governors or legates to share the burden of jurisdiction, and sometimes none. With their legates, they were responsible for all the administration and jurisdiction that could not be left to the municipalities, and the whole of the serious criminal jurisdiction came to the governor alone. He had no permanent secretariat to help him, though he could form an office staff for routine correspondence from the provincial soldiery or his own servants. For advice on the spot, he relied on friends whom he invited to accompany him from Rome, or upon the provincial gentry. This had its dangers. Pliny advises a friend who was going out to govern Spain not to be too familiar with the provincials. He himself, when governor of Bithynia, took out an elderly centurion whom he had known thirty years before when on military service, to manage his provincial troops, and two Roman knights who had some administrative experience.

The governor was not concerned with finance. The collection of taxes, the provincial expenditure, and the management of state property were in the hands either of a young senator entitled 'quaestor' or of two or three imperial procurators who, like the procurators who governed provinces, came from the social class of Roman knights. This 'equestrian' class increasingly provided the upper administrative personnel of the Empire, and the staff officers of the armed forces, apart from the senatorial legates and proconsuls. The procurators of all grades were a more professional body than the senatorial officials. They maintained permanent bureaux and record offices for their financial operations and documents, manned by imperial slaves and freedmen, at the provincial capitals. As chief assistant they usually had an experienced imperial freedman. These procurators were not the subordinates of the governors, though socially they ranked lower. They were appointed directly by the Emperor and were immediately responsible to him.

Equestrian procurators and senatorial legates alike held their appointments for some three or four years. But while the knights normally proceeded without interruption from post to post until retirement, the senators held office more irregularly, and resumed their life at Rome between appointments. There as members of the Roman Senate they were nominally the chief council of the Roman State; also, if they were the Emperor's 'friends' (*amici*), they were summoned from time to time to sit as advisers on his Privy Council.

A provincial would find himself dealing with the equestrian procurator and his staff for public business involving finance, and with the senatorial governor in matters affecting his personal status, property rights and municipal affairs. Since they were independent of each other and had different functions he could not play them off against each other or secure redress from one at the hands of the other.

The Roman Army and the Provincials

The Roman army was mostly concentrated along the boundaries of the Empire, facing the unconquered barbarians of northern Europe along the Rhine and Danube. In the east it kept watch, in Syria and eastern Turkey, against the civilized oriental empire of the Parthians, who lay beyond the river Euphrates. The army also garrisoned the half-conquered territory of Britain with substantial forces, and controlled the uncertain loyalties of the semi-nomadic tribes of north-west Africa in modern Algeria and Morocco. Some thirty legions under the command of junior legates were distributed in corps of three or four legions each under the control of senior legates. With the legions there were brigaded independent units known as 'auxiliaries', which in total manpower equalled the legions. Altogether the imperial army numbered some three hundred thousand men at its greatest strength.

Because of its peculiar recruitment and organization this army played a large part in the social development and unification of the Empire. The legions were divisions of some five thousand infantrymen, recruited in the first century A.D. among Roman citizens of Italy and the more civilized provinces. Later the recruits came increasingly from military townships of veteran settlers that sprang up in the frontier provinces. The auxiliaries were units recruited among the peoples of the more recently conquered regions, such as northern Spain, Britain and the Balkans. The whole of the Roman cavalry was raised in this way, mostly from northern Gaul. These auxiliaries were formed into independent units of 500 or 1,000 men. They had the same training and equipment as the legionaries and fought alongside them. They served for twenty-five years before discharge, and could gain promotion through a series of grades to the well-paid post of centurion or company officer. On discharge they received the Roman citizenship for themselves and their children. Their units were commanded by Roman officers, the language of command was Latin, and their organization and community life, with its cults and ceremonies, was Roman. Hence the auxiliary army was a rough school of Romanization. The auxiliaries, who were provincial peasantry by origin, took back to their villages what they had learned in the army and spread it around. The 6,000 auxiliaries who were being discharged annually throughout the first two centuries A.D. formed a considerable pro-Roman element throughout the Empire. They seem to have given wholehearted loyalty to Rome once the system of reward by citizenship was established.

The Roman Citizenship and the Provincials

Roman citizens of high and low degree alike were a class possessing great privilege and great prestige. They were the nominal lords of the world, though the real power was in the hands of a very select group, to which the citizenship gave the possibility of access. The rest of the world were the ruled, and they were in Roman law not only subjects but foreigners and citizens merely of their local city or tribe. Yet the Romans at all times were ready to give their citizenship to subjects who had been of service to the Roman State. This in the period of conquest usually meant helping the Romans to master one's own country, and later to keep it under control by collaborating in the job of government. The local aristocracies that ruled the provincial communities, and the common folk who served in the auxiliary army, alike found the door to the Roman citizenship wide open. Not only individuals but whole communities could gain the Roman franchise. The whole of the free-born population of the townships and villages of a community and their descendants would then become Roman citizens. This separated them from all other communities in their province, and the individual from all other individuals, that did not possess the citizenship.

There was some awkwardness in this. In strict Roman law a citizen could not make effective legal compacts of certain sorts, notably marriage, with non-Romans. Hence property and status did not descend to the children of mixed marriages, who would be non-Romans and lack the civic position of their fathers. The difficulty was much less when a whole community received the franchise and changed status together. There was then a total change in the private law of the community, and of its public life. The citizens must all order their affairs according to the rules of Roman civil law, and the community must substitute the complex Roman system of local government, including the use of Latin as the official language, for their former way of life as Celts, Iberians or Dalmatians. This might mean a great local upset. But frequently the cities that were given Roman status had already begun to adopt Roman usages unofficially, and also contained a nucleus of Roman citizens among their leading gentry.

The impact was less upsetting because it was voluntary. The Roman government did not impose its citizenship or its customs. The initiative came from the provincials themselves who either as communities or as individuals petitioned the government. Sometimes the government offered the franchise as a reward for some service. But the decision to accept was then left to the local inhabitants in the council or civil meeting. When the Roman

annexation of the former dependent kingdom of Mauretania in
A.D. 40–1 provoked a local rebellion, the local potentate of the
semi-Phoenician township of Volubilis stood by the Romans.
The man was already a Roman citizen, and later he secured the
same status for the whole of his rather barbaric community. For
the benefit of local gentry at Volubilis who had married wives
from other districts these foreign marriages were specially allowed
to count as valid. The Roman lawyers were frequently inventing
similar devices to solve the problems that arose from the grant
of the Roman citizenship to remote provincial units. Though
Roman wills were supposed to be written in Latin, gradually
other languages were allowed to count, including 'even Celtic',
as one lawyer writes. The Romans did not insist on certificates
of proficiency in Latin or in Roman usages before granting their
franchise. They assumed that if the loyalty of the provincials
was committed the rest would follow.

That the Romans were not mistaken appears from the spread
of Latin language and literature among the middle and upper
classes of northern Europe. This is still shown by the dominance
of Romance languages from the Alps and the Rhine to the Atlantic coast of Spain and north of the Danube in Romania. Latin did
not spread as the language of commerce or of the army. Trade
remained in the hands of the local practitioners – the Romans
were not a commercial people – and the army was too restricted
in its cantonments, mostly confined to the Rhine and Danube
valleys, to have more than local influence. The recruitment of
auxiliaries, however, helped Latin to percolate the peasantry, as
did military colonization also, mostly in the coastlands of the
Mediterranean provinces. The clue lies largely in the remarkable
connexion between Roman administration and the art of public
speaking, or 'rhetoric'. The provincial gentry came into contact
with Roman officials mostly at their tribunals and at official ceremonies such as those of the provincial councils. Here the spoken
word ruled supreme, like the printed word in modern times. The
effective speaker was the man trained in the Roman art of advocacy or 'rhetoric'. This was developed into a fine art in antiquity
through a training in literature, and formed the hard core of

Roman education.* Hence the men of property and the magnates required these arts, or else they needed the services of those who had them. The schools of rhetoric also opened the doors of promotion to the politically ambitious. Tacitus speaking of the spread of Latin in Britain remarks : 'There was no need of compulsion; ambition served instead, and Latin rhetoric became the popular study.'

So the Roman policy of opening their citizenship and their public service to wealthy provincials led to the establishment of schools and universities of Latin literature and language throughout the great cities of the western provinces. Fashion and imitation did the rest. The native languages gave way to Latin as the public language even of the non-Roman communities. Not even a local civic alderman could make his mark if he could not dress up his ideas in the best Latin rhetoric. Examples survive of the ornate and fulsome addresses of small town orators, and at its peak this educated society produced serious literature. The Spaniard Seneca, son of a professor of rhetoric, wrote philosophical essays about life and behaviour. The great historian Tacitus (c. A.D. 100) was of Celtic descent. Apuleius, author of the famous novel called *The Golden Ass*, came from North Africa. So too did two great Christian writers, the fiery Tertullian, defender of the faith, and Augustin of Hippo, whose *City of God* was an attempt to identify the Roman Empire with the Christian Church. These writers were products of the great amalgam of the barbarian cultures with the Latin civilization. All are alike in that in different generations they accepted the Roman order as the basis of society. Even Tertullian, who championed Christianity in the age of persecution, insists again and again that : 'We too are Romans – and better Romans than those who persecute us.'

The spread of Latin language in its most polished form, percolating downwards from high society, met a vigorous and vulgar Latin that forced its way upwards from the working population that provided recruits for the Roman army and servants for the upper classes. This was probably a slower business, and languages

* *See* on Roman oratory pp. 201–9.

such as Celtic, in the form of Breton, and Welsh and Basque (though diluted with much Latin vocabulary) survived the fall of the Roman Empire in some sizeable areas.

Provincials in the Service of the Roman State

The practical advantages of being a Roman citizen in a state which lacked democratic forms were material and social rather than political. For the common man enlistment in the army opened a continuous path of promotion through a series of 'non-commissioned' ratings to the post of centurion or company commander in a legion. The ablest of these in middle life secured advancement to the 'equestrian' class, and after commissions as staff officers entered the administrative service of the Emperor as procurators and frequently reached the very top of the ladder. These various posts were increasingly well paid, so that through the army humble men of ability could achieve both fame and fortune. Otherwise the most obvious benefit of Roman citizenship was that it protected a man against the absolute power of the provincial governors. Technically a Roman citizen might not be enchained or beaten in any circumstances or put to death on a criminal charge by a provincial governor, but could claim trial before a court at Rome. This was a valuable privilege in a system which put the ordinary provincial entirely at the mercy of the power of governors who were apt to follow the lead of influential pressure groups. The Christian leader Paul of Tarsus, who was a skilled craftsman in social status, used his Roman citizenship to avoid the machinations of his enemies in Palestine, by securing the transfer of his trial on a charge of subversion from the province to the court of Nero at Rome.

For the wealthy upper classes there were greater privileges. They could secure equestrian status at an early age, and after serving as staff officers of legions and the auxiliary army secure imperial procuratorships, including the fattest plums of the profession, such as the governorship of Egypt and the command of the Praetorian Guard at Rome. The sons of such men could enter the Roman Senate, and as senators hold the highest posts in the

Roman army and the provincial administration. The Emperor Nero for the first eight years of his reign left imperial policy in the hands of the Spanish senator and man of letters Seneca and of the Praetorian Prefect Afranius Burrus, who came from the township of Vasio (Vaison-la-romaine) near Avignon in Provence, and whose grandparents were Celtic peasantry. They had received the Roman citizenship from the governor Afranius in the time of Julius Caesar, and had taken his family name, as was customary. The great general Julius Agricola, who conquered Scotland in A.D. 77–81, came from Forum Julii (Fréjus), also in Provence. His grandfather had been a procurator of the first Emperor Augustus, and his great-grandfather may have received the citizenship from Julius Caesar.

The number of provincials in the Senate and the equestrian class increased steadily. All the great Emperors of the second century were provincials – the Spaniards Trajan and Hadrian, the Provençals Pius and Marcus Aurelius, and the African Septimus Severus whose sister was said to speak Latin badly. By the end of the second century A.D. half the Senate and most of the procurators were men of provincial origin. Such men, unless they had risen from the ranks, were by origin great landowners and magnates of their provinces. They sat as deputies on the provincial council, where they met and entertained the Roman officials with whose help and recommendation they secured entry to the imperial service. The senator Pliny the Younger, had connexions through his uncle, a former procurator of Spain, with that province. So he recommends Voconius Romanus of Saguntum to the Emperor Trajan for admission to the Senate, and also writes to Priscus, the army commander of Syria, to secure Voconius an appointment on Priscus' staff, as follows :

Voconius is the son of a distinguished equestrian . . . he has been head of the provincial council of Spain . . . he is a man of brilliant intellect and a skilled advocate in the courts . . . his Latin style is impeccable . . . his personal fortune is considerable . . .

Through this network of recommendations the Emperors could select the most promising candidates for public office, and so satisfy the ambition and secure the support of influential provincials who might otherwise have fomented sedition. Hence provincial rebellions, when the protracted wars of conquest were finished, were few and ineffective. In northern Gaul, a century after the conquest, there were two considerable risings, partly stirred up by excessive taxation but with some undertones of a nationalist movement against Rome. Both collapsed because the majority of the Gallic nobility refused to support them.

The Limits of Tolerance

The Romans ruled successfully because of their remarkable and positive tolerance. Their claim was that 'conquerors and conquered share the rights of community on the same terms, provincials rule provinces and subjects are in command of the armies that control them.' Their one great failure was in dealing with a people who did not welcome or share this tolerance, the Jews of Judaea. These staged three bitter insurrections, two in their native country, and one in the Jewish settlements of the eastern provinces of Cyprus, Cyrene, and Egypt between A.D. 66 and 136. The rebellions arose from the internal development of Judaism, the violent and passionate exclusiveness of the Jewish sects, and their equally violent belief in the establishment of a Messianic or theocratic kingdom on earth. The severity of Roman governors of Judaea sparked off the first rebellion, but this severity was the inevitable reaction to the refusal of the Jewish national and religious leaders to accept the compromises that were accepted throughout the rest of the Roman Empire. The Romans deserved better of the Jews. They had always consistently supported the local Jewish communities, scattered through the Greek cities of the eastern provinces, in their claim to freedom of religious practice, against the local Greek municipalities, which objected to these alien colonies, and harried them. A hundred years of Roman edicts defended the Jews against the Greeks.

In Judaea itself the Romans had taken over the government in A.D. 6 at the request of the Jewish leaders who at that time disliked the rule of the unorthodox house of Herod. But they found that the ordinary usages of Roman government and military discipline offended the strict practices and taboos of Jewish monotheism. The Jews had, for example, like Moslems and Protestant Christians later, an abhorrence of cult images, which were used in the religious ceremonies of the Roman army. The governors were generally at pains to avoid offending such susceptibilities. But they made mistakes, which provoked riots and hence countermeasures. In Judaea the Romans had the bulk of a fanatical population against them, and were far less successful than elsewhere in securing support from the upper classes. The result was the destruction of Jerusalem in A.D. 70 and the settlement of a Roman military colony on the site in A.D. 136.

Yet Roman tolerance is normally most notable in the sphere of religion. The Romans followed the system of civic or national gods. The welfare of communities was thought to depend on the goodwill of their protecting deities. Hence they respected all local cults, and expected everyone to fulfil his duties to his local gods. The attitude was reciprocal. There was no question of imposing Roman gods on the members of foreign communities. But equally provincials were expected to respect the Roman gods in a Roman setting. Jews, and later Christians, as monotheists, were unable to do this. Because Judaism was concerned with what the Romans considered a local diety, the Romans extended their tolerance to it despite the lack of reciprocity, and went to great lengths to enable Jews to maintain their national worship. It was even possible, and not uncommon, for Jews to become Roman citizens with special exemption from partaking in the Roman cults. But after the great revolts the government reinforced an ancient rule that forbade Roman citizens, who were not Jews by birth, to adopt the Jewish faith and customs, because of the incompatibility of religious duties.

It is remarkable that the Romans, who were so flexible in dealing with the Jewish problem, found it impossible to come to terms with the Christians, who had the same intolerance as the Jews towards the cults of other peoples. In Roman eyes they were not practising a national or civic cult which was obligatory on them, but were members of particular communities, caught out trying to evade the obligations of their birth on which the safety of the community depended. Hence, unlike the Jews, they undermined the common weal by their practices. This was the only religion which the Romans finally proscribed as a religion. Other cults of a personal sort were disciplined or suspended from time to time, usually on the grounds that some particular custom, such as the human sacrifice practised by Druids and the priests of the Phoenician Baal, were criminal actions. But with Christianity it was the basic belief that conflicted with a basic principle of Roman statecraft. The religion came to be a forbidden cult. Yet the Christian Churches survived under the protection of the administrative inefficiency of the provincial government, and its lack of an organized police. For two centuries Christians were only prosecuted when some private enemy thought it worth his while to make trouble for a particular group.*

BIBLIOGRAPHY

A more detailed discussion of the topics contained in this chapter can best be found in the two chapters of H. M. Last, 'The Principate and the Administration', 'Rome and the Empire', *Cambridge Ancient History*, Vol. XI, Ch. X and XI (Cambridge University Press).

For the spread of the Roman citizenship *see* A. N. Sherwin-White, *The Roman Citizenship*, Parts II and III (Oxford University Press, 1939).

An interesting account of a province under Roman rule will be found in the geographer Strabo's chapter on Gaul (Book IV, Chs. 1–6) which may be read in translation in the Loeb edition.

See further, Chapter 10.

6

ROMAN LAW

F. H. Lawson

IT is a commonplace that Roman law is the greatest contribution that Rome has made to Western civilization; and again it is often said that Roman law is one of the main structural elements in the modern world. These statements are for the most part accepted by persons who do not know what they mean and, perhaps, because they do not know. In fact it is difficult to define the historic importance of Roman law, more difficult to see what is peculiarly Roman in it and still more difficult to explain either its importance or its Roman character.

Certain statements at least can be made without much fear of contradiction.

The Roman world is a dead world existing only in the past, a mass of fragments to be dug up, seen, read, inspected, or copied. Even the Latin language no longer survives as a means of communication used naturally in ordinary intercourse, and capable of idiomatic development; its standards of correctness are all in the past. To this generalization Roman law provides a solitary exception. Less than a century ago it was completely alive in important parts of the Western world. Even now it is applied in a few places, and elsewhere it has suffered a change of name rather than of substance. Before 1900 over large parts of Germany Roman law was in active operation. In 1900 it was superseded by a Civil Code, but that code contains in scarcely modified form much that had previously existed as Roman law. Similarly in France those topics which under the *ancien régime* were governed by Roman law are still governed by the same rules and principles, though they are now integral parts of codified French law. Moreover, they remain Roman in a way that the French language does not.

103

Of course the Roman law in force in the modern world is not the same as that of the early city state of Rome. Such identity as Roman law has preserved throughout its history is like that of the human body, in which cells are constantly being replaced by other cells, an identity preserved by continuous development. Roman law likewise developed continuously with only one clean break at the end of the ancient world, which, however, was healed after a long interval by what was substantially a resurrection of its old self, in the condition to which it had attained before the break. Accordingly the debt which the modern world owes to Roman law cannot be understood without some knowledge of its history.

We have little direct evidence for Roman law before the time of Cicero; and indeed systematic knowledge begins in the second century A.D. with an elementary textbook written by an unknown author who went by the name of Gaius. Any attempt to describe Roman law in its earliest state must take the form of a hazardous reconstruction. There can indeed be little doubt as to its general structure, though we are probably led to think of it as neater and more logical than it really was.

The republican constitution, while it protected the citizen against the abuse of power by magistrates, conferred on him no rights which he could assert against the sovereign people. Yet it seems that although the State never admitted any limits to its power over its citizens, it interfered very little in the relations between them. A sharp distinction was always made between public law, which regulated the structure and powers of public authorities and their relations to the individual citizen, and, on the other hand, private law, which regulated the relations of citizen *inter se*. The State provided means for the settlement of their disputes and, while it allowed the administration of domestic justice by the head of the family, it had already, before historical knowledge begins, suppressed anything that may have existed in the nature of a blood feud. But although murder and treason were already crimes against the State, most of what would now be treated as criminal offences were redressed by way of civil action brought by the victim against the wrongdoer. Moreover, a person seeking justice against another person got no help from the State in bringing him before the courts. Nor was private law for the most part the product of legislation, though the Roman people could in its assemblies modify private law if it chose.

For the Roman Republic was organized on lines in many respects closely resembling, though in miniature, those regulating the Federal Republic of the United States. It was a group of families, each composed of a man who, having no surviving ancestors in the direct male line, exercised an unlimited jurisdiction over his slaves and his own issue in the male line, in short, a number of patriarchal families, corresponding in their main outlines to the constituent states of the American Union, the subordinate members of the family corresponding to American citizens in their capacity of citizens of their particular states. But just as the national government of the United States exercises power directly over those citizens in certain matters without the intervention of the states, so the Roman State, in matters of public law, dealt directly with all its citizens and took no notice of the subjection of some of them to a family head.

Thus we have to take account of three kinds of relations: that of the citizen to the State, that of the subordinate member of a family to its head, and that of one family head to another. That of the citizen to the State, in principle one of absolute subjection, came to be governed by public law; that of the subordinate member of a family to its head remained one of absolute subjection, tempered not by law but by public opinion and an official censorship of morals; that of one family head to another was the subject-matter of private law.

Now while the power of the State over the citizen or of the family head over his subordinates was not in fact exercised irresponsibly, each appeared too arbitrary to attract the serious attention of the jurists who turned Roman law into an object of scientific study. On the other hand, the disputes between family heads, like the disputes between nations in modern times, had to be decided on principle, with state officials doing little more than hold the ring; and this remained true even after individuals became legally important in their own right. It may be said here, once and for all, that since the Roman jurists did not subject either public law or criminal law to profound study, modern students of Roman law also have usually left them to the ancient historians and confined themselves to private law.

The rules then of private law determining a decision could not, given the essential structure of Roman society, be established by the arbitrary act of a public officer; but there had to be some persons whose business it was to 'interpret' the law; those persons would have somehow or other to reduce it to a rational system; and they would be likely to find it altogether more worthy of intense study than the arbitrary commands of a superior. If we may employ a distinction familiar to students of legal theory, private law would be the product of reason, not of will. Those familiar with Roman habits of thought would doubtless prefer to speak of common sense rather than reason; and the history of Roman private law may be described as the application of organized common sense to a whole range of problems which were in principle removed from the exercise of arbitrary authority.

How that was done was in many ways very remarkable. It was for an elected magistrate, a praetor, to supervise the initial procedure under which the parties to an action arrived at an 'issue', that is to say, sorted out the question to be tried. Then a private citizen, chosen by the parties from a select list and empowered by the praetor to give a binding decision, tried the action. But since he had not necessarily any knowledge of the law to be applied, he had to depend for such knowledge on others whose business it was to know the law and to interpret it. At first that function was performed by the College of Pontiffs,* who kept their knowledge to themselves. In due course, partly by the enactment of the Twelve Tables in 451–50 B.C. and partly through what appears to have been a calculated indiscretion, their secrets were laid open to the general public, only to become the speciality of a few artistocrats who took a peculiar interest in studying and interpreting the law and, by discussing with their pupils the legal questions raised by actual or hypothetical cases, created a

*On whom, *see* p. 185.

lasting tradition. These secular jurists (*jurisprudentes*) were followed by others in an unbroken succession which lasted until the end of the third century A.D., who, directly or indirectly, did almost all the work of developing private law. As far as we can see, the secular jurists simply assumed authority to interpret the law and had no official authorization until, by an obscure provision characteristic of his general method of acquiring power, Augustus apparently authorized selected jurists to give opinions on his authority. By that time, however, the general development of Roman private law was set on permanent lines, and the jurists of the Principate seem to have done little more than fill in the necessary details and make such minor adjustments as were required by social and economic changes.

We do not know why this authority of unofficial jurists was accepted. We can only infer, first, that it was in line with the 'influence' which commonly plays so great a part in an aristocratic system, and, secondly, that the general public found the quality of their work as satisfying as it has proved to later ages. For they did not trouble to give the real reasons for their opinions; at most they showed that they were consistent with pre-existing law. But no doubt another reason for their success was that they were willing to take trouble off other people's hands and were trusted as experts usually are unless they obviously go wrong.

Their influence was probably enhanced by a detachment from the actual results of litigation. They left advocacy to professional and paid orators, hoping to gain for themselves only prestige and support in a political career. Thus they did not concern themselves with the proof of facts, but gave their opinions on the assumption that the facts laid before them were correctly stated; and the outcome of litigation was, it would appear, a matter of indifference to them, a great aid to impartiality and breadth of judgement. While they cultivated the practical experience of the man of the world, they were able to see legal problems in an exceptional degree *sub specie aeternitatis* and give to their writings a universal significance applicable to far distant times and places.

So far the development of Roman private law has been indicated in such a way as to make it appear to have been entirely due to the jurists. That is an overstatement, for although legislation was resorted to on comparatively rare occasions, its intervention was important and even decisive. Thus the Twelve Tables were traditionally regarded as in some way or other the origin of most of the law, and the law of damage to property was always based in great part on the Lex Aquilia (of uncertain date). So also resolutions of the Senate (*senatusconsulta*) made important changes, especially in the law of intestate succession.

Finally, a person who had suffered loss of a novel kind might induce the praetor for the time being to afford him redress by means of a new action, not included in those authorized by the old civil law or in those promised by him in the edict he issued on entry into his praetorship; and, once the new action had been incorporated in the edicts of his successors, a new right would be seen to have come into existence by the mere fact of its having been protected by the new action. The history of private law cannot be understood without constant reference to the praetor's edict.

Nevertheless, it will not be wrong to see in the activity of the jurists the mainspring of legal change, at any rate during the six centuries from about 300 B.C. to about A.D. 300. For they alone had the necessary expert knowledge, and their services were not confined to interpreting the law. Praetors were not necessarily, perhaps seldom, learned in the law. Moreover, like other men in public positions, they were accustomed to take advice from a council, which would assuredly contain jurists. Again, the grant of a novel action would in the first instance be asked for by a litigant, who would be advised by a jurist to make the application.

In short, improvements would be sought from a praetor, from the Senate or from a popular assembly only where interpretation would not suffice, and it may fairly be inferred from all the circumstances that they would be suggested by the jurists.

We can be no less certain of their influence even when legislative power passed to the Emperor, for we know that jurists were important members of his privy council. In fact most imperial action on private law was only formally legislative and consisted of answers to questions referred to the Emperor for his decision, in much the same way as jurists gave opinions on questions submitted to them. Juristic activity persisted anonymously behind the curtain of imperial quasi-legislation.

The jurists did not create laws out of nothing; they started with certain customs, partly codified in the Twelve Tables, and modified by a few other statutes (*leges* or *plebiscita*), most of which marked settlements agreed upon between patricians and plebeians during the Struggle of the Orders. An important part of them regulated the succession on intestacy of the head of a family and accepted the principle according to which the family of a person leaving several sons was not kept intact but was divided among all the sons so as to create several new families; Roman law had already rejected the large joint family and insisted that each family should have a monarchical head exercising power over all his descendants in the male line. Otherwise the law provided a number of methods by which actions could be brought to remedy wrongs or by which heads of families could acquire property or modify their relations among themselves. The actions were all dominated by formalities, the non-observance of which rendered them invalid. So also were some contracts or modes of acquiring property, but along with them were informal acts which had a remarkable future before them.

The law may say to a person, 'If you want this particular result, you must act as follows.' If so, it will probably prescribe a particular formality. Or, on the other hand, it may accept what a person normally does in order to achieve a particular result and attribute to it the result that is normally aimed at; the act will then usually be informal. Where an act is required to be formal, the person doing it is made conscious of the fact that he is doing something to which the law attaches a legal consequence. If there is no such requirement, it is more than possible that he may be unaware of such a consequence and be quite without any intention of producing it. He appears to himself to be acting on the business or social, not on the legal plane. He will be like M.

Jourdain in *Le Bourgeois Gentilhomme*, when he was surprised to find that he was speaking prose.

There is of course a place for both informal and formal acts. Although the modern world prefers to act informally, there may be situations where it is very important to bring to a person's notice that what he proposes to do will have a particular legal effect. Moreover, it may be necessary to be able to recognize a particular act by its outward form, especially when effect has to be given to it with extreme rapidity, as when a strictly defined form given to a cheque permits a bank cashier to pay without having to ask unnecessary questions. However, the more one requires formalities, the more one tries to canalize human activity according to preconceived ideas. There ought to be room for people to experiment, to invent ways of doing business which do not conform to predetermined forms.

The problem that then faces the jurist is one of interpreting the informal acts that are thus rendered necessary. It seems clear that the Roman jurists were more interested in solving such problems than in anything else, and moreover that this part of their activity has been of greater influence and of greater value than any other in the development of medieval and modern continental law.

It looks as though in handling these questions they made a major 'breakthrough'. Interpretation means for us elucidating the meaning of words. This task was of course one with which the Roman jurists were familiar from an early date. They were also capable of interpreting tendentiously in order to achieve a result never intended by the draftsmen. But it seems that they did something quite new in accepting as valid and legally efficacious the ordinary informal acts of everyday life and in working out their legal implications on a basis of common sense. Here a few interrelated examples will do much to explain the nature of their achievement.

The Romans used the names Titius, Maevius, and Seius as English lawyers use John Doe, Richard Roe, and William Styles to denote the *dramatis personae* of legal problems. Now suppose that Titius, out of the goodness of his heart, gratuitously lends

Maevius a horse for the afternoon and Maevius returns the horse in a damaged condition. Will Maevius be liable to compensate Titius for the damage? Will Maevius have a claim against Titius if the horse throws and injures him? Or again, if Seius, as a friendly act, lets Titius leave a jar of wine in his house for a short time because Titius wants to lighten the load he is carrying home, and when Titius calls for it he finds that it has been damaged and some of the wine has been lost, will Seius be liable to compensate Titius? Will Seius have claim against Titius if the wine has leaked and spoilt a valuable rug? Would the answers to any of these questions have been different if Titius had charged Maevius for the hire of the horse or Seius had charged Titius for the storage of the jar? We must assume that, as would probably have been the case, nothing had been said by any one of the parties about the possibility of damage.

It seems probable that the original answers to these questions were (1) that Maevius would be liable to Titius without proof of any fault on his part, unless indeed the damage was done by the sort of extraordinary accident which English lawyers call an act of God; (2) that Titius would be liable to Maevius only if he knew of the horse's dangerous propensity; (3) that Seius would be liable to Titius only if he had intentionally damaged the jar; (4) that Titius would be liable to Seius if he either knew or ought reasonably to have known that the jar was leaky; and (5) that if it had been agreed that the use of the horse and the storage of the jar were to be paid for, the damage would in each case have to be paid for if caused by the intentional or careless conduct of Titius, Maevius or Seius.

These are all common-sense solutions arrived at by asking what was meant by gratuitously lending or taking a thing on deposit or by letting it out on hire or storing it for reward. But although the Romans did not express themselves in that way, it has long been recognized that they constitute a mass of systematic doctrine, according to which, if both parties stood to receive reciprocal benefits, both should show reasonable diligence, but where one party alone stood to receive a benefit, that party was liable for careless or even accidental damage, whereas the other party was liable only for damage which he had caused intentionally. Many of these and similar solutions later underwent modifications, which need not be discussed here; they too were made on common-sense grounds.

Perhaps in the long run the fact that the jurists should have asked themselves what was implied in such informal acts and should have given a series of common-sense answers to the question has been of greater importance than the answers they actually gave; for they created a method of developing the law which has been a pattern for all future ages.

The republican jurists had subjected the ordinary contractual dealings of everyday life to a certain amount of analysis and classification, distinguishing, for instance, sale from hire or partnership, and, what needs to be specially mentioned, providing each of them with its own action or pair of actions if enforcement were needed. In doing so, they contrived to give to each so-called contractual figure a specific recognizable shape, while covering with only a few such figures almost the whole range of social and commercial intercourse.

It is easy to see that such a technique could be very fertile, that one solution of a problem could lead to another by a process of generalizing from a number of cases and applying the principle so arrived at to new cases, or even by mere analogy. By a cruel misfortune legal historians cannot see the republican Roman jurists at work as they made their most crucial innovations in handling private law. For the necessary steps were taken during the two or three centuries before Cicero, a period of enormous importance in the history of Roman law, but of which we can say little more than that when it started the law had hardly passed its primitive stage and it ended in an atmosphere of rationality and even sophistication.

How much of this was original and how much derived from Greek sources it is impossible to determine. We do know that the Romans attributed no importance to outside influences and regarded other people's notions of law as 'almost ridiculous'.

The importance of informal acts was enhanced by the need to deal with the business relations of foreigners. It seems certain that Roman law at first governed only Roman citizens; we have at any rate clear evidence that early statutes did not govern foreigners. Now although the Roman people could remain indifferent to the family relations and succession rights of foreigners, they had to provide for the settlement of business disputes between Romans and foreigners. Thus by the first century B.C. all informal acts could be effectually done by foreigners as well as by Roman citizens, the most important formal contract, the *stipulatio*, was available to them, and the courts were open to them as well as to Roman citizens, the procedural stage before the praetor, which had hitherto been formalistic, having become informal.

Thus on the one hand, the law was subjected to forces which tended to make it more and more universal, and, on the other, the informal acts came to prevail over those that were formal, even when Roman citizens were dealing among themselves. In order to become universal, Roman law had to pay particular attention to informal acts, since foreigners could not be expected to know the Roman formalities; and any advantage that informality could confer on foreigners had to be accorded to Roman citizens too.

This part of Roman law available to citizens and foreigners alike became known as the *ius gentium*, in contrast to the *ius civile* available to citizens alone. It did not bear the meaning it acquired in modern times, that of International Law, for it was in no sense a law between states. There is, however, this much to be said for the transference, that what common sense prescribed for the business relations between private persons, some of whom might belong to different states, might properly govern the relations of one state to another; and indeed many of the principles of International Law were originally taken from the Roman *ius gentium*.

In the end substantially all Roman law, with the important exception of those parts which governed the family and succession on death, were made applicable to foreigners as well as to Roman citizens, and when early in the third century A.D. Caracalla extended citizenship to almost all the free inhabitants of the Empire, the whole of Roman law came to be of universal application. Moreover, such need as still survived to use the formal acts gradually disappeared and eventually those acts were themselves abolished.

The activity of the jurists culminated under the Severi in the writings of Papinian, Paul and Ulpian, all of whom served as heads of the imperial civil service. Although all of them became famous as great lawyers, Paul and Ulpian owe their prominence in part to the fact that they summed up what their predecessors had achieved. After them came the collapse of the central government known as the Anarchy, and then Diocletian's reorganization under an absolute monarchy, which historians call the Dominate. In those circumstances the summing-up of the Severan jurists proved to be final, and all subsequent legal development was by so-called *constitutiones* issued in the Emperor's name. The old law which had had its source in common sense came to be known as *ius*, or law *par excellence*. The new law emanating from the sovereign will of the Emperor usurped the title of *lex*, which had once dignified the enactments of the sovereign people. The distinction bears a rough resemblance to the English distinction between common law and statute.

The period of the Dominate is also marked by a strange phenomenon. Although the substance of the law was on the whole greatly improved by contact with the Hellenistic East, there was a serious decline in legal proficiency from the high level of intellectual mastery shown by the great jurists of the Principate. Moreover, however necessary recourse to their works might be in the practical conduct of affairs, it became increasingly difficult to consult and understand such a vast and, one may conjecture, not wholly accessible mass of legal literature, the more so because it comprised for the most part actual or hypothetical cases discussed separately and with little or no explanation of the doctrinal connexions between them.

In the sixth century Justinian decided to enact or re-enact in legislative form all the existing law, from every source, that he wished to preserve. There was no question of rewriting the law; all that could be done was to make selections from the decisions and orders of the Emperors and from the writings, the latest of which were now over two hundred years old, of the jurists, in both cases with such omissions, alterations or additions as the lapse of time had made necessary.

The various committees that Justinian appointed for this purpose produced three works, (1) the *Codex*, a new edition of the imperial constitutions, including some issued by Justinian himself, (2) the *Digest*, or *Pandects*, edited fragments from the works of the jurists, and (3) the *Institutes*, an introduction to the law for students, which was a new edition of the *Institutes of Gaius*, supplemented by extracts from similar works of roughly the same date and by new material provided by the compilers. Once promulgated by Justinian both *Codex* and *Digest* and, oddly enough, the *Institutes* also were given legislative force.

The *Institutes* are easily read and understood. They are arranged according to an order which, though it can be criticized on many grounds, is clear and perspicuous. The task of reading and understanding the *Digest* is formidable. It is of the same order of size as the Bible, and is divided into fifty books containing in all 432 titles. The titles are the important units, each of which purports to contain all the juristic material on a particular topic, such as marriage, the contract of partnership, or damage to property. The order of the titles, though unsystematic, is not in practice an obstacle to understanding. Inside each title the order is often so unintelligible that the first thing the student must do is to rearrange the various fragments of which it is composed, in the knowledge that there is quite possibly something essential to a full understanding of the topic in another, quite remote title, coupled with an apprehension that it may conflict with what he has already read. Fortunately a study of the *Institutes* greatly lightens the task of understanding the *Digest*. The *Codex*, being in a sense a supplement to the *Digest*, would be approached last, and consequently with less difficulty. In any case it is much less important for private law.

Justinian's legal activity did not cease with the publication of these three works. He continued to issue constitutions, a very few of which contained important modifications of private law. They were later collected together under the title *Novellae Constitutiones*, and are known to the modern world as the

Novels. *Codex*, *Digest*, *Institutes* and *Novels* are collectively called the *Corpus Juris Civilis*, or the *Corpus Juris* for short.

With a few exceptions, far the most important of which is the *Institute of Gaius*, contained in a palimpsest discovered in 1816, all that we know of the Roman law of the ancient world is contained in the *Corpus Juris*. It may be said that without the *Corpus Juris* later ages would have had an extremely jejune acquaintance with Roman law, and even if everything but the *Digest* had been preserved, Roman law could not have exerted much influence on the development of modern law. Whatever sins Justinian's compilers may have been guilty of in mauling the original texts of the jurists, they performed an inestimable service in transmitting the real Roman law to medieval and modern times.

The later history of Roman law in the eastern Mediterranean may be briefly dismissed. The knowledge of it was never lost, though only from time to time could the *Corpus Juris* as a whole be put to profitable use in a Greek translation. It was theoretically in force until the last generation in the Kingdom of Greece. There was, however, no substantial development apart from a slight sporadic legislation.

Roman law in the West has a much more interesting and more important history. But first came a phase of acute degeneration; a systematic and detailed body of law was inappropriate to the abject conditions of Barbarian Europe. Moreover, the new problems of a declining economy received no answer from it. It is probable that the *Digest* was never put to practical use for several centuries after its promulgation. The *Institutes* never fell out of use; they were short and simple enough to be understood. However, for the most part Roman law, where it remained in force, seems to have operated as a sort of custom, as was indeed natural in a society where hardly anyone outside the clergy was literate.

The revival of Roman law studies from about the middle of the eleventh century was therefore substantially a rebirth. It was part of an intellectual reawakening which extended also to philosophy, theology and Canon law, and for which it is impossible to assign any clear single cause. The lawyers of any country that had once been governed by Roman law must always have been under a duty to study the *Digest*; the Italian lawyers were under a special duty, for were they not subjects of the Holy Roman Empire, and was not the Emperor of their day the legitimate successor to Justinian? Why were they so slow to do their duty? A legend was once current that the Florentinus, the manuscript of the *Digest* from which all others are derived, was discovered almost miraculously at Amalfi in the eleventh century. That legend is no longer believed, and we may prefer to think that although the text of the *Digest* was always there to be read, no one before that date had enough courage and intelligence to undertake the task.

Much of the attractiveness which Roman law possessed for the man into whose hands the *Digest* now came had little relation to its inherent qualities. Almost all other law, apart from Canon law, was unwritten custom. Roman law was contained in books; and the men of the twelfth century were starved of reading matter. It is well known to medievalists that in the Middle Ages almost any book possessed some measure of authority. The Bible came first, followed by the Fathers, but Aristotle, in a Latin translation of an Arabic translation, enjoyed an authority not far behind theirs. Classical antiquity as a whole was regarded with veneration, extending even to the frivolities of Ovid. A parallel can easily be found in the tendency of uneducated people even today to believe everything they see in print; but medieval man was unaccustomed to verify statements by experiment. First, then, the *Digest* was attractive merely because it was a book.

Secondly, it was in Latin. The knowledge of Latin had never disappeared; it had survived in a sufficiently pure form alongside of the Romance languages into which it had broken down in ordinary discourse. The Western Church needed it in order to use its patristic literature, and had to maintain a means of communication intelligible to the clergy in every country. Latin remained the *lingua franca* of the literate world. Thus the *Digest* was readable to anyone prepared to take trouble.

Thirdly, there came a time when someone appeared who wanted to see what was in the *Digest* – that was probably bound to happen sooner or later – and was not put off by the difficulty of the task. There was, first of all, the difficulty of the language itself, for *Digest* Latin does not read like the simple narrative Latin of the Middle Ages. Secondly, the order in which the various topics are treated in the *Digest* is extremely unhelpful, not to say exasperating. On the other hand, to use the jargon of the present day, the *Digest* presented a challenge to anyone who wished to master its contents, and men were found who had the necessary intelligence, energy and intellectual curiosity to take it up. Moreover, the greater the difficulty, the more insistent was the challenge. For this was the age of the earlier scholastics who founded the University of Paris and were determined to employ reason to solve the riddle of the universe. Bologna produced men prepared to pit their brains against this most difficult law book, and, once a start had been made, nothing could stop the onrush of Roman law studies.

It soon became evident that, even with the help given by the more logically arranged *Institutes*, this was no task for amateurs. The men who studied the *Digest* rapidly became professionals and trained others in a professional skill. Moreover, they acquired a proprietary interest in their knowledge and skill, which they were determined to defend against all comers. Had the task of understanding the *Digest* been easy, it would have been, in the first place, intellectually unsatisfying and therefore not attractive to men of first-rate ability, and, secondly, open to all the world.

Accordingly all the cards were stacked in favour of Roman law, irrespective of its intrinsic merits. These were, however, substantial.

Not only did it provide medieval lawyers in great abundance with the detailed solutions of practical problems, but it possessed a powerful structure based on clear distinctions. It distinguished for instance between property and obligation, protecting the former against all comers, but treating the latter as a mere bond between two persons, giving the one rights only against the other or creating reciprocal rights and duties between them. In contrast to feudalism, it did not impose on the owner of a thing a duty, merely by reason of his ownership, to perform positive acts in favour of another private person. Nor did ownership of itself imply negative duties beyond a very small number which hardly diminished its economic value. An owner was indeed allowed to create rights over his property which could be enforced against anyone into whose ownership it came. Such rights exceeded merely personal rights created by obligations, but they were jealousy limited so as to encumber ownership as little as possible. One variety, known as praedial servitudes, corresponded to the easements and profits of English law, more particularly rights of way or of digging lime. Since they could be exercised only by owners of neighbouring land, they were allowed in order to enhance the value of one piece of land at the expense of another. The other variety, which conferred on a person the right to the income derived from property, could last at most for his lifetime and could not be alienated. The pattern of property rights was much simpler and more easily recognized than in customary law. Such simplicity and sharpness of outline are of immense value in teaching untutored people to think clearly about law.

Most important of all to an age of rationalists was the intensely rational character of Roman law as portrayed in the *Digest* and its freedom from relativity to any particular time or place, once such readily detachable topics as slavery and the family were put on one side. That it was law laid down by a Roman Emperor made the study of it necessary, but its sixth-century origin in no way made the doctrine contained in it out of date. Even to this day, however absorbing the study of its history may be, it is still possible to treat most of the law comprised in the *Digest* merely as good law, which H. A. L. Fisher in his little book on Napoleon described as 'organized common sense'.

Thus we come back by a broad circle to common sense.

Perhaps the greatest contribution made by Roman law to world civilization has been its demonstration that it is possible to construct a body of law upon a basis of common sense that can be accepted by different peoples at different stages of their development. It has been said that the difficulty with natural law is to get any detail into it. But this is what, as has already been shown, the Romans achieved by a converse process, by working out in ample detail the common-sense implications of certain institutions and gradually getting rid of the less rational elements in their law. Moreover they extended what had been the law for the citizens of a small city state to all the inhabitants of a large empire, irrespective of the language, literature or religion in which they had been nurtured. Roman law could not have become the universal law of the Mediterranean world without also becoming rational; rationalism might not have been so appealing to the jurists who imparted to the law its dominant character if they had not felt the need to extend it throughout the Empire.

We must be on our guard against exaggerating the extent of common sense, so acceptable to those who revived the study of Roman law in the Middle Ages. Not every irrational element was expelled from even the most rational parts of the law. Most Romanists would consider the law governing the contract of sale to be one of the most rational parts of Roman law, yet it contains rules the survival of which is hard to justify, however rational we might judge them once to have been did we know their history. Moreover, some of the most well-established institutions of Roman society, such as the *patria potestas*, the power exercised by a father over his issue in the male line of whatever age, continued even in the time of Justinian to resist the sapping operation of common sense; and throughout antiquity a strange inhibition prevented the Romans from admitting the legal possibility of such an indispensable part of modern life as direct agency in contract. Perhaps the need to conform to some irrational elements is necessary if law is to be obeyed as such and not merely in so far as each man considers it reasonable.

However, once medieval lawyers had seen the possibility of using common sense as a test of legal validity, there was no reason why they should always respect the inhibitions of jurists who lived a thousand years earlier. Rationalism operates by fits and starts, gaining momentum and then losing it as what is happening dawns on those with conservative prejudices and they proceed to organize their defences. But once the taste for the common-sense solution of difficult problems is acquired, it is never entirely lost.

In this connexion regard must be paid to the distinction between policy and technique. The purpose of private law being to organize civil society, effect is given to fluctuating views of what is right and proper; the determination of such views is the function of policy. How they are to be put in operation is the function of technique. Now we may say metaphorically that the law itself fixes the policy governing large portions of human intercourse; and in that department technique signifies the means afforded by the law to turn policy into rules of conduct, to ascertain those rules and to enforce them when necessary. However, over a very wide field the law has no opinion as to what ought to be done, but leaves the choice of policy to individuals acting solely or in concert; it contents itself with providing a technical apparatus of instruments or devices, the operation of which is governed by legal rules and principles, but which have for their object to enable men to act purposefully and to obtain results which would otherwise depend entirely on the goodwill of their fellow men. They are told how to act in order to attain certain ends and are guaranteed success so far as is humanly possible.

That kind of technique, dealing as it does with such matters as the making of contracts or wills, the acquisition of property and the judicial protection of rights, is what peculiarly exercises the minds of lawyers, who strive by working out its logical implications and reducing them to a system, to furnish more and more exact and efficient instruments of social intercourse. If the technique is well suited to its purpose it can be adapted and developed so as to meet new circumstances in accordance with the demands of common sense. In contrast, where the rules and principles governing conduct are the product of a policy laid down by the law itself, they can be adapted to new conditions only by a deliberate change in the law, usually a difficult and hazardous process, and one that lawyers are on the whole reluctant to undertake. Accordingly they often come to represent the common sense not of the present but of a past age.

That the Roman jurists conformed to this pattern of lawyerly activity is shown by the apparently disproportionate amount of space in the *Digest* devoted to some topics at the expense of others.

Those which are most extensively discussed are precisely those on which argument on a basis of common sense is likely to be most fruitful. Thus there is a limit to what can be got out of discussing intestate succession, whereas the interpretation of wills has no end. Marriage, though it is entered into voluntarily, does not admit of variations, whereas contracts, though most of them fall into established classes, can present innumerable problems; hence the law of marriage attracted less attention than the law of contracts.

For about two hundred years the first school of medieval jurists took whatever came into their hands, and expounded it as though it was existing law, although some parts of the *Corpus Juris*, such as those dealing with slavery, marriage or intestate succession, had no relevance to the circumstances of their own time. They were concerned to understand whatever they read, and since cross-references were needed and sometimes one text had to be contrasted and if possible reconciled with another, they wrote in the manuscripts marginal notes known as *glosses*; hence they acquired the title of Glossators. The next school, that of the *Post-Glossators* or *Commentators*, which lasted in one way or another until the seventeenth century, took a more practical view of Roman law, paying attention only to what was profitable to them and reconciling it with existing practice. They carried further the process characteristic of the Roman jurists, that of working out the implications of the existing law, each generation adding new courses to what its predecessors had built. This very practical way of dealing with Roman law roused the scholarly ire of the so-called *Humanistic* school, mainly in France, who insisted, though without convincing practical lawyers, on the need to go back to the original Roman texts.

Of all the Roman law that was expounded and studied in the universities only part became 'received' into the actual law of the various countries of western and central Europe. Everywhere it had to compete with varying regional and local customs and naturally with varying results. Moreover the uniform Canon law of the Catholic Church had pre-empted certain fields of activity. It would be dangerous to generalize; much historical research needs to be done before we can fully understand the reception of Roman law in any one country. There is, however, reason to believe that by and large it was the Roman technique that was received rather than the Roman policy. It was used when people wanted to do things they had not done before and had therefore no way of doing them, or where the current ways of doing them were awkward and obviously inferior to those provided by Roman law. More often, perhaps, use was made of the Roman ways of interpreting words or acts. In countries such as England and Germany, where Roman law was refused admittance, these technical aids could not be used. In England, it has been said that the law received in the twelfth and thirteenth centuries an inoculation of Roman law that preserved it from further infection. Once Englishmen had learnt from a cursory study of Roman law how to think like lawyers they reacted against it and built up in the Inns of Court a powerful profession trained on non-Roman lines which was able to find its salvation by developing a technique of its own; and, except where a specialized group of lawyers used Roman law to administer the law of wills and maritime law, the ban remained. In Germany, where there was no such profession, use had to be made by the princes of persons who had been trained in Roman law, and who had no knowledge of any technique other than the Roman; and for that and other reasons the dam was burst and Roman law came flooding in.

This is not to say that the policy of Roman law had no influence; but there is more than a suspicion that the persons or classes dominant at any time took what they wanted of it and allowed it to lead them where they wished to go, disregarding it when it ran counter to their desires. In this they were aided by the fact that the *Corpus Juris*, by imperfectly reconciling texts from different ages, could be made to yield evidence of different and even contradictory policies. Thus some modern generations were able to use Roman technique, devised to effectuate the policy of the last centuries of the ancient world, in order to make property inalienable and keep it in a family for a long period, whereas later generations, in their desire to keep property as far as possible alienable, appealed to what was almost certainly the prevailing policy of the late republic and principate. Moreover, non-Romanized English law could favour some of the same fundamental policies as the Romanized law of France. It has, for instance, been almost an article of faith with continental capitalists and socialists alike that Roman law was an essential factor in the emergence of modern capitalism; yet the economic changes came just as easily, and sometimes faster, in England than on the Continent.

In the end Roman law helped to dig its own grave. It has been well said that 'Like the arch, Roman Law never sleeps'; it is always subject to strains and stresses. It has always strained towards the rational and the universal. Eighteenth-century lawyers on the Continent, sharing the rationalistic spirit of the age, sought to find a way out of the intolerable disorder of their laws. Their predecessors had, over many generations, attained to a sufficient mastery of the Roman texts to see that they could be purged of their remaining irrationalities and anachronisms and rearranged in a rational order together with the non-Roman elements in each country's law. And here the *Institutes of Justinian* came into their own, as showing how general principles could be detached from their detailed application. The disorder of the *Digest* could be made to yield the necessary materials, the elegant arrangement of the *Institutes* the form. The solution the jurists everywhere demanded was the creation of a common law by selecting the best elements from the regional and local customs and fusing them with the received portions of Roman law, followed by its enunciation in a civil code. The earliest such code that is still in force is the French Civil Code (the *Code Napoleon*) of 1804. It was adopted wtih modifications by most countries in western and central Europe, except Germany and Switzerland, each of which resisted on various grounds for about a century and then enacted a Civil Code of its own on more modern and systematic lines.

This amalgam of modernized Roman law with non-Roman elements is known to English lawyers as the 'Civil Law', a term which has in due course been accepted by all who are engaged in the comparative study of law; and its practitioners and students are often called 'civilians'. The non-Roman elements are not always of customary origin or even of very modern development; in many countries they are a part of religion, for instance Islamic, Jewish, Hindu. What is distinguished from Civil Law under the name of Common Law has very much the same general structure, the place of Roman law being taken by a body of doctrine based mainly on cases decided by judges, at first in England and later also in countries to which English law has from time to time been taken.

If Civil Law and Common Law are understood in these broad senses, they now divide between themselves the whole world outside the Scandinavian countries, Afghanistan and Arabia. The Common Law has hardly gone outside the countries in which English is the *lingua franca*, that is to say, most of what is or was the Commonwealth and the United States. The Civil Law, with its hard core of Roman law, has the rest, including such Asian countries as Japan, Thailand, Indonesia, Iran and Lebanon, such African countries as Egypt, the Congo and the former colonies of France, and the whole of Latin America. Behind the Iron Curtain too, in the restricted sphere still governed by private law, the Civil Law prevails.

Lawyers in all these countries are conscious enough of differences which keep them apart, but to English lawyers they look very much alike, because they think in a Roman way which is alien to us; and their minds are set in such a common direction as to enable an Egyptian student to study law with profit in Paris or Rome or a Greek in Lausanne or Bonn.

An important group of countries were originally civilian, but have since been subjected to such powerful influences from England or the United States that their laws are now properly called hybrid systems. Such are Scots law, the Roman-Dutch law of South Africa, the laws of Quebec, Louisiana and the Philippines.

Reference to the original Roman texts is now almost confined to one or two countries such as South Africa, and even there is uncommon. The study of Roman law is now purely academic, though it may serve the practical purpose of introducing students to general legal ideas and, in Common Law countries, of preparing them for the study of modern Civil Law systems. It may be doubted whether any more help can be got from Roman law in the solution of modern problems, for not only have the best parts of it already been absorbed into existing law, but the world is turning away from the kinds of society to which it has been found appropriate. We may not wish for a return of the conditions which caused the reception of Roman law.

BIBLIOGRAPHY

The foregoing is one man's selection of what he thinks are the most important contributions Roman law has made to the modern world. It by no means conveys a complete picture of Roman law.

For a fuller and more systematic account the reader whose interest has been captured may turn to either Barry Nicholas, *An Introduction to Roman Law* (Oxford University Press, 1962) or to *Leage's Roman Private Law* (3rd ed., by A. M. Pritchard, Macmillan, 1961), both of which contain short bibliographies.

7

ARCHITECTURE AND ENGINEERING

Sir Ian Richmond

IN the modern world architecture and engineering are on the whole two distinct professions. The Roman made no distinction between them, using the word *architectus* to mean either architect or engineer. So it comes about that, writing in the very early days of the Empire, Vitruvius, whose work has acquired the somewhat exaggerated importance which attaches to a sole survival, finds himself equally at home in describing the Orders, or concrete mixing, or the mechanical devices of his day, such as torsion-propelled artillery, a double-acting force-pump, a water-organ or a water-mill; and he will consider with equal aplomb questions of town-planning or tests for a good water-supply. But, as in so much ancient literature concerned with factual knowledge, breadth of scope is matched by lack of experimental data and to an extent which would alarm either an architect or an engineer of the present day; while by contrast the surviving works, confined indeed principally to architecture, give an impression of soundness the more emphatic because in the nature of things only sound work can endure for so many centuries.

It would, however, be wrong to suppose that, because the experimental basis of textbook knowledge was not the Roman approach, no experiment in fact took place. The very nature of Roman architecture is based upon an evolving skill, first, in the employment of a new medium, namely, concrete, and, secondly, in the use of the curved form of bearer for thrusts; that is, the arch or vault in the vertical plane and in the horizontal the niche, viewed as an arch on its side. It is the habitual use of these characteristic structural devices which divides Roman architecture from its predecessors; for, even if anticipations are to be found, it must be recognized that the Roman architect used these media with familiarity and a skill of which the repute still resounds in history. But an inquiry into the actual use of the material and its methods reveals how gradual was the evolution and how cautious the approach. This is the effect not of experiment but of experience: for experiment, successfully operated, facilitates and promotes rapid advances, while experience moves the more slowly because it is feeling its way in the realm of unknown risk. In no field, moreover, is the union or fusion of architect and engineer more complete, and it becomes evident how the very nature of the work called for the qualities of both trainings.

Vitruvius takes this duality of approach for granted, but also lays much emphasis upon the function of the architect as the producer of seemly and beautiful form appropriate to the situation, function and nature of a building and of adornment suited to these. That adornment might be subsumed in the broadest outlines of a design itself is an idea with which Roman architecture cannot be credited, although its articulation, as surviving in such gaunt and massive skeletons as the Baths of Caracalla or the Basilica of Maxentius, has sometimes induced this supposition or even inspired its application to other materials in other ages. But the circumstances of the ancient world, its traditions and its strongly conservative attachment to them, dictated that, however stark the framework or shell of a building might be, its surface must be covered with decoration in the classical convention. Here, as in literature, fancy might indulge in conceits which startled or variations which surprised, but tradition reigned supreme. Indeed, although a resemblance has often been indicated between Roman architecture and the Baroque, it must be realized that the Baroque far exceeds the Roman in its abandoned fluidity of form and, so far as is known, in the boldness of its illusionism. Yet moments exist in Roman architecture, and particularly in its forms of interior decoration, when painted illusion is employed wholesale, as in *trompe l'œil* architectural vistas or in the backgrounds of mead and bower set within an architectural framework which mimics actual voids. It is possible and indeed likely that these and other comparable decorative developments owe their inspiration to the Hellenistic world, which Rome had absorbed and in so doing had become cosmopolitan without shedding her own individuality. But what this inspiration produced was something as markedly Roman as Sir Christopher Wren's borrowings from the Baroque are English, and something, too, which was no less rich in its variety. Nor were Roman contributions lacking. It is often claimed that Rome added little or nothing to the Classical Orders. But, in the first place, her own Tuscan Order, in mature Roman work generally used in combination, was a dignified and appropriate application of restraint to the composition of an architectural frame, less bulky than the Doric and less emphatic in vertical line. This form offered little room for variety in surface treatment. Developments in surface decoration are associated rather with the second and more important Roman exploitation of the Orders; by which the Corinthian Order, based upon the acanthus, was treated with an ingenuity which gave it entirely new life in its own right, or, again, was combined with new motifs or with the Ionic style to produce the Composite Order. This new projection of the Corinthian was to introduce in architecture a decorated column capital of sufficiently powerful and bold enrichment to hold its own in buildings of the vast scale demanded for Roman public works. Here, as in other fields of decoration, the cosmopolitan mason or designer came into his own; but this did not mean that eclecticism in Roman architecture became a welter of foreign copy and mannerism like that in which Victorian architecture lost itself. Whatever Rome might borrow was shaped and subordinated to Roman needs and Roman idiom with a compelling sense for dignified line and composition.

The instinct which endowed Roman architecture with an innate visual dignity or *gravitas* was even more evident in terms of planning. In this field of the profession Roman public works called for elaborate and not seldom intricate planning on a scale generally unequalled thereafter until the later nineteenth century. Attempts have been made to link this manifestation of Roman skill with solemn principles of spatial theory or ritual, and there is no doubt that the Roman ritual insistence upon the augur's division of space, both for ritual observation and for planning, created a fundamental predisposition towards axial lines and a balanced composition about them. Once the principle was granted, its manifest utility in practice favoured its automatic adoption, and there can be little doubt that its practical use and value soon eclipsed the ritual or religious thought on which it had been based. This will explain why Vitruvius has virtually nothing to say about augural dispositions, but more about proportion and utilitarian reasons for choice of site or aspect than would be written by most architects of today. Again, just because the Roman world had begun to resemble the modern in its division into specialisms, Vitruvius omits all mention of military practice in the principles of planning and layout. Yet the Roman practice of constructing regular camps, even in campaigning, which so startled the contemporary world, was in effect a seasonal expression of practical design in the service of the Roman state militant, and must have imbued the citizenry at large with a sense for balanced and intricate planning. This influence had been brought to bear many generations before the Roman conquest of the eastern Mediterranean carried Hellenistic architectural inspiration to Rome or Italy; and the importance of this priority lies in the fact that it ensured that, when these influences came, they entered a field in which they could be not only received but cross-fertilized, to produce a new and altogether better class of building or plan. The capability of planning in the grand manner for large bodies of people thus emerged as a peculiarly Roman qualification, and in architecture it affected every field. The great temples, whose plans and elevations were full of variety and minor ingenuities, were placed axially at the focal point in a grand vista of courts and porticoes. The public square received its architectural frame, no longer of haphazard growth but of unitary plan. The *basilica* evolved in Roman hands from the Hellenistic portico of several longitudinal bays lacking in focus into a stately and symmetrical enclosed public hall, with a focal point at one or both ends of its great nave. The market-hall, again of Hellenistic origin, became a new thing in Roman hands through the application of vaulting to its roofing and lighting problems. There were, however, other major buildings and developments quite specifically Roman. Great houses and palaces were now of a scale unimagined in communities of less wealth and splendour, and to their planning went both the innate genius for organized symmetry and the new possibilities offered by faced concrete in the exploitation of vault, dome and niche. Comparison of the broad outlines of the plans of Nero's Golden House (*Domus Aurea*), Hadrian's villa near Tivoli and the great country house of Piazza Armerina in Sicily reveals a progressive skill and a lively changing world, wherein both practice and fashion can be seen to evolve. Vaulting and the elliptical plan, brilliantly applied to problems of access and auditorium, produced the amphitheatre, whose imposing external aspect was due to the Roman combination of the Orders, and notably the Tuscan Order, with the arcade. The culmination of architectural achievement comes in the great public baths or *thermae*, whose design had to suit not only large crowds but rooms of graded heat, used in forward and reverse order and with fundamental variations, all fitted in turn to an unseen high-capacity service of heat, drainage and water-supply. To fit such demands into a symmetrical plan, soundly adapted to the needs of the public which it was to serve, evoked in the Roman architect the highest skill and most brilliant design. The genius displayed in the handling of crowds in relation to planning here again recalls Roman military organization, which was distinguished so early and for so long by exactly this flair for disciplined system.

It would have been impossible to execute most of the greater schemes except in the new material, of which something in general may here be said. Roman concrete owes its durability and its strength to no secret formula, nor does analysis support the popular belief that its ingredients were elaborate or complicated. The first-class quality of the material was determined by the choice of really good and unadulterated lime, excellent sand, often of volcanic origin, and a carefully selected aggregate which varied much from district to district. There is no doubt that the material was originally invented through the medium of the mud or *adobe* wall into which limestone, which abounds in many parts of Italy, was introduced in comminuted form. But such material was not habitually used to bear the principal weights and stresses. These were carried either by timber framing or by masonry, while the composition was used for panels of infilling. Nor was the face of the composition panel habitually exposed to the weather: it was waterproofed, or at least treated to throw off water, by a coating of lime-wash or plaster; and in due course an outer face of small rubble, between which the mixture or composition was laid wet, was found to provide a more effective and durable face. It is clear that all these discoveries, well illustrated in the oldest houses of Pompeii, were made during the fourth and third centuries B.C. They cannot be regarded as the result of experiment, in the true sense of observed and recorded single or serial tests or observations: but they may properly be considered as the application of a body of experience, from which grew an *expertise*, in building. Another important factor was the increasing size of State building contracts, from the third century B.C. onwards, which must have encouraged the establishment of contracting firms with an experienced staff, whether slave or free, capable of handling a contract when undertaken. These are the nameless necessities which appear in no history, but which are implicit both in the increasing size of public works and in the moves towards standard practice evident from the second century B.C. onwards.

If it is in the fourth and third centuries B.C. that the development of concrete as a material takes place, it was the following two centuries that saw the development in its handling. This is characterized by great caution in the distribution of stresses, so that masonry is employed in preference to concrete at all crucial bearing points, while concrete is liberally used for vaulting, for niches and for long runs of walling, particularly those retaining walls which in the Italian *praeruptis oppida saxis* – 'towns on sheer cliffs' – had so important a structural function. As the structures grew in size and ambition, so it became of increasing importance for the contractor to arrive at a facing which would throw off the weather, could be produced quickly, in material cheap and easy to work, and would adhere well to the mass behind it. Hence came the exploitation of tufa facing in forms which steadily become more standardized, from the *opus incertum*, of small, roughly fitted rubble, to the cuboid form with long tail, which ultimately becomes uniform in size and is set diagonally so as the better to throw off water, the famous *opus reticulatum*. Here can clearly be detected standardization not only of practice but of materials in order to meet the problems of costing and quantity surveying which must for long have exercised the keen contractor. It is very evident that at this juncture in the fortunes of Roman building practice an experimental inquiry into materials, their strength, crushing power and durability would have been of the greatest value : but it must be realized that the whole structure of ancient society and labour organization militated against such research. The lack led to the retention of cautious and conservative methods and estimates, particularly in relation to margins of tolerance and safety, which has much in common with large-scale structural practice of the early nineteenth century, when exactly the same dearth of experimental data obtained.

An excellent example of the effect of the consequent reliance upon experience rather than experiment is afforded by the next and final development in faced concrete. The problem of obtaining a cheap and durable waterproof surface had been in large measure resolved by the invention of *opus reticulatum*. But the Roman architect had also to consider fire-risk as a serious danger, the more formidable in an age where fire-fighting devices remained primitive and wholly unequal to dealing with conflagrations. At the close of the first century B.C., when Vitruvius was writing, a beginning had been made in the use of sawn or broken roof-tiles for facing in the manner of thin brickwork, the narrow, flat edge of the tile being the exposed surface, the diagonally broken or sawn faces furnishing an effective bond with the concrete packed or poured in behind them. Vitruvius recommends the employment of old roof-tiles, not for cheapness, though this must in fact have counted, but because weathering had seasoned the tiles and made it possible to distinguish good ones; furthermore the material had the merit of being fire-proof. This discovery revolutionized Roman building. Although facings of *tufo* or *selce* were by no means rejected, facing in tile or brick now became so widely used as to be typical, particularly in Rome itself, though the cost and the capacity of transport always played an important part in the choice.

The new use of tiles was even more important in relation to the articulation or framing of buildings; for the same caution that was applied to the margins of tolerance and .safety reigned also in the treatment of concrete in relation to stresses or struts. As already observed, in walling or in foundation-work, if weight was unevenly distributed, its main stresses were confided to stone framing or piers, the concrete being treated as infilling, very much as in a modern steel-framed building. But whereas in modern building the steel framing is not only vertical but also horizontal, in Roman building horizontal ties could be achieved solely by ribs or arches, whether curved or flat. So long, then, as the principal weight-bearing material was restricted to stone, its own weight and its relative clumsiness imposed strict limits both on the size of buildings and their structural development. Within these limits schemes of complication and a certain grandeur were being achieved from the second century B.C. onwards. The Porticus Aemilia and the Tabularium in Rome, the Temple of Hercules Victor in Tivoli or the Amphitheatre at Pompeii indicate what could be done in public architecture to meet the needs of commerce, administration, religion or entertainment. But the evident limitations of space and form which materials imposed gave scope only for the deployment of units in the plan, while a wide choice in size and variation of the units themselves remained out of the question. The use of tile for facing, for aggregate and for ribs, made possible entirely new developments. Tile afforded a facing with much improved resistance to weather or fire, and, when broken or crushed, an aggregate which dried and set more quickly. Moreover, the ever-present doubts concerning the strength and stability of concrete could be assuaged by the use in walling of tile bonding-courses, lacing-courses and relieving arches, while in vaulting the lighter and more tractable ribs of tile could be much more easily erected and then sustained while setting, whereupon they were ready themselves to contain and support appropriately comparmentalized panels of concrete. In this way an articulated building could be designed with a view first to controlling its own stresses, then to distributing these successfully by means of the articulation until the concrete finally set, and, finally, to ensuring that the stresses could be taken up yet again if the building was subjected to an exceptional strain, such as seismic shock. The classic example of this is the Pantheon of Hadrian in Rome, built six generations after Vitruvius, to a size and plan of which he would not have dreamed. The walls of this vast rotunda, 144 feet in internal diameter, are symmetrically compartmentalized, horizontally by niches and vertically by relieving arches, so that they resolve into eight immense tied piers, on to which the weight and thrust of the dome is delivered by a complicated series of interlocking arches and ribs. It is well known that the building has more than once withstood very substantial earthquake shocks, but less often remembered that before the repairs and consolidation of a generation ago, the cracks induced by the tremors could clearly be seen and traced to vanishing-point along its great relieving-arches, which had first made the structure possible and ultimately saved it from ruin. While, however, the vast scale of the Pantheon demanded a highly complicated articulation, its form was essentially simple. Its stresses were not widely distributed across a series of voids, but concentrated and interlocked about a single tied and continuous circle. The building thus had a coherent structural unit which many other types lacked. Only when the designers of a great dome combined it with a skilled disposition of vast arches and piers did such a building as Justinian's Sancta Sophia in Constantinople become possible. This vast metropolitan church, though more vulnerable to earthquake shock, represented a structural advance at least as great again as that for which in its time the Pantheon had stood, and the experience which made it possible was derived from the great halls of the Roman world, and in particular from the building of *thermae*. These were indeed enormous halls, now barrel-vaulted and now cross-vaulted, planned in ever-varying association with vast domed hot rooms and niches containing heated baths. The largest examples, in Rome, display a last concession to ancient prejudice; for, instead of concrete piers, gigantic stone columns are employed to carry the principal vaulting ribs, a conservatism completely absent in Constantinople. Here must also be taken into account the decorative tradition current in the older capital, in which the whole exterior of such buildings as the Baths of Caracalla or Diocletian, or the Basilica of Maxentius, was rendered in stucco treated to imitate ashlar, while the interior was clad with marble veneering or painted plaster and ceiled in coffering which imitated stone. The columns thus served as an especially telling and emphatic enrichment of the interior decoration at its most significant points as well as supporters of the principal vaulting-ribs, so much so that the ordinary spectator will hardly have looked beyond their decorative function. No buildings indeed illustrate more effectively than these the divorce which the new materials had inevitably induced between structure and decoration. It had not always been so. Decoration of this scale and richness had first been applied in the Near East, where the exceptionally fine building stone and the cheap and countless labour-markets of Lebanon and Syria enabled the wealthy caravaneer patrons of Baalbek or Palmyra to encourage building of a scale and a richness unexampled in its age. Here material and decoration were one : and so also in Rome, the Forum of Trajan, which was renowned in antiquity for its sumptuous splendour, and was the work of Apollodorus of Damascus, reflects in its vast size, its polychrome marble columns and its large-scale decoration, that Eastern world to which Apollodorus belonged. In contrast with later days, the East was not yet a world of building with domes, and this fact illumines the outspoken remark by Apollodorus to Hadrian on 'pumpkin-building'. Hadrian, however, in reality adopted the Eastern mode on his own terms, in the internal wall-decoration of the Pantheon and its columned niches. It was evident that this bold decoration in the grand manner proved as well suited to the great vaulted hall as to the rotunda. The fact that there was now a divorce between the material and its decoration had no influence upon design since the basic conception of form remained the same.

An entirely different effect is conveyed by the use of the new materials for urban domestic building, in the form of blocks of flats. Such blocks had already existed in republican Rome, as early as the third century B.C., but speculation and jerry-building made them a heavy risk, particularly in the matter of collapse and fire, so that once again only the introduction of tile provided a sound material for their construction. This made possible the simple and attractive lines of the well-known domestic blocks which were to be created after the fire of A.D. 64 at Rome and a little later at Ostia. They were either flats or private houses, but all were constructed with clean lines and sound materials, the contrast being with the sea-front dwellings of Pompeii, to which the tirade of Vitruvius against timber and lath-and-plaster construction (*opus craticium*) would still have been wholly appropriate. Both public and private urban building thus took on an entirely new aspect.

The landscape scenes in wall paintings of the so-called Fourth Style, while Hellenistic in inspiration, met a taste for natural scenery reflected in the letters of Cicero or the Younger Pliny. In actual architecture the results were notable, and the fashion lasting. Italian sunshine and the problem of lighting large and complex buildings always favoured the courtyard plan, partly because it produced coolness, and partly because it served as a light-well. But the appreciation of landscape and the long view favoured also the exploitation of façade or wings, and in the great country houses all these elements are combined to produce plans of an ingenuity and splendour certainly matched both in external appearances and landscape gardening, though these have not survived. Thus, the Golden House of Nero made its impact by the boldness and variety of the ensemble rather than by any single part : the great vestibule on the Velia, with its colonnaded approach from the ancient Forum, attracted rather than dominated; while the main block, looking across the lake on the site of the later Colosseum to the vast fountain-façade against the Temple of Claudius on the Caelian, surveyed an operatic landscape cut out of the heart of densely crowded Rome. This imperial whim, a ruthless Sans Souci which did not survive, in the end serves best as a reminder of what was possible on the hillsides of the Campagna or on the sea-coast. Hadrian's Villa near Tivoli, itself the successor of a fine republican house, lay extended in the sunshine of an enormous hillside park, overlooking its own secluded glade, with room to indulge every fancy of that much-travelled Emperor's taste. Audience-chambers, water-pavilions, spacious porticoes of fixed lengths for exercise, Egyptian gardens, theatres and conservatoires again form no vast design, like a Versailles or a Caserta, but a series of individual conceits, in themselves coherent, but as various as the moods to which they ministered. These vast palaces, which represent the caprice of unlimited wealth, were imitated on smaller scale by the larger country houses or villas, whose distribution had an extent which the world was hardly to see again. With all the variety which so wide a distribution might entail the general type was common to the whole Empire. The greatest country-houses, such as Val Catena in Istria, Chiragan in Narbonensis, St Ulrich in eastern Gaul, or the riverside governor's palace in Cologne, even Fishbourne or Woodchester in Britain, mirror the same tastes with an infinite variety of execution, but with always a sense of planning which bears the coherent stamp of Roman architecture.

New opportunities for the development of purely decorative monuments were presented by the concentration of glory in the single person of the Emperor. The triumphal arch, which had republican antecedents, now became not merely the basis for statues but a frame for the display of large-scale historical reliefs. Closely akin was the four-way arch or *tetrapylon*, of which the Arch of Galerius at Salonica is an outstanding example. Yet another conception inherited from the Hellenistic world and the Republic was the monumental *tropaeum*, a huge tree-trunk in stone, hung with arms and begirt by captives, which was set upon a vast decorated drum, as at Tropaeum Traiani, now Adamklissi in Romania. No antecedent, on the other hand, is known for the great war-memorial Columns of Trajan and Marcus Aurelius, round the shafts of which continuous narrative friezes wind in a spiral from bottom to top. If the first three types of monument represent a lively and inventive reshaping of earlier forms to new purpose, the last remains a uniquely daring and imaginative invention.

It might be thought that in the pre-eminently conservative field of religion architectural designs remained more stereotyped and traditional and a review of the material might at first sight appear to confirm the notion. But in fact both the needs of an Empire and the revolution in building methods dictated that important changes should take place in this sphere also. The point may be illustrated by three temples from Rome itself, where the Campus Martius or the Fora had become the pre-eminent monumental quarters. Their areas were so crowded that much ingenuity was required in devising forms to suit buildings that were often of multiple purpose and at the same time severely cramped. Here the strong Roman sense for frontality and axial treatment played an important part in design, with striking results in both plan and elevation. In the Forum Romanum the Temple of Divus Iulius, dedicated in 29 B.C., had to serve the triple purpose of a shrine for the cult, of a decorative official speaker's platform, and of a setting for the altar already erected on the spot where the corpse of the assassinated Dictator had been cremated. The temple rose on its own lofty base, high above the orator's platform, which pushed the steps of the temple to both sides of it and presented a front broken by a prominent niche containing the altar. Access to the temple was obtained by a second flight of stairs rising from the back of the platform to a porch diversified by an extra wide middle intercolumniation which displayed the cult statue. This extremely neat solution to a highly complicated problem has a compact efficiency which a modern architect might envy.

The temple of Mars Ultor, in the Forum of Augustus, presents yet another new and ingenious design, with owes its basic conception to Julius Caesar's adjacent Forum, in which a large monumental enclosure serves as the setting for a great temple placed at its back and forming the axial feature. In the Forum of Augustus the rearward irregularity of the enclosure, formed by a huge screen wall as a protection against fire, is disguised by the vast scale of the temple and its apsidal sanctuary. The enclosure then expands, to form an opposite pair of very large semicircular bays (*exedrae*), intended to house statues and tablets commemorating famous citizens; and the bays are screened, and thus prevented from destroying the axiality of the plan, by colonnades which were heightened by the addition of an exceptionally tall attic embellished with elaborate circular shields set between Caryatids. The western colonnade terminates in a hall containing a colossal statue. This is another instance of a multiple-purpose design, combining a temple with two Halls of Fame and with colonnades which served as courts of justice, all on a restricted site.

Both examples so far cited belong to days before the new structural methods resulting from the introduction of tile. An extreme case of what this might mean is indeed provided by the Pantheon. But a more sober indication of how the new materials might affect temple architecture is afforded by the Hadrianeum, dedicated to the deified Hadrian, which stands in the heart of the Campus Martius. This remarkable building has the outward aspect of a colonnaded temple, but the sanctuary, like that of Mars Ultor, is apsidal, and its main hall is covered by a large coffered barrel-vault. How the roof was treated externally is unknown, but, in order to take up the extra height involved, the entablature was crowned by a large attic decorated with the famous reliefs of personified provinces of the Empire to which Hadrian had devoted much energy and thought. The conception of the vaulted temple hall may indeed be of Hadrianic rather than Antonine origin, if it goes back to the interesting double temple of Venus and Rome on the Velia; but that building in its present form belongs to the time of Maxentius (A.D. 306–12), though it is likely that the fourth-century architect copied the form of the Hadrianic original. The vaulted hall, however, transformed the whole aspect of the building by concentrating attention upon the terminal apse. The result was the creation of a divine audience-hall whose resemblance to the palace audience-hall of the semi-divine Emperor cannot escape notice.

The boundary line between architecture and engineering is difficult to demarcate, but it is certainly crossed by military architecture. Development in this sphere, to meet the differing needs of Roman army units, from the legion of between five thousand and six thousand men to the auxiliary units of thousands and five hundreds, whether mounted, part-mounted or infantry, was the distinctive achievement of the Imperial standing army. It called for precision and standardization combined with flexibility and, in relation to materials, stockpiling and quantity-surveying on a hitherto unexampled scale. Some idea may be gained of the concentrated effort and organization involved in the rapid creation of a fifty-acre legionary fortress, when it is considered that in such an establishment over eight miles of walling will be required for the barracks alone; and that, apart from fortifications, themselves a mile and a quarter in perimeter, the buildings of greater complication range from administrative headquarters to drill-halls, granaries, hospitals, construction shops, officers' houses of great variety, baths (*thermae*) and blocks of colonnaded stores. Compared with this the effort involved in erecting an auxiliary fort of three to five acres is small indeed, but it must be realized that thirty or more forts may go with one legionary fortress. All this structural work was planned and organized, often at considerable distance, from the offices of the legionary *praefectus fabrum*, which must have enshrined a body of practice in quantity-surveying and skill in execution second to none in the Roman world. It goes far to explain the earlier career of Vitruvius as a military engineer and the affinity which has often been noted between provincial public building and military architecture. Manifestly, army engineers must often have retired into civilian practice in their profession, in its many aspects. In no field is this more evident than in the public baths or in the urban *basilica* combined with a courtyard *forum* which so closely resembles the headquarters building of a legionary fortress. Much ink has been spilt upon the question of which derives from the other, but what is much more striking is the ease with which the military architect could transfer to this type of civil architecture.

Road-making was another field in which the military and civil engineer might be equally skilled. This had indeed not always been so; for the lack of a standing army during the Republic meant that the great roads of Italy were put out to contract. These massive highways were built in country where a long dry summer demanded a durable surface which would not disintegrate in dust, so that hard stone, often blocks of volcanic *selce*, was employed and lasted long at the expense of comfortable driving. But under the Empire the great embanked provincial roads and lines of penetration were military works, with a substructure of such bulk and solidity as to defy destruction and to serve as a lasting base for a surfacing which might itself be relatively slight. Between these two extremes, and predominant in the large picture, come the macadamized roads founded upon a sound bottoming. In all the types great attention is paid, first to drainage, with the object of keeping the road dry against winter damage to surfaces which had no bituminized medium to hold them; secondly, to providing a substructure strong enough to form a permanent basis for repairs. In choosing the course, the natural predilection of the engineer for a straight line, or a point-to-point series of straight lines, is manifest, but the tendency was not carried to extremes. In hilly or mountainous country, where gradients were in question or a straight course inapposite, the Roman engineer, with that common sense which in general distinguishes his work, will choose the contoured or valley-side course, or, again, the zig-zag. What impresses is the selection of route, especially in relation to natural obstacles and surface drainage, and the brilliantly incisive reconnaissance which lies behind it. Allied to this is the solidity of the main elements in the work and the relative infrequency of repairs. The engineering is fundamentally simple, calling for heavy labour applied *en masse*, and suited to the capabilities of local unskilled labour working under skilled direction. At necessary points, reduced to a sensible minimum, elaboration was required, in the embankment, the bridge or even the tunnel. Here entered the pile-driver, the caisson (kept dry by bucket-and-chain pumps or by force-pumps) and the crane, operated by compound-pulleys and windlass or treadmill. Sometimes such building schemes may seem too grandiose, and their astonishing permanence, enduring beyond all presumable expectation of their authors, lends force to such a view. The great Tagus bridge of Alcántara, for example, is forty-eight metres high from river-bed to roadway, and this seems excessive;

but a sight of the river in high flood suffices to vindicate the judgement of its builder, Julius Lacer. Hardly less impressive, if in a minor key, is the resourceful use of local materials and ready adaptation to local conditions, all resulting in a variety of structural practice so fascinating as almost to obscure the fundamental principles here outlined.

Tunnels are much rarer than bridges, yet in the relatively soft tufa rocks of Italy they have a long tradition going back to Etruscan practice, as exemplified by the tunnel which linked the Veii hinterland with the Tiber valley by piercing the ridge which later carried the Via Flaminia, seventeen miles north of Rome. On the Via Flaminia itself the tunnel in the Furlo Pass is a well-known Augustan example, and was no doubt the prototype for the short tunnels cut through various Alpine spurs; but it is greatly surpassed in length by the contemporary road-tunnel of Cocceius at Cumae, which survives and is a little under three-quarters of a mile long, and that between Naples and Pozzuoli, about half a mile long, which filled Seneca with trepidation in the first century A.D. and through which Petrarch travelled in the fourteenth. The planning of such enterprises, particularly in relation to light-shafts, was perhaps more remarkable than their execution, though they were double-track tunnels intended for simultaneous use in both directions. A rare but certain instance of single-line traffic occurs in the Alpine Gorge du Covatannaz where the road is cut along a precipice in the living rock and is furnished with deep grooves deliberately cut in order to keep the vehicle wheels on the road.

Less common than roads, but not less remarkable for their engineering, are canals, usually dug either to regulate or to modify natural water-courses in favour of transport or to serve as vast catchment drains, when consideration of transport facilities became incidental. In the former class come the republican canal of Marius, which circumvented the blind mouths of the Rhône delta; Agrippa's canals which linked Lake Avernus through the Lucrine Lake with the sea and so created a landlocked training-ground for the preparation of the Augustan war fleet; the Canal of Drusus, which linked the Rhine and the Zuyder Zee and afforded a sheltered passage for naval operations in north Germany; and the Fosse Dyke connecting the rivers Witham and Trent. To catchment drains belong the Pomptine canal, whose barges were immortalized by Horace, and such works as the Lincolnshire and Cambridgeshire Car Dykes. Some notable schemes remained abortive. The Corinth canal, whose construction was contemplated by Julius Caesar, Gaius Caligula and Nero, and that which was to link Rhône and Rhine by their tributaries Saône and Moselle, were both killed by politics rather than by technical failure.

But drainage was not always by means of the canal. Outlet tunnels or *emissaria* were an ancient device, exemplified by the Etruscan diversionary tunnel at Veii; while the Cloaca Maxima, one of the most ancient of Roman sewers, was in fact intended to drain and to evacuate the pent-up waters of the valley later occupied by the Forum Romanum. In Imperial times the drainage tunnel of the Fucine Lake, which rendered a natural basin fit for agriculture, was opened with much ceremony by Claudius, with unexpected accidents at the opening. But all in the end went as the designers planned, and the tunnel itself was no mean feat of engineering. Nor were river tunnels unknown. The twin tunnel which carried the ancient Caicus below the monumental area of the city of Pergamum offers us the impressive existing counterpart to the similar work commended by the younger Pliny at Amastris when he was governor of Bithynia under Trajan.

Allied to canals and drainage were the great ports. Those of Ostia are well known, and represent famous attempts to by-pass the mouth of the active delta-forming river Tiber and to provide good docks on the west coast of Italy, which was hereabouts notoriously deficient in good harbours. To this work went not only all the experience gained in bridging and draining, but also that acquired in the building of retaining-walls and in embanking. The hill-top towns of Italy had given opportunity for long practice in the erection of retaining walls in order to meet their requirements of fortification or of substructures for monumental buildings on the edge of declivities. Much valuable experience had also been gained in the erection of monumental round tombs, which, in linear descent from the earthwork tumulus, had enveloped and divided the mass of earth with an articulated structure which converted it into a stone monument resistant to all the unequal internal stresses to which it was liable. The greatest of such monuments is the Mausoleum of Augustus in Rome, whose circular funeral chamber was constructed round the solid core which carried the central crowning statue, and was separated from the articulated peripheral mass by an annular corridor reached by the entrance passage. Embanking developed more slowly, but skill in retaining a steep lakeside liable to slip is admirably illustrated in the elaborate sheaths and groynes discovered on the shore of Lake Nemi, while the embanking of a great river liable to high and swirling floods is exemplified at Mérida, the capital of Lusitania, on the south bank of the Guadiana, the ancient Anas. This embankment is linked with the system of sewers, flushed by surface water, but carrying also the town sewage in the manner common throughout the Roman world. This was a field in which Roman practice was more haphazard, probably owing to ignorance of how infection was carried or how it might be related to casual sewage-disposal.

In no field of engineering, however, has the Roman achievement been more famed than that of water-supply. The aqueducts of ancient Rome itself make the deepest impression of all. No capital was ever supplied with so lavish a quantity of running water, nor did any metropolis put it to more spectacular public use. But while the long procession of arched substructures bestriding the Campagna tends to stand for the entire achievement, the earliest line of development sprang from a very different source. The beginnings lay in the Etruscan method of soil conservation by the capture of eroding streams in underground conduits; and the experience of driving tunnels between shafts sunk at a series of set levels below the valley floor was exactly what lay behind the Aqua Appia, the earliest aqueduct in Rome, which served only the low-lying area of the republican city. Only the need to supply the high-lying regions drove the aqueduct builders to erect the arched conduits, and these may be judged as saving material and reducing wind-stress rather than as designed for an elegance which is fortuitous rather than intentional. Had the lie of the land permitted, the engineer would naturally have preferred the hillside contoured course, which demands neither tunnelling nor high substructures and, in the later and longer aqueducts of Rome, represents a high proportion of the course. The instruments used for surveying the course were a large water-level, the *chorobates*, which must have been useful in the detail of tunnelling between points of fixed depth, and in fixing a series of horizontal points. Surveying at relatively long distance could be undertaken by means of the *dioptra*, which was a water-level fixed on a tripod stand with vertical and horizontal movements and cross-line sights which were capable of fine adjustment. The instrument was used with a graduated levelling-staff up which moved a large sighting-disc, so that readings were taken at the staff itself in default of telescopic sights. This was perhaps the most ingenious instrument that the ancient world produced.

The bridges across the valleys and the arched substructures remain in reality the exception, but rightly and inevitably capture the imagination. The two most famous provincial examples are the great valley-bridging aqueducts of Segovia and of the Pont du Gard, which carried the aqueduct serving Nemausus, the modern Nîmes. While the Spanish monument impresses by the size and relative slenderness of its two superimposed sets of arches, the Pont du Gard, carried across the powerful river Gardon, represents the more difficult task of engineering since it has not only to attain height but to meet pressure at its base from the seasonally variable river current. These requirements account for the design of the bridge, whose unequal spans are due to the choice of rock-platforms in the river-bed as the basis to the main pier foundations, while the strength of the river and convenience in erecting the structure accounts for the sturdy lower bridge which must have been in effect a platform from which to build the higher stages. The middle stage in relation to its height and spans has very wide and massive haunches and it is to avoid increasing the resistance presented by these to wind-stress and to permit an easy adjustment of the top to the fall required for the channel that the crowning stage is built on the series of small stout arches which incidentally so appropriately balance the greater voids in the design. The strength of the work is best illustrated by the fact that, before the modern road bridge was built alongside it, the piers of the second tier had been cut back in order to accommodate a medieval road without causing their collapse. The aesthetic effect is due solely to the functional design and aptly illustrates the sheer elegance of straightforward engineering. In Rome itself the rustic masonry of the Arches of Claudius, which carried the Aquae Claudia and Anio Novus across the Viae Praenestina and Labicana, conveys an equally striking aesthetic effect of pure engineering, again due purely to practical considerations : for the rugged aspect of the masonry which gave the work its primitive grandeur owes its survival for our appreciation solely to the fact that it was erected rough hewn, as it came from the quarry, and never, for this or that reason of economy, received in full the trimming which had begun to adorn it with smooth and conventional architectural ornament.

The universality of public water-supplies, especially in hilly lands or in towns or cities isolated from the source of supply by deep valleys, invited and received alternative methods of treatment. Rome knew only one inverted siphon, running from the Caelian to the Palatine, in which the water was conveyed in a depressed conduit and was delivered to its destination by rising to its own level. The principle was already employed at Alatri in the early first century B.C., where a siphon dealt with a depression some three hundred feet deep. But the most remarkable examples are the four Lyons aqueducts, which were laid in this manner across the rift valleys which cut off the height occupied by the great Gallic capital from the hills which furnish the waters. Here depressions of up to 390 feet are negotiated, as at Beaunant. These remarkable structures, in which pressure is reduced by the use of multiple pipelines and blow-off towers, illustrate two important points; first, that the conception of a high-pressure supply was wholly outside Roman practice, and, second, that extreme caution was exercised in relation to any build-up of pressure in the main supply. Any pressure that existed lay in the pipes between the *castella* or distribution-tanks and the customer's delivery-points. Here becomes significant the Roman view of the economics of water-supply. This was conceived as a public service supplied by the State and paid for by capital acquired as war-booty or given by an individual benefactor. When the supply was installed the private customer might use only such residue as existed after public needs were served, and there was no idea of developing the system to the extent of making the supply a paying or profit-making concern. Again, the existence of what was in effect a low-pressure gravity supply meant that the principal conduits were running continuously and that there was in fact a steady flow of water running to waste (*aqua caduca*). This was, indeed, of great value for flushing latrines and sewers, or for working simple mill-machinery on its course towards them. The State mills for grinding cinnabar were thus worked by the waste water from the Baths of Caracalla, while the flour-mills and fish-nurseries of Rome were run by the overflow of the Aqua Traiana on the Janiculum. A drop in the feed-channel might be used on the aqueduct of Arles for the needs of flour-mills at Barbegal. But the entire conception of water-supply, its economics and its use belongs to a social world whose organization and thinking precluded the further advances which private enterprise might have developed in another kind of society. Just as the social organization did not favour the experimental attitude in building, so in engineering it tended to inhibit progress.

Such inhibition is very well illustrated by the history of machinery. Although mass production was not unknown in the Roman world for commodities such as pottery, tiles or even certain classes of metal objects, it did not advance beyond the stage of the hand manufacture. The idea of accurate standard sizes, which came in with the production of repetitive machined goods, may have existed in individual concerns, though there is little evidence for it; but it had no place whatever in the wholesale production of goods. The first necessary step in the production of machinery is the existence of standard tools, but in the age of the hand-made tool – and there are few hand-made tools of any kind

which the Roman world did not possess – the imposition of accurate standards was out of the question. Thus, while the Roman
engineer could produce such a machine as the double-acting
force-pump, a comparison of the bronze examples in the British
Museum or in the Archaeological Museum of Madrid will show
how much difference might exist between types, while the Silchester example in wood, lead and leather comes in as an example
of crude efficiency. Individual workmanship can be admired, but
standard production was out of the question. Accordingly, such
discoveries as depended upon high accuracy in workmanship,
such as the Hellenistic inventions in the field of pneumatics or
steam, which are adumbrated in the literary sources, remained
beyond realization. Only in the realm of water-power, where the
machinery can remain relatively rough, were developments possible. These, however, were much restricted in the Mediterranean
world owing to periodicity of flow in so many streams, and it is
only north of the Alps that thin and fragmentary evidence exists
for more regular recourse to the water-mill for flour-milling and
for marble-sawing, which might reasonably be thought to imply
saw-mills for timber though these are not attested either by
literature or archaeology. For the rest, advances depended upon
the individual ingenuity of small concerns, and this should not
be discounted. It could provide, for example, the turn-tables connected with apparatus on the Nemi galleys of Caligula. One of
these was operated on ball-bearings, the other on conical bearings;
but neither the balls nor the cones were packed so as to run free
in their races, but were each held on a spindle set in sockets at the
side of the race. The full advantage of the design was thus only
half realized and was certainly not widely known or applied,
despite its usefulness. The whole device aptly illustrated the
limitations of ancient technique in the engineer's field, and makes
what was achieved within such limits the more remarkable.

BIBLIOGRAPHY

ARCHITECTURE

Anderson, W. J., Spires, R. P. and Ashby, T., *The Architecture of Ancient Rome*, Batsford, 1927.

Blake, M. P., *Ancient Roman Construction in Italy from the Prehistoric Period to Augustus*, Carnegie Institute, 1947.

Blake, M. P., *Roman Construction in Italy from Tiberius through the Flavians*, Carnegie Institute, 1959.

Boethius, A., *The Golden House of Nero*, University of Michigan Press, 1960.

Delbrück, R., *Hellenistische Bauten in Latium*, 1907–12.

Fasolo, F. and Gullini, G., *Il tempio della Fortuna Primigenia a Palestrina*, 1953.

Gentili, G. V., *La villa Erculia di Piazza Armerina*, 1959.

Krencker, D., Kruger, E., and others, *Die Trierer Kaiserthermen*, 1929.

Lugli, G., *La tecnica edilizia romana*, 1957.

Robertson, D. S., *A Handbook of Greek and Roman Architecture*, Cambridge University Press, 1954.

Vigni, R., *The Pantheon*, 1957.

Vitruvius, *De architetura libri decem*.

ENGINEERING

Ashby, T., *The Aqueducts of Ancient Rome*, Oxford University Press, 1935.

Choisy, A., *L'art de bâtir chez les romains*, 1873.

Cozo, G., *L'ingegneria romana*, 1928.

Durm, J., *Die Baukunst der Etrusker; Die Baukunst der Römer*, 1905.

Germain de Montauzan, C., *Les aqueducs antiques de Lyon*, 1909.

Giovannoni, G., *La tecnica della costruzione presso i romani*, 1928.

Merckel, C., *Die Ingenieurtecknik im Alterthum*, 1899.

Ucelli, G., *Le navi di Nemi*, 1940.

Van Deman, E. B., *The Building of the Roman Aqueducts*, Carnegie Institute, 1934.

8

TOWNS AND HOUSES

M. W. Frederiksen

ONE of the most enduring legacies of Rome's rule were her towns. Ghost towns, like Pompeii or Timgad or Verulamium (St Albans), give us indeed much information about social life; but the skill and understanding of the Romans, both in selecting sites and in planning, is shown most strikingly by the towns that have survived into modern times. In many cities of Italy and the western provinces the street-plans still indicate their Roman origins, from Florence and Turin to Trier and Cologne, from Arles and Barcelona to Gloucester and Lincoln. The Greek East was already a land of cities, and the Romans inherited the institutions and habits of architecture that were there. But in the remoter districts of Asia Minor and above all in the west, towns had to be created afresh. After Caesar, all Italy beyond a mile of Rome was administered by municipalities; in the early Empire the same system was extended to the provinces. Many towns were colonies of Roman citizens or veteran soldiers, but even native peoples – the great Gallic tribes or the smaller Spanish peoples in their anarchic hill-forts – were taught trade and settled agriculture, given charters that laid down administrative duties, and were educated in the seductive amenities of town life. Towns were the centre of civil life and the focus of ambitions; though created by the conqueror's action, they were proud to administer themselves and might even resent interference. To ordinary men the system of provinces and legions was remote, and the Empire seemed rather a myriad world of cities.

Towns and Town-planning

The planned town of the Romans, with its chequerboard pattern of streets, had a long history, but certain developments may be seen. The earliest type was the *castrum*, a simple rectangular enclosure with a central cross-road, and it appears mainly in the early Roman colonies, as in Ostia (*c.* 338 B.C.) and Minturnae (296 B.C.). These were small garrisons of some three hundred families guarding a highway or an exposed coastline, and were too small to be towns proper. They were apt later to expand, as at Ostia, in an uncontrolled fashion beyond the original walls.

A later phase was the Hippodamean town, so called after the Greek architect who developed it; it is easily recognized by its rectangular street-plan, and quickly became the commonest type in all cases where a self-sufficient town was intended from the start. The earliest examples known are in the Latin colonies of Alba Fucens (303 B.C.) and Cosa (273 B.C.), in which the street-grids are plain although the walls are still irregular and follow defensible contours. Where the terrain allowed, the whole city formed a rectangle. At Aosta (Augusta Praetoria, 23 B.C.) this was divided mathematically into sixteen repeating rectangles, each further divided into four building-blocks; the town gates were sited in an odd and asymmetrical fashion that suggests (as probably also at Aix-en-Provence and Trier) that it originated as a *castrum* and was extended systematically when a temporary camp was converted into a city. Another variant appears in later towns, especially in the military provinces, which clearly imitated the layout of a legionary camp; often indeed they had begun as such but later became veteran colonies and look like a camp solidified into stone and endowed with the elements of civilian life. Carnuntum and Lambaesis are famous excavated examples, but, in Britain, Lincoln and probably Gloucester represent the same type. The Hippodamean plan remained the standard ideal, even though asymmetries and local variations occur, as they were bound to, in the numerous examples that survive.

The Roman preference for a plan having symmetry and diagrammatic simplicity is most evident in the new towns that were created. In this they contrasted sharply with Rome itself; the capital had grown, too early for planning, in a complex site of seven hills and a river crossing. Much of it was a chaos of tall, rickety houses and winding, narrow streets, and it was only at enormous cost that order was imposed upon the central political buildings to gratify Roman tastes for symmetry. By the time of Sulla some harmony had been given to the archaic Forum by flanking porticoes and the Tabularium, a large architectural façade at one end. In 54 B.C. Julius Caesar, with calculated egoism, bought up a densely peopled quarter nearby to lay out a fine colonnaded forum of his own, and his example was followed later by the Emperors. Augustus, Vespasian, Nerva added new forums, but Trajan's great work of gigantic proportions and superb coloured marbles surpassed them all; to a Persian prince who visited Rome in the fourth century A.D. it seemed more than human work, worthy to be admired by the gods – he was surprised that men in Rome were mortal. But it was the Campus Martius that contained some of the earliest and boldest experiments in planned building, political gestures by the magnates of the late Republic. Here were the great gardens, theatre and colonnade of Pompey; among the temples and porticoes lay the great Saepta or voting-enclosure of Caesar surrounded by its double colonnade and works of art. Strabo much admired the Campus Martius, and Ovid from his exile in the Black Sea remembered it above all. Although, however, the Emperors brought many improvements and sumptuous prestige buildings, much of Rome continued to present the acute problems that stemmed from its unplanned growth.

It is likely that, from early times, the Roman insistence upon schematic planning derives in part from a desire to prevent the same problems from arising elsewhere. Scholars have, indeed, produced other reasons. Some have derived it from the augural rituals of the Etruscans, who also showed some knowledge of planning in their colonial sites like Marzabotto near Bologna; but Roman thinking about towns remained firmly unmystical and astrological influence is badly attested. Others suggest that the planning of towns resulted from military needs and was modelled on that of the army camp. Yet even though defence was important, existing remains do not support the idea: at Cosa, for instance, the street-scheme is pinned down by the main gates but bears little relation to the defensive towers of the circuit walls. Even Vitruvius knew that rectangles were hard shapes to defend. Most likely the idea came from the Greeks, for they had already made much progress in the regular planning of towns, conspicuously influenced by Hippodamus, who gave his name to the new style. The Romans needed to look no further than Paestum, Naples or Capua for examples of such plans and their advantages to urban living. There can be little doubt that it was the benefits of a civilian, not military, kind which inspired Roman planning. They were not such militarists as to believe that towns were army camps writ large – indeed Polybius reverses the relationship in describing a legionary camp 'with streets and buildings regularly planned *like a town*'. Above all, a properly independent town needed well-sited temples, demarcation of property, drainage and a water-supply. The veteran colonies in newly conquered provinces rarely, in fact, had to function as garrisons; every schoolboy knows that in Britain's first colony, Colchester, when destroyed by Boudicca, there were a senate-house, theatre and temple – but no walls. To writers like Cicero and Tacitus it was self-evidently true that conquest required the acquiescence of the conquered, and that towns, being 'mirrors of the Roman people', were uniquely successful in winning former enemies into civilized submission.

While a plan alone conveys something of Roman ideas of a town, the sites themselves show how the ideas were realized in detail. In Pompeii the Forum finely expresses the religious and political functions of a town. At one end stood the Capitolium or main temple; at the other the three halls for senate and magistrates; while on either side lay the basilica, the voting-enclosure and public temples and the Macellum or enclosed food-market. The whole was surrounded by a two-storeyed colonnade and was barred to wheeled traffic. There is little here of the Greek *agora* with its broad spaces and horizontal porticoes; rather the oblong space directs the eye to the vertical façades of the Capitolium and the municipal offices at either end. In other towns the same elements occur in slightly varying forms – Vitruvius had, indeed, ordained that an ideal forum should have the proportions of three to two, but there is no evidence that such strict theory was applied. The political forums of Lambaesis and Wroxeter are different again, and they may owe something to military architects and the severer symmetries of an army camp. But Pompeii not only contrived to give a systematic form to the solemn succession of public edifices, but also, with its airy colonnades and backcloth of Vesuvius, has earned the praise of Le Corbusier as a real achievement of spatial architecture.

The practical advantages of planning were manifold. Markets were confined to special buildings, as in Pompeii, or were banished from the Forum to special enclosures; in Rome's harbour town of Ostia there was the great Square of the Guilds where foreign traders had their offices; control and supervision were thus made easy. The bigger amenities like baths, theatres and amphitheatres could be rationally sited and their needs predicted – the more necessary since Roman law made no provision for compulsory purchase. At Ostia great foresight was shown in claiming the whole riverside area as state land for the organized siting of docks and warehouses. Nor were the demands of sanitation ignored. Livy stresses the difficulties in Rome where uncontrolled building meant that 'sewers originally laid down in public soil now everywhere run beneath private houses; it is like a city that has been created by squatting rather than properly apportioned'. Thus it was that under the streets of the new towns, available for repair or inspection, lay a grid of drains; and with aqueducts there came a parallel system of lead water-pipes, again under the streets, that served public fountains and – at a fee – private houses. There is hardly a site that fails to reveal Roman concern – Pompeii, Ostia, even Mauretanian Volubilis show the care lavished; indeed, the vanished street-plan of Augustan Carthage has been wholly recovered from its buried sewage-system, so intimately were planning and sanitation linked. Moreover, the Romans took a robust pride in their public latrines. Modern visitors to the famous specimen at Ostia (a roomy affair with accommodation for thirty) are apt to feel inhibited not merely by the lack of privacy, but by the very idea of marble seats. Such things were, of course, part of the Roman wry image of themselves; rather than the 'useless though celebrated works of the Greeks' to prefer the great serviceable aqueducts, as did Frontinus; to concern themselves with 'what the Greeks had neglected, paved highways, aqueducts and sewers' (Strabo).

And yet, to avoid the unplanned horrors of Rome, did not the Romans strive too hard? To modern architects the new towns seem a formula, monotonously the same, east and west; the objection would hardly have made sense to the ancients, few of whom were much-travelled connoisseurs. In fact Roman builders avoided the sense of geometrical rigour by adding secondary features – colonnaded streets, fountains, decorative archways and statues according to a town's wealth; and nowadays archaeological sites all too often conceal the part once played by vegetation and formal gardens in attracting and holding the eye. In terms of pure architecture, admittedly, there were drawbacks; Roman temples, for instance, compared with those of Athens or Pergamum, are less adventurously sited, are rarely peripteral, and are apt to be mere façades on a square. Their architects made assumptions that to an English town-dweller may seem strange: that much public life happened in the open, that private affairs were settled strolling in a portico, that streets were for pedestrians (for wheeled traffic was allowed usually only at night), that spaces were to contain crowds. Inevitably in such towns, architecture is a backdrop; pure architecture, like those 'celebrated works of the Greeks', was not the aim, but the urban life that architecture subserves. It was a deliberate choice, and it is presumptuous to blame them. Their bridges and aqueducts are in many places still in use; had they known that Lewis Mumford would describe the Cloaca Maxima, in continuous service after more than twenty-five centuries, as 'one of the cheapest pieces of engineering on record', they would have been delighted. Besides, to strive to emulate the Parthenon – was not that a waste of labour?

Private Houses and Private Lives

In their nature Roman private houses followed many different patterns that varied with the climate and were modified by the tastes or position of their owners. Nothing reflects social position more intimately than domestic architecture, and its interest lies in the glimpses it gives us into other lives.

The earliest Roman house, which is best known from Pompeii, was of a low-built, spreading form of one or two storeys, that was centred round an *atrium* (hall open to the sky) and a colonnaded garden or peristyle. Its plan was firmly centripetal; the rooms opened into the atrium which was the sole source of light and exit for smoke, and the outer walls were blank and forbidding as though shutting out a hostile world. The origins of this singular house, which is quite un-Greek, are obscure, but it may be conjectured that the atrium, which housed the central hearth, the altar of the household gods, and the effigies of ancestors, had religious connotations and was thus retained as a traditional feature. Certainly it was a style that was favoured by the earlier aristocracy and municipal classes, and to later writers carried with it an aura of the old-style paterfamilias with his household of children and domestic slaves. Examples of such houses that were owned by the aristocrats of the first century B.C. can now be seen on the Palatine in Rome, and were still relatively modest in size and decoration.

A parallel development was the apartment-house or *insula*. This type, it is true, is best known to us from the fine examples at Ostia, and consisted of large well-built blocks of several storeys, strongly reminiscent of many modern blocks of flats; but the Ostian *insulae* are the end of a process, and the origins lay in the harsher economic conditions of metropolitan living. From early times Rome suffered from overcrowding and shortage of space, and had many areas of poor-class tenement houses; they were rickety structures largely of timber, and were insecure and insanitary. This was hardly a style of architecture at all; rather it was a spontaneous growth produced by a large urban proletariat and slum landlords, and could no doubt have been found in some of the teeming cities of the Hellenistic world. But in Rome, where the population swelled to about a million inhabitants, they were a painful administrative problem; in the end Roman builders evolved an answer that was, perhaps, Rome's chief contribution to urban living.

Such were the main types of housing, but town and capital differed sharply in the style and standard of living. Pompeian houses vividly reflect the comfortable, middle-class conditions of a prosperous municipality, wherein some fifty leading families mingled on terms of tolerable amity with the rest of the population. There was no spectacular wealth; the walls were painted in flat primary colours to give the effect of light, since the windows were small and darkened by wooden shutters. The figured wall-paintings are not great art, but many of them are based on Greek masterpieces and are copies (in some cases recompositions) by not unskilled groups of painters. Basic furniture is quite simple, though there is some elegance in the ornamental tables of wrought bronze; more typically Roman is the profusion of tableware, silver banqueting sets and many kinds of ornate cauldrons and casseroles of bronze. In general, the spectrum of style varies widely; the House of the Silver Wedding is cool and elegant with Corinthian columns; the House of Menander is richer in decoration and unusually spacious; the famous House of the Vettii is startling in its *nouveau-riche* expensiveness and dubious taste. Nowhere else can we get such an intimate, and at times unfortunate, insight into the minds of their owners.

It is more in the dwellings of the poor that Pompeii displays the rapid effects of peace and prosperity. Increasingly, from the time of Augustus, the old houses were adapted to meet the needs of a rising commercial and artisan class. Some were converted into bakeries, fulleries and wine-shops, but were apt to retain the faded ornament of a nobler past. The Villa of the Mysteries began as the rich residence of an imperial freedman; within a generation it had become a centre of agricultural industry, and we find oil-presses, flour-mills and rows of storage jars in its lavishly painted rooms. Other houses were taken over, subdivided into shops and flats, and sublet. The fine old House of Pansa bore the following notice: 'The Insula Arriana Polliana, property of Cn. Alleius Nigidius Maius. To let from July 1 next: shops with attached upper rooms, gentlemanly upstairs apartments, and the main house. Agreements to be made with Primus, slave of the above.' In these changes we see the rise to affluence of a middle class of freedmen, artisans and craftsmen; the simplest housing units might well be envied by many a Neapolitan of the twentieth century.

As public amenities developed the houses of the aristocracy grew larger. Senators in Rome laid out huge gardens on the hilly outskirts of the city with trees and fountains, made possible only by aqueducts that now brought copious water in on a height. Others built farther out, in the Alban Hills or (like the Younger Pliny) by the sea. Terraced gardens, colonnades and fish-ponds were demanded by fashion; veneers of brilliant variegated marbles soon became a middle-class necessity, though in Sulla's time they had seemed a scandalous extravagance. The change in architectural conceptions that could be inferred from remains is seen even in literature. In building a library, Cicero amusingly tells of trouble with his learned architect, Cyrus, and complains that the windows were too narrow: 'when I spoke to Cyrus, he told me that views on to the garden through wide windows were less agreeable; for let the eye be α, the visible objects β and γ, and the light-ray δ, ϵ... you know the rest.' Not surprisingly, Cyrus got his way. Yet a century later the Younger Pliny and Statius describe their villas overwhelmingly in terms of light, space and vista. By the second century A.D. the new techniques in concrete had broken further barriers; Hadrian's villa at Tibur (Tivoli) set a new fashion, and the villas of the wealthy grew lively with curvilinear movement – domes, vaults, apses, and all manner of wilful romantic effects.

But in Rome itself there were cruel social extremes. Its ancient tenements and slums have disappeared without trace, but Martial and Juvenal have preserved the indignant voice of the urban poor. It was a city of tall buildings and narrow streets in which the poor rented teeming apartments and landlords grew fat. The noise at night was terrible; collapses were frequent, and fire a constant hazard from timber buildings and oil lamps. Beginning with Augustus the Emperors took firm measures to limit its sprawling growth and improve it. Fresh aqueducts were built and public fountains multiplied; there was now stricter policing and a fire-brigade, armed with hand-pumps and wet blankets, became a state charge. The Emperors took on responsibility for the corn-supply; the city proletariat grew increasingly parasitic upon imperial largess, first of corn, then of bread and wine, until in the third century a praetorian prefect exclaimed sourly, 'It only remains to serve them chicken.' But doles and spectacles were mere palliatives to what Juvenal graphically called a life of competitive squalor. Housing was a much harder problem. Although Augustus fixed a maximum height for houses of seventy feet (later reduced by Trajan to sixty), and there were some attempts at rent control, his measures and others to the same purpose seemed to do little to curb the rapacities of speculative builders and landlords; governments in other ages should find the scene uncomfortably familiar.

The only answer possible in Rome was not to abolish the *insula* but to improve it. By the mid first century A.D. builders had discovered the advantages of brick-faced concrete as a medium that carried more weight and withstood intense heat. The great fire of Rome in A.D. 64 gave Nero a chance to rebuild many parts of Rome, and he seized it with what seemed suspicious enthusiasm. The 'new city' of Nero with its wider streets and solid apartment houses was a beginning; the next two generations saw its completion, for by then the Ostian *insulae* show that an answer had emerged that avoided the worst of the terrors. Space, light and basic sanitation could be secured, and there was no hesitation in building up to five storeys. Since floors and partition walls were still of wood, the perils of fire could not be wholly prevented, and running water and sanitation was unusual except on the ground floor; but there can be little doubt that Rome's habour town offered a level of physical security to a wage-earning population that was hardly equalled before the new techniques released by the Industrial Revolution. We cannot know how far the capital itself was so improved, but much of it took on a new aspect; the plan of the city drawn up under Severus shows a large predominance of regular *insulae*, and it has been calculated that there were thirteen miles of colonnaded streets – not to mention the ubiquitous public lavatories, one hundred and forty-four of them. In fact the diseases of Rome were probably beyond the powers of the administration to cure, and were inherent in her position as ruler of the world. But were there not compensations? None are warmer than Martial and Juvenal in their praises of country life and rustic innocence; yet after a while in the backwaters of Bilbilis or Aquinum, they seem to have found pressing reasons for plunging again into the iniquitous metropolis.

In the provinces, Roman houses tended to follow the native forms that were suited to local climates, but they were improved and embellished beyond recognition. The first country villas in Britain, often the successors of round native huts, show a quick employment of Roman timber and masonry building styles, and in separating residential and workers' quarters followed the practice of smaller farms in Italy. In a second stage, for instance at Chedworth or Northleigh, the owners (whether Romans or natives of eminence) avail themselves of a large repertory of architectural luxuries, and few can have felt those regrets for a lost simplicity that Roman writers sometimes felt on their behalf. Bath quarters with hypocausts, drainage, piped water, imported marbles and decoration of all kinds were there for those that could pay; apart from a Celtic element in some sculpture and personal ornaments there is nothing very British about these villas. Mosaics give some idea of standards, and compare with the upper ranges, if not with the best, from elsewhere. The finest are of the fourth century: Verulamium has a good range, and such examples as those from Woodchester or Lullingstone are effective and often beautiful. Britain indeed lacks the dazzling pictorial mosaics of the African and German villas; even the remarkable series of scenes out of the *Aeneid* from a late villa at Low Ham in Somerset is more eloquent about the pretensions of its owner than the skill of the mosaic worker, who fitted it rather clumsily into a large chamber of the baths. Since many British farms were small or middle class and the population relatively scattered, British patrons may have been too few to support the 'schools' of mosaic artists found elsewhere; but the remains do not suggest that they lacked enterprise.

The Structure of Town Life

Although Rome's towns are, like people, only knowable as individuals and hard to sum up in a word, life within them had some uniform features. To hold a magistracy one needed to meet a property qualification that varied from town to town; the council (*curia*) was filled with ex-magistrates, so that control of affairs gravitated towards wealthier families and tended to become exclusive. A 'new man' boasted of the fact on his tombstone; and by the second century A.D. the pattern had solidified further into a hereditary magisterial class, the *curiales*, distinguished by privileges and subject to duties. Below them stood the powerful freedmen, men of talent who were too rich to ignore. Laws prevented them from holding office, but the problem was met by Augustus in his creation of the boards of Augustales to which wealthy freedmen could belong; ostensibly these were ministers of the Emperor cult, but they also provided posts of prestige for freedmen, and the Augustales tended to form a kind of aristocracy within the freedman class. Their influence might be resented, but their role was a large one and they were often hard to distinguish from the freeborn. Their sons moved smoothly enough on to the town council, their lowly origins forgotten, and such offspring often abandoned trade and became respectable members of the local *bourgeoisie*. In commercial towns like Ostia and Puteoli they dominated the trading guilds, and could thus exercise a power effectively larger than the town's officers.

Below the wealthy came the ordinary citizen; he had his vote and used it keenly at election time, as the brisk painted propaganda of Pompeii shows. 'Bruttius Balbus for duovir: he will maintain the town treasury' – 'Helvius Sabinus for aedile: recommended by the united bakers, they and the neighbours want him.' Elections tended to die out as they lost real political content, but they existed in the towns long after their suppression in Rome, and are still mentioned as usual in African towns under Constantine. Yet even when formal elections disappeared, the voice of the people was heard; a fracas in the theatre, or some shouts at the games, could alarm the town elders and produce a prompt reaction. Beneath the townsfolk was the rural population, whose lot was often unenviable; slaves lived in cells and worked in gangs, and in farmhouses near Pompeii shackles have been found; even the free labourer was at the caprice of his employer, and if he lived at a distance shared none of the amenities and entertainments that were showered upon the towns. In the provinces the land was often worked by natives who were barbarian in speech and without rights, to the profit of their town-dwelling masters. As in the capital itself, a whole system of social gradation and classes, each with its distinct privileges and duties, was encouraged in the towns, as can be detected in the extant charters of the Spanish towns. The class structure with the *curiales* at the top was frankly avowed: Pliny is studiously broad-minded in suggesting that Virgil, even though not a municipal senator, was yet morally respectable; at the other end of the scale, Galen, who was court physician to Marcus Aurelius and a humane man, prescribed a cure for a labourer 'as for a mule'. The Romans did not know their Marx, and approved of the class hierarchy as a challenge to ambition; but the hard edges of class division were to some extent softened by the enforced intimacies of town life.

To the magistrates fell, as a rule, the duty of maintaining a town's amenities. They had some powers to keep order – St Paul was summarily imprisoned at Philippi. They supervised markets and checked weights and measures; they controlled the renting of public property, the upkeep of drains and water-supply, and, later, had to guarantee the prices of food; every town worthy of the name had its basilica, baths, theatre and porticoes. The expenses naturally were borne by the curial class, either as liturgies apportioned as in the Greek cities, or in the west as the fees paid on entering office or as election promises – which in the competitive atmosphere were often staggeringly generous. Italy has eighty-five known amphitheatres, Gaul a like number of aqueducts: these were overwhelmingly the result of private generosity. An African notable gave 600,000 sesterces in one election – a rich man's fortune. Other such offers came from freedmen seeking the position of Augustalis. Yet in this surprising display of municipal altruism was there not an element of fever? The Younger Pliny certainly struck trouble in Bithynia where pretentious schemes ran aground through jerry-building and dishonest contractors; but this was probably not general, since the charters for new towns in Spain were strict about peculation and graft, and it is hard to see how under them the Bithynian situation could have arisen. Indeed the Greek cities were notoriously proud and factious, always prone to confuse limited rights to administer themselves with the sovereignty remembered from their own history, when freedom had meant power. 'Leave the battle of Marathon and past glories to the rhetorical schools,' writes Plutarch in his advice to those who would govern cities – it was safer to fulfil one's smaller duties as conscientiously as one might. It is true that such un-Greek ideas of dutiful subordination were better grasped in the western provinces; yet the words are the first straws in a wind of growing disillusion. Generosity was not liked, it was endured; without their games, their festivals, cheap corn and bread, would not the people riot? Was the fierce bidding for esteem worth it? Many had doubts, but nevertheless dug deep into their pockets to pay for gladiatorial shows or libraries or schools, and were honoured in death like heroes with statues and fulsome inscriptions.

Perhaps such world-weariness was rather premature, for the cities had varying fortunes, not all of them predictable. Little Panopeus in Greece could hardly be denied town status, but it had no public buildings, no theatre and no piped water – 'if you can call it a town,' said Pausanias. Yet Syrian Antioch was a proud and beautiful city that boasted a much-envied system of street lighting. Where Rome expected so much of a spontaneous local initiative, the results were colour and variety – but also great inequalities. The shifting of trade-routes brought prosperity to some and ruin to others, and the small town had few hopes of gaining better amenities unless it could attract the eye of an emperor or senatorial grandee. In Britain, the veteran colonies of

Colchester, Gloucester, Lincoln and York were bound to succeed. For the natives, the first experiment was Verulamium, a full *municipium*, which meant that its residents became full Roman citizens; although in its first phase timber-built (the techniques suggest that army builders were used), it adhered almost absurdly to a formula of colonnaded streets, shops and rentable apartments – which had indeed already been applied in the Gallic town of Vaison, but to the Belgic inhabitants of Prae Wood must have seemed distinctly novel. More realistic were the tribal capitals, planned city centres for a tribe that were laid out often with great pretension. Good examples are Cirencester and Wroxeter, where towns on the plain succeeded to native hill fortresses and created a flourishing new life – striking witnesses to the Roman methods of de-feudalizing by architecture. Silchester was perhaps a miscalculation, for its large town-plan seems never to have been built over, as was the case also with Autun in France. On the other hand, London seems never to have been granted the status of a town, though it was the largest urban complex in Britain. It was well planned and its domestic architecture and appurtenances were in excellent condition; but its traders were probably mainly Romans and could look after themselves. Generally town life in Britain remained somewhat superficial, for tribal feelings were still strong and country estates were predominant. But in France, Spain and North Africa, the abundant remains show how deep urbanization went; wealthy landowners lived in the towns and helped to sustain and encourage a productive class of craftsmen and shopkeepers.

In the third century A.D. there begins a period which historians have called somewhat portentously a time of municipal decline. Certainly the legal writings suggest a sharp increase in central interference and something of the old freedom had gone; it was now an imposition to belong to the curial class who were made legally responsible for policing and taxation, and its members had to be forcefully restrained from retiring to country estates, or escaping altogether from the burdens of local government into more lucrative sinecures – mainly, we note, the civil service and the Church. The causes were many, the chief being the ravages of barbarian invasions and the decline of country populations. Yet the generality of these complaints may be delusive. Chiefly affected were the smaller towns whose capacity for survival had passed, and the Emperors had to recognize their abandonment or wink at their pillaging. But Constantine was still hailed as the creator of towns, and Africa and Asia show new foundations until the fifth century. Big cities like Milan, Arles and Aquileia flourished still in something like the old style; and a surprising number of sites – the British cities among them – show signs of building in the fourth century, public and private, of high quality. Although the final fate of British towns is uncertain, Roman foundations survived in the Byzantine East, and in Frankish Gaul. In Italy, documents speak of *curiales* still in the seventh century A.D.; and Verona and Pola, which can yet give a visitor much visual testimony of their past as Roman cities, have been occupied without interruption.

As late as A.D. 527, Cassiodorus in a famous letter spoke eloquently of the education and the *civilitas* that only town-life could provide; even if this was in his time largely a romantic ideal, a society without towns was still unimaginable. Little, in fact, can have survived the Dark Ages. But when, with the stimulus of trade, towns began to reappear in northern Italy and Germany, they bore resemblances to the towns of late antiquity that were more than accidental. Many Roman sites were reoccupied; others had maintained some vestigial life throughout. The men who planned medieval Aigues Mortes eand Winchelsea assuredly knew of these surviving towns. The Italian *palazzi* which first appeared in the eleventh century, and in some measure town houses in Germany, show a pattern of street-front shops, first-floor apartments and inner *cortile* that had been remarkably foreshadowed in the architecture of the Roman *insula*. Walls, even aqueducts, were repaired. Behind the Classical Renaissance, when artists and poets turned to the imperial ruins of Rome and pondered giddily about the fall of empires, there lay humbler traditions and more concrete experiences, of lives lived in the old towns of northern Italy and France. In many small ways, material continuity helped to mould the habits of urban living in later ages; and by then Cassiodorus' words would have been appreciated once more.

BIBLIOGRAPHY

On the administrative and social life of Roman towns, *see* M. Rostovtzeff, *Social and Economic History of the Roman Empire* (Oxford University Press, 2nd ed., 1958), Chis. V–VII, a brilliant survey; A. H. M. Jones, *The Greek City from Alexander to Justinian* (Oxford University Press, 1940); and on late antiquity, by the same author, *The Later Roman Empire* (Blackwell, 1964), Vol. II. Ch. XIX.

The city life of Rome is described by W. Warde Fowler, *Social Life in Rome in the Age of Cicero* (Macmillan, 1908, paperback, 1963); for the later period, J. Carcopino, *Daily Life in Ancient Rome* (Pelican, 1956) is good on the seamy side; and also the encyclopedic work of L. Friedlaender, *Roman Life and Manners under the Early Empire* (London, 1907).

On town architecture in general, A. Boethius, *The Golden House of Nero* (University of Michigan Press, 1960) is a well illustrated survey of planning and housing. On the Greek background of town-planning, *see* R. E. Wycherley, *How the Greeks Built Cities* (Macmillan, 1949); and F. Haverfield, *Ancient Town Planning* (Oxford, 1913) is still useful; J. B. Ward-Perkins, 'Early Roman Towns in Italy' in *Town Planning Review*, XXVI (1955). For private houses, apart from Boethius, use A. Mau, *Pompeii, Its Life and Art* (trans. Kelsey, London, 1902); A. Maiuri, *Pompeii* (Novara, 1957); H. Tanzer, *The Common People of Pompeii* (Baltimore, 1939); R. Meiggs, *Roman Ostia* (Oxford University Press, 1960) is instructive on *insulae*; and for painting, A. Maiuri, *Roman Painting* (Cleveland, 1953). Modern architects' views are given in F. R. Hiorns, *Town-building in History* (Harrap, 1956); and sometimes wilfully in Lewis Mumford, *The City in History* (Secker & Warburg, 1961).

On Roman Britain: I. A. Richmond, *Roman Britain* (Pelican, 1955; 2nd ed., Cape, 1963); A. L. F. Rivet, *Town and Country in Roman Britain* (London, 1958); J. M. C. Toynbee, *Art in Britain* (Phaedon, 1963) – an excellent picture-book; and by the same author, *Art in Britain under the Romans* (Oxford University Press, 1964) is an authoritative survey. The following articles are central: I. A. Richmond, 'The Four Coloniae of Roman Britain' in the *Archaeological Journal*, CIII (1948); S. S. Frere, 'Verulamium, Three Roman Cities' in *Antiquity*, XXXVIII (1964). On medieval practices, M. W. Beresford and J. K. S. St Joseph, *Medieval England* (Cambridge Air Surveys, 1958).

On other provinces: O. Brogan, *Roman Gaul* (London, 1953); and T. Wiseman, *Roman Spain* (Bell, 1956).

9

WORK AND SLAVERY

P. A. Brunt

AGRICULTURE was the chief source of income and the chief occupation in all ages and lands of the ancient world. Trade and industry were by modern standards little developed. For this there were many reasons. Technology was backward and fuel scarce. Legal and social institutions did not favour the accumulation of liquid capital. Above all, transportation was slow and costly. Under Diocletian's tariff of maximum prices the cost of moving a bushel of grain fifty miles by wagon would have absorbed two-fifths of the permitted retail price. It was less expensive to move goods by sea or inland waterway. But ships were small and slow, there were few navigational aids, and voyages were normally suspended in the winter. Italy, in particular, has few good harbours or navigable rivers. As most people lived near the subsistence level, there was no effective demand for most goods that had to travel a long distance. Some indispensable raw materials like iron might have to be imported despite the costs, but consumer goods could not have found a world-wide market, as Lancashire cottons did in the nineteenth century, and this alone can explain why there were no large factories. Industry catered for local needs or for the production of high-class goods which could stand the costs of transport. Trade was chiefly in luxuries or semi-luxuries. One great exception must be noted. The large population of Rome and later of Constantinople was fed with grain imported from overseas, especially from Africa and Egypt. But much of it was paid for by the Imperial treasury out of provincial revenues. Other cities without similar resources could not rely on imports of food. In general each community, indeed each large estate, aimed at self-sufficiency, and the result of a local failure of crops was famine.

Even by ancient standards Italy was not important for industry, nor, except for a short period, for commerce. Rome itself was never a manufacturing centre; it was only some Campanian, Etruscan and north Italian towns that were noted for armaments and certain fine products. Thus in the time of Augustus the ware of Arretium in Etruria was the most prized in the Mediterranean world; but it was soon imitated elsewhere, and lost its imperial market. In the first century B.C. Italian business men were dominant in the east. As a result of the great conquests Rome had made, enormous capital flowed into Italy, and Italians became the financiers of the Greek cities. They also traded in grain which the Italian tax-farmers had collected in kind. These were temporary advantages which faded when Rome ceased to exploit her subjects so ruthlessly; Syrians or Gauls replaced Italians in imperial commerce. Italy herself had little to export except wine and oil; her available surplus of timber had vanished with deforestation, and she had virtually no mineral wealth. It is for the fertility of her land that the highest praises are heaped upon her by ancient writers.

The Romans and the other Italians were thus primarily agriculturists. They themselves were convinced that they owed their empire to their hardy peasant stock. They loved to tell how in the early days of the Republic Cincinnatus was called from the plough to command the army. 'It is from the farming class,' wrote Cato in the second century B.C., 'that the bravest men and sturdiest soldiers come, their calling is most highly respected, their livelihood is most assured ... and those who are engaged in that pursuit are least inclined to be disaffected.' It is characteristically Roman that Virgil's great poem, the *Georgics*, is devoted to describing the hard, almost unremitting labour and rustic festivities of the farmer's life:

But still the farmer furrows the land with his curving plough:
The land is his annual labour, it keeps his native country,
His little grandson and herds of cattle and trusty bullocks ...
Such was the life the Sabines lived in days of old,
And Remus and his brother: so it was beyond all question

That Tuscany grew to greatness, Rome became queen of all the world,
Ringing her seven citadels with a single wall.*

The old-style peasant had just enough land on which to raise
and support a family; he was not producing for the market, except to the extent that he needed to buy tools and a few other
things he could not make for himself. The women spun and
weaved; even great ladies in later times are commended for their
wool-making, and the Emperor Antoninus Pius was proud to
wear home-spun clothes.

Of course there were also skilled craftsmen. The second of the
Roman Kings, Numa, is said to have organized guilds of flute-
players, goldsmiths, carpenters, dyers, cobblers, tanners, copper-
workers and potters, and of the 193 centuries into which the
Roman people in arms were divided (the Comitia Centuriata)
two were appointed for the makers of arms, who enjoyed, it
seems, a position of some honour. In the early period such craftsmen in Rome were evidently for the most part free citizens, and
presumably this was true elsewhere.

The great majority of Romans and of other Italians, however,
must have lived on the land. Their life was never easy. In a bad
year they had to borrow, and if they could not repay, their
creditors could reduce them to a form of bondage. Roman conquests in Italy probably did more than remedial legislation to
improve the position of the small man. Rome confiscated part
of the territory of the Italian cities she subdued and used it to
settle her own citizens, a policy which at once increased her
population and military strength and provided the poor with
lands. But from the beginning of the second century B.C. onwards wars overseas contributed to ruin the peasantry. While
the ploughman was doing military service, perhaps for six years
on end, in Spain, his farm was neglected. Other factors helped
to promote the concentration of landed property in the hands of a
few rich men who sought to accumulate it because it was both
the safest and the most honourable investment and who did not
scruple to secure it even by force or fraud. Pasturage, which required relatively little labour, was often the most lucrative way

*C. Day-Lewis's translation.

of exploiting their lands, and they often preferred slaves to free workers.

Thus the old yeomanry gradually diminished. Many displaced farmers sought shelter in the city of Rome. We must not exaggerate the extent or speed of the process. At the lowest and probably correct estimate the free population of Italy under Augustus did not exceed five millions, and probably under one million lived in Rome. In 37 B.C. Varro spoke of large numbers of the poor who tilled their lands with the help of their children, smaller owners, or, perhaps, tenants of the great proprietors, who were recommended by the experts to lease farms, if they could not supervise them closely or if they were situated on unhealthy land, where slaves would suffer heavy mortality. It was also uneconomic to maintain enough slaves for seasonal operations, harvest or vintage for which gangs of free labourers were employed, probably men who eked out subsistence at other times on their own little plots or by casual work in the towns. In the late Republic some two hundred thousand free Italians were often under arms; these soldiers came from the country and sought allotments of land as a reward for their service. But numerous assignations of land to the rural poor seem to have done no more than retard the concentration of property. The process went on, and in the late Empire we hear of enormous estates in Italy called *massae*.

It is indeed generally held that under the Augustan peace the supply of slaves dwindled and that the large proprietors had to rely more on free labour and, in particular, on leasing farms to tenants. This is dubious. Certainly fewer slaves were made by war, piracy and brigandage, but we cannot be sure that Italian slaveowners did not then breed them in large numbers, like the owners of plantations in the Southern States. Even tenants often worked their farms with the help of slaves, who might be supplied to them along with other expensive equipment by the landlords. Nor were the tenants themselves prosperous; they were often in debt, and by the time of Constantine they had come to be tied to their lands and were little better than serfs. Probably, in most periods of Roman history, there must have been perennial under-employment and near starvation among the agricultural poor.

Driven from the land, what could the Roman peasant do? Unlike his successor in the England of the Industrial Revolution, he could not readily find alternative employment in the towns. This was not merely due to the absence of a large-scale industry; there was also slave competition. The freeborn poor in the towns had to depend in large part on public corn doles and on the bounty of the great houses. There were also casual earnings, especially in the building trade, where the operations were not sufficiently continuous to warrant the employment of slaves who had to be fed and clothed, whether they were working or not. The Emperor Vespasian was a lavish builder; once when an engineer came to him with a labour-saving device, he was rewarded – but Vespasian refused to adopt his invention. 'You must let me feed my poor commons' he said. The Colosseum and his other great monuments were evidently constructed by free labour.

One result of the impoverishment of the masses from the second century B.C. onwards was decline in the birth rate. Many of the poor were unable to raise children. This was a source of concern to many statesmen from Tiberius Gracchus to Trajan. That Emperor made public funds available to feed poor children under a scheme which endured for a century. Its success is uncertain; plague, endemic malaria and famine helped to reduce the population, and in Marcus Aurelius' reign parts of Italy were desolate and could be used for settling barbarians.

What has already been said indicates the importance of slavery in Roman society. As in all other ancient lands it was an institution of immemorial antiquity, which no one ever proposed to abolish. Greeks who were accustomed to question everything had challenged its legitimacy and evoked a powerful defence from Aristotle; the slave was in his view a man who had only enough rationality to understand and obey orders, and it was as much in his own interest as the master's that he should be subject to rational government. (Slightly modified, this argument is familiar today from the writings of imperialist apologists.) But this controversy was in the realm of theory. Even when slaves rebelled, they did not object to slavery as such: they merely wanted to be free themselves. A Roman jurist said that by natural law all men are born free, but he hastened to add that slavery existed by the law of nations. The Stoics, who were influential at Rome, taught that all men were brothers, including slaves; but in their philosophy man's welfare is purely spiritual, and material conditions irrelevant to it; true misery lies in being a slave to one's own passions, and legal servitude does not stop a man from being master of himself in the moral sense. The Christian attitude was much the same. Slaves, according to Paul, are not to worry about the condition in which they were called; and he did not recommend Philemon to liberate Onesimus. Hence it is no surprise that when Christianity became the official religion, the Church did not advocate abolition: on the contrary, it acquired slaves of its own. In the break-up of the Empire slavery gradually dwindled, for reasons that are not clear; but as great numbers of free men were reduced to serfdom, from which it was often harder to escape, the net gain to human freedom was not large.

The children of slave mothers were born slaves, but free men could be made slaves by capture in war, by piracy and by kidnapping. Legally a Roman citizen or a free subject of Rome could not be reduced to servitude within Rome's jurisdiction, but this rule may have been often evaded; in particular, exposure of free-born infants was not forbidden until Christian times, and when such foundlings were reared as slaves, there would seldom have been evidence of their original status. In primitive Rome, a poor community, there can have been few slaves, but there was a vast influx as a result of Rome's wars of conquest from the middle of the third century B.C. In one campaign in 167 B.C. the Romans are said to have made 150,000 slaves in Epirus. Trade across the frontiers always swelled the numbers, and so did piracy by sea and brigandage by land until the time of Augustus. In the heyday of piracy the mart at Delos was reputed to be capable of handling 20,000 in a single day. Never before had slaves been so cheap and plentiful as in Cicero's Italy, and nowhere else in the Empire did the economy become so dependent on slave labour. A comparison may be drawn with the Old South in the United

States. There, in 1850, only eleven owners had more than 500 slaves apiece. But in Nero's reign one senator had 400 serving him in his own town house – and how many more working in the fields to support this establishment of unproductive mouths? Augustus thought it necessary to forbid owners to manumit more than a hundred by testament. It can be conjectured that in his time there were three slaves for every five free men in Italy.

The slaves were of all nations, including Celts and Germans from the north and Asiatics from the east; many, born in slavery or illegally enslaved, came from Italy or the provinces. These were not only sturdy labourers for the fields or mines, but craftsmen or men with professional talents who brought new skills to Italy. Shrewd owners trained slave boys to be secretaries, accountants and doctors. It was such trained scribes in Atticus' publishing house who copied the works of Cicero. The master and preceptor of a young mathematical genius records with sorrow his death at the age of twelve. The fine pottery of Arretium was made by slaves. Hundreds of epitaphs prove that in such industries as the making of lamps, pipes, and glassware eighty per cent of the workmen were of servile stock; the same is true of goldsmiths and jewellers. Most of these men died as freedmen; they had been presumably employed in the same way as slaves, but manumission was the normal reward for their services.

In Roman law the slave was a chattel. Varro classifies the equipment of the farm as articulate, inarticulate and mute, that is to say, the slaves, the cattle and the ploughs. The slave can be bought, sold or hired out, mated or not (the Elder Cato allowed no women to his farm-hands), fed, clothed and in general punished at the master's will. All that he earns is legally for the master's account. The child of the slave mother is the master's property.

From the first, however, the law was not consistent, and could not be. It had to take account of the slave's humanity, if only in the interests of the free citizens themselves. He might commit a crime; the State would then punish him and more severely than if he were free. He might witness a crime and then he should give evidence. The slave might denounce a plot against the State, and then the State would free him. Moreover the law provided formal procedures under which the master himself might manumit his slave. Manumission is always a concomitant of slavery, but under Roman law, unlike Greek, the freedman of a Roman citizen became a citizen himself, if he was emancipated by the proper formalities.

The interests of the master too required him to care for the slave's welfare. He had to be fed and clothed even when the free poor went hungry and naked. The harsh Cato recommends for farm-hands about as much wheat as the soldier got, with a little wine, oil, olives or pickled fish and salt; they should have shoes and a tunic and cloak every other year; blankets may be made of the discarded clothes. The master was for long empowered to put his slave to death, but only a very capricious owner would destroy his property without strong cause. He could have him flogged, but Varro, for one, preferred verbal rebukes – if they were equally effective. Rewards often served the master's interest better than punishments. He might pay his slave a wage or set him up in business and let him retain part of the earnings. The money or other property he then acquired, though legally his master's, was in practice treated as his own (*peculium*); it might even include other slaves. With his savings he could buy his freedom, 'defrauding his belly', as Seneca puts it. But freedom often came as a gift. Owners, especially if they died without natural heirs, were particularly ready to emancipate slaves by their wills; this gave them posthumous acclaim for generosity. But manumission in the owner's lifetime was also frequent – astonishingly at first sight, but it is not hard to explain. Freedom was the greatest spur to good work, and probably no other incentive sufficed for slaves employed in skilled work and trusted posts. Moreover the former owner now became the patron of his old slave and retained a right to respect and services of many kinds; he might actually impose on the freedman the obligation to work for him without pay to an extent limited only by the proviso that he must either maintain him or allow him enough time to maintain himself. We do not know how usual this practice was; certainly it was not universal, for many freedmen became rich.

Of course kindly, humane feelings and the philosophic doctrine that a master was custodian of his slave's welfare often fortified the self-interest which by itself dictated good treatment of the slave and even his emancipation. But the chief beneficiaries from all these motives were the skilled slaves and the domestics whose duties brought them into close contact with the masters. Farm-workers on distant estates did not benefit; they were often chained together in work or sleep, and Pliny calls them men without hope. Even the farm manager was normally a slave, not a freedman.

Jefferson, writing from experience, declared that

the whole commerce between master and slave is a perpetual exercise of the most boisterous passions, the most unremitting despotism on the one part and degrading submission on the other.

How far was this true in Rome? We cannot generalize either from instances of kind and friendly relations or from recorded atrocities. But Seneca says that masters notorious for cruelty were pointed at in the streets, and the development of the law, which is apt to lag behind the best opinion of its day rather than lead it, is significant. From the first century A.D. for instance it was murder for a master to kill his slave without cause, and a slave who was starved or subjected to savagery and debauchery could take asylum at one of the Emperor's statues and had a right to be sold to another master. It is not likely that the protection of the law was very efficacious, any more than in the Old South, where masters accused of slave-murder were always acquitted by their peers. The Christian Emperor, Constantine, moreover, ruled that where a master was charged with murdering his slave, it had to be proved that he intended to kill him; it was not enough if he died under a flogging. But the provisions of the law do at least reveal the moral climate of opinion.

Humanity was not indeed the only reason for protecting slaves against the cruelty of individual masters. Antoninus Pius declared that such protection was in the interest of masters and designed to prevent uprisings. Centuries before, the philosopher-historian Posidonius had pointed out that ill-treatment of some slaves had been the cause of the great revolt which desolated Sicily from 134 to 132 B.C. This was not the last slave revolt. In the seventies before Christ, slaves led by Spartacus devastated many parts of Italy and routed Roman armies. The Principate was better able to keep order, but the sense of insecurity persisted. *Quot servi tot hostes* – 'Every slave is an enemy' – was a Roman proverb. Slaves were always running away, and the murder of masters was a constant danger. Under a savage Augustan enactment, which gave rise to much case law, when a master was murdered, all his slaves 'under the same roof' were to be executed; if not accomplices, they were at least guilty of not preventing his death. One slave-girl pleaded that the assassin of her mistress had terrified her into silence; Hadrian ruled that she must die, for it was her duty to cry out at the cost of her own life. Still, harsh repression was at least accompanied by some attempts to curb the excesses of masters.

For many who could attain freedom slavery was not a hopeless lot. Petronius depicts a Sicilian who sold himself into slavery (illegally) because he preferred the chance of becoming a Roman citizen to remaining a provincial taxpayer. The freedman could more easily be integrated into society because there was no colour prejudice; there were seldom marked differences of skin to give rise to it. His rights were indeed limited; he could not serve in the army, nor hold state or municipal offices, and he might have onerous obligations to his patron. But if he had economic independence and some little talent and enterprise, he might grow wealthy. His political disabilities, like those imposed in later times on Jews or Quakers, channelled his energies into business, where freedmen were often dominant. They might be assisted by their patron, like the freedman of an Augustan nobleman who managed all his business affairs and received from him ample gifts for himself, a dowry for his daughter and a commission in the army for his son. Another freedman of this time boasted in his will that he left 4,116 slaves, 3,600 pairs of oxen and 257,000 head of other cattle. Petronius' Trimalchio, whose estates in Italy stretched from sea to sea, is no mere figment of a novelist. These are extreme examples, but many other freedmen secured a modest competence, and were able to advance their children, who suffered no legal disabilities, further in the social scale. The poet Horace was the son of a freedman who could give him the education of a gentleman and help to make him the court laureate, and Horace was not ashamed to recall his origin. In Nero's time it could be alleged that most senators had servile blood in their veins and a century later, Marcus Helvius Pertinax, the son of a freedman, rose by military and administrative capacity so high that in 193 he was proclaimed Emperor.

The most favoured of slaves and freedmen were the Emperor's, who were employed in the Imperial administration. Under Tiberius a slave who was paymaster in Gaul took sixteen of his own slaves with him on a visit to Rome; of these two were needed to keep his plate. Claudius' freedmen secretaries are said to have been the wealthiest men of their day and the real rulers of the Empire; the brother of one was that Felix who governed Judaea in Paul's day and married a descendant of Cleopatra. In some later reigns, chamberlains, often eunuchs, who had the Emperor's private ear, were to exercise power no less great.

The enormous importance of slavery in the economy of ancient Italy raises a large historical question. Obviously if the technical advances of even the early modern period of European history had been anticipated in the Graeco-Roman world, the Empire must have been too strong for the barbarians, whose invasions were at least the proximate cause and the necessary condition for its disruption. Can the extensive use of slavery be held responsible for technological backwardness and economic stagnation?

It has been argued that because slave labour was abundant and cheap the ancient world had no incentive to technological invention and that slavery so far abased the dignity of labour that the best minds turned away in disgust from everything connected with manual tasks; hence the backwardness of the Greeks and Romans in all scientific investigations which, unlike mathematics, demanded any approach other than that of abstract thinking. At the same time, to quote Cairnes' famous judgement on

American slavery, slave labour 'is given reluctantly; it is unskilful; it is wanting in versatility'; it must therefore be assumed that it was inefficient.

Even on these premises slavery cannot have been a prime cause of Rome's decline. After Augustus the Empire drew its strength increasingly and in the end exclusively from the provinces, where slavery was not predominant as it was in Italy. Not only did the provinces furnish soldiers; some of them, notably Gaul and Egypt, were economically more prosperous, and it is certain of Egypt and probable of Gaul that slavery there was on a small scale. Yet these regions were no more inventive or progressive than Italy. We must therefore look elsewhere for reasons that will explain scientific or technological stagnation. Some have already been given; and we must add that progress was to depend on the formulation of fertile scientific hypotheses or on crucial inventions like optical glass; it is perhaps no more easy to understand why these happen in one age and not in another than to account for the flowering of poetical genius.

And was slave labour so inefficient? Roman experts on agriculture assumed that on good land and adequately supervised it brought in higher profits than free labour. We lack ancient evidence to test this assumption, and modern analogies yield no clear conclusion; the latest analyses of the economy of the Old South seem to show that its backwardness compared with the North cannot be certainly ascribed to slavery. In trade and industry the slaves were skilled workers spurred on by the hope of freedom; they are actually credited with minor inventions (like American Negro slaves) and, if other factors had permitted mechanization, they were clearly capable of minding machines; indeed Negroes too were used successfully in factories, although they were at a lower cultural level and lacked such strong incentives. (Similarly in the last world war German productivity actually increased with the extended use of what was in all but name slave labour.) However cheap Roman slaves were, and we do not know just how cheap, the owners still had no motive to be indifferent to devices that might have increased their output.

It is thus on moral rather than on economic grounds that

Roman slavery merits opprobrium. And many Roman slaves were no worse off than the mass of the peasantry who, though free in name, found it hard to assert their rights or defend their interests and never lived far from starvation. In a pre-industrial and poor society, of course, the poverty of the masses is the price to be paid if even a few are to enjoy leisure and civilization and the opportunity of promoting further progress. But in the Roman world such inevitable inequality was carried too far, further, for instance, than in democratic Greek communities. Hence, in the first century B.C. agrarian discontent in Italy helped to bring the Republic down, and in and after the third century A.D. the peasantry, unconscious of the benefits that accrued even to them from the Roman peace, often showed themselves indifferent and sometimes hostile to an empire in which the interests of the wealthy, *beati possidentes*, were always preponderant. This was no doubt one reason why despite its immensely superior resources the Empire succumbed to the inroads of barbarians.

BIBLIOGRAPHY

Much of the evidence is collected and translated in *An Economic Survey of Ancient Rome*, 5 volumes, edited by Tenney Frank (New York), and interpreted by Frank in his *Economic History of Rome* (New York), and by M. Rostovtzeff, *Social and Economic History of the Roman Empire* (Oxford University Press, 1957). For agricultural labour see W. E. Heitland, *Agricola*; for freedmen, A. M. Duff. *Freedmen in the Early Roman Empire* (Heffer, 1959). The useful but inaccurate compilation of W. L. Westermann, *The Slave Systems of Greek and Roman Antiquity* (*see* my criticisms in *Journal of Roman Studies*, 1958) has not wholly superseded H. Wallon, *Histoire de l'esclavage dans l'antiquité* (1879). Some valuable essays are republished in *Slavery in Classical Antiquity*, edited by M. I. Finley.

ROME AS A BATTLEGROUND OF
RELIGIONS

J. P. V. D. Balsdon

To a Roman of the best days of the Republic religion represented stability in the State and in the home; it was the foundation of public and private life, the oldest thing of all. The temples of the gods were the noblest buildings that existed; the temple of Juppiter Optimus Maximus on the Capitol watched over the city as the great dome of St Peter's watches over it today. The rules governing the relationship of the gods and the Romans themselves, the citizens, were the city's very charter. These rules were in fact a codification of the various religious practices of the different communities which combined to form the city of Rome;* and legendary tradition, with its liking for individuals and personalities as law-givers, ascribed its formulation, as if it was a single act, to King Numa.

The regulations were not concerned with ethics. The State religion whose origin was ascribed to Numa was, anyhow in the third century B.C., a matter of regulations for various sacrifices and, at the foundation of it all, was the belief that the gods would not desert Rome as long as they were fed with the proper sacrifices in the proper manner at the proper times. More than that, they could be relied on to issue warnings when danger threatened. A rainstorm of blood, a swarm of bees in a temple, the monstrous birth of a calf which spoke with a human voice – these were the signs, the portents. They meant trouble, unless the correct apotropaic action was taken, in which case danger could be averted.

At times of national disaster it was to the gods that the Romans went. Days of public intercession (*supplicationes*) were proclaimed. And when the danger was surmounted, they went to the gods again. There were days of public thanksgiving (also called *supplicationes*).

The gods were just as important for the family as for the State. For continuance a family has two needs, a full larder and, generation after generation, a supply of vigorous young children. The Lar Familiaris, the protecting spirit of the house, and the Penates, who watched over the larder (*penus*), were the real spirit of every family, together with the spirit (*genius*) of the master of the house – the house which once had had his father as its master and which one day would have his son.

The well-being of the city depended on the correct performance of their duties by the priests and priestesses, who were citizens, members of eminent families, particularly chosen. The priests were normally men active and prominent in public life; they were not professional clergy, ordained and set apart from other men, except in the few cases in which they were shackled by religious taboos. The three major priests, for instance, the Flamen Dialis (the priest of Jupiter), the priest of Mars and the priest of Quirinus, originally the god of the Quirinal communities (who by the third century B.C., through a development which we cannot trace, had become Romulus turned after his death into a god), must be the sons of parents married by an antique ceremony (*confarreatio*) which, divorce being difficult, had by the second century B.C. gone out of fashion; they must have wives whose parents had been married in the same manner. The wife of the Flamen Dialis became a priestess, Flaminica Dialis, at the moment when her husband became a priest. He must not look on blood, and so in the late Republic he was denied the profits and the glory which came from provincial administration and fighting; and if his wife died, he must at once resign his priesthood. How different might history have been if, as came near to happening, Julius Caesar in his youth had been made Flamen Dialis.

Though the Pontifex Maximus was head of the State religion in historical times, his priesthood was less ancient, and he was hampered by no taboos at all.

Even the Vestal Virgins, whose chaste discharge of their varied and exacting duties was at the very core of the city's good health and prosperity, were bound by no perpetual vow of chastity. There were only six members of the College, varying in age between six and ten (when they were 'taken' by the Pontifex Maximus) and thirty-six to forty, when their assignment was completed unless they chose to remain within the College. If a Vestal Virgin returned to private life when her thirty years of duty ended, she was free to marry, though it was believed that good fortune did not attend such marriages. If, while a member of the College, she failed in any of her duties, she was punished, for her shortcoming could spell catastrophe for the State: thrashed by the Pontifex Maximus if she had let the fire go out in the temple of Vesta, buried alive in an underground chamber under the Campus Sceleratus by the Colline Gate if she had been found unchaste.

The priesthoods and the established religion of the State had once been a bastion of patrician power. The plebeians were not enemies of religion, for then they would have been enemies of the State; they only wanted to belong themselves to the Establishment. In this they succeeded and by the end of the Struggle of the Orders, though the major Flamines must be patricians, the plebeians had secured full eligibility for election to the priestly Colleges.

Since the public acts of the State depended on the gods' approval, it was necessary to make certain of the gods' consent before an assembly of the people (the Comitia) started its business and on the battlefield before the general engaged the enemy. With the expansion of Roman power in Italy new methods of divining the intentions of the gods were acquired. One form of divination came from the Etruscans – divining by the flight of birds, by thunder and lightning and by scrutiny of the inwards of animals which had been sacrificed. The technical experts in this field were Haruspices, men whom Etruria continued to train but who, though they were constantly consulted by the Senate, were never held in the highest esteem at Rome. Different from the Etruscan was the Roman practice of augury, the field of the eminent Augurs, who constituted one of the three major Roman priestly Colleges. Their venerable records contained the history and precedent of augural 'science', in relation particularly to the public activities of the State. In 49 B.C., for instance, when the consuls had fled from Italy and it would have suited Julius Caesar's convenience that in their absence a praetor should conduct the election of consuls for the following year, the Augurs could inform him that what he wanted was something which the Roman constitution did not allow.

Rome's first expansion (or earlier, perhaps, her government by Etruscan Kings) brought divination to Rome. Her expansion to the south brought from the Greeks in Campania the art of divination by the sacred books. These were carried to Rome from Cumae, and a College of priests, first Duoviri then Decemviri and later Quindecemviri Sacris Faciundis, had the responsible control of them, and knew how to open them and read them on any occasion at the right spot. So when alarming prodigies were reported to the Senate, the Senate normally submitted the reports to the expertise of the College, and was told what apotropaic action must be taken – an appropriate sacrifice perhaps, or the introduction of some novel cult – to avert disaster.

The third and most important priestly College was that of the Pontifices, to which, in addition to ordinary members, the three major Flamines and the Rex Sacrorum belonged. Here was the repository of the best legal knowledge in the State. Its expert advice was often requested by the Senate, to which, if old enough, its members, like the members of the other Colleges, naturally belonged. It was before the Pontifices that a Vestal Virgin was arraigned.

The Pontifex Maximus was chairman of each of these three Colleges, and in addition he presided over the Vestal Virgins.

Contact with Greek civilization, first in the south of Italy and then in the eastern Mediterranean influenced religions as it did every other branch of Roman thought. New cults, like that of Liber Pater, were introduced, and existing Roman gods and goddesses came to be identified with their Greek equivalents, Juppiter with Zeus, Juno with Hera, Minerva with Athena. But the

Greek gods, though superhuman figures, were yet fashioned in the image of men. The Greek world was full of these images. So now in its turn was the Roman.

No country has ever survived a great and critical war with its social structure unchanged. More than any other, the Second Punic War was critical for Rome's survival and religion was an important element in the social structure of Rome. At the end of the Second Punic War the firm wall of conservatism which surrounded Roman religion was breached when, in the form of a black stone, the Great Mother (Cybele) was brought from Pessinus in Phrygia to Rome. Her importation was respectably authorized by the Decemvirs' consultation of the Sibylline books, as a specific for victory, and she was housed in a temple on the Palatine and worshipped *more Romano*.* But, though she might be Romanized, other similar cults were to come unauthorized the way that she had come from the east, explosives and not the sedatives that Romans liked their gods to be. They were to come at first with Roman armies returning from service in the east.

The war ended in 201 B.C. Fifteen years later the first explosion occurred. Information was laid that Bacchic worship (an importation from Greece through Etruria) had become a cover for disruptive conspiracy and debauch. There was a witch hunt† and a spate of executions, and then the Roman government, to whose mind it would have seemed incongruous to forbid any form of religious cult, took what seemed the proper corrective measures for the future. It brought Bacchic worship under the supervision and control of public authority. There were to be no more than five worshippers at any one time; the Urban Praetor must be approached for leave, and he in his turn must consult the Senate at a meeting attended by a necessary quorum of members.

Up to the middle of the second century B.C. the traditional religion of Rome held its ground. That was when Polybius lived in Rome, looking at its government with the eyes of an intelligent

*See pp. 192f.
† See further, pp. 28f.

Greek. Nothing impressed him more strongly than the integrity of the Roman governing class (an integrity which would not survive much longer) in their handling of public money; he ascribed it to their religious faith, particularly to their respect for the vows which they made to the gods.

Religion being at the very foundation of the ancient State's existence, it was a natural thing that in the kingdoms of the turbulent Hellenistic world the King should be made a god, and his divinity recognized. The Athenians sang to Demetrius Poliorcetes in 291 B.C.:

He stands, his friends round him, like the sun among the stars. Welcome, son of the god Poseidon and Aphrodite. Other gods are far away, have no ears to hear with, or do not exist, or have no care for us, but you we see, a very present and true god, no piece of wood or of stone. So we pray to you.

The Hellenistic Kings went down like ninepins, vanquished by Roman proconsuls. The word 'Rome' in Greek meant 'strength', and the Roman proconsul, encompassed by his legions parading with full-dress ceremonial, was often more impressive and worshipful than the Kings had ever been. Proconsuls could have worship for the asking, and bad ones did. Good proconsuls were shocked, explaining that they were servants of Rome and of the Senate. So Rome became a goddess – Dea Roma – with temples and altars in many places in the Greek world of the eastern Mediterranean from the second century B.C. onwards. Cult was even paid to the Senate. In Rome itself, Rome was not a goddess until the second century A.D.

Ethics were no significant part of Roman religion; nor was speculation on the problems of life and death and of survival after death. These were questions for the philosophers, and it was left to the philosophers in antiquity to preach sermons. The two philosophies which touched the lives of the largest number of people were both Greek, Stoicism and Epicureanism. Their language was different, the Stoics advocating 'life according to nature', the Epicureans 'the pursuit of true pleasure', but there was little difference between the two different conceptions of the truly moral life. They had no room, either of them, for the tenderer virtues of compassion which Christianity was to rate so highly; but otherwise the good life which they both described and advocated was life in conformity with the highest standards of austere morality. Stoicism allowed for the possibility of the spirit's survival after death, survival by absorption into the world spirit, of which in life it was a part. Epicureanism taught the atomic theory and believed that death was utter disintegration of body and spirit alike. This, preached by Lucretius at the end of the Republic, was a message not of despair but of hope; nobody's life need be clouded by apprehension of torment after death.*

The best Roman was a natural Stoic. Stoicism was the philosophy of the younger Cato, of Thrasea Paetus, of Helvidius Priscus, and had Epictetus and the Emperor Marcus Aurelius as its distinguished exponents. Epicureanism was suspect. It was easy to take its language at face value, and to maintain that it advocated hedonism as the noblest form of life. So Romans who were Epicureans tended to be bad Epicureans or else bad Romans.

Philosophy did little to arrest the disintegration of Roman morals in the century which followed the fall of Carthage in the middle of the second century B.C. Sallust, a reformed sinner himself, was later to describe the conquest of Rome by selfishness, greed, base ambition and simple lust. Even the holiest ceremonial was smirched when in December 62 B.C., as people believed, P. Clodius, disguised as a female harp player, penetrated the High Priest Caesar's house during the festival of the Bona Dea, from which men were rigorously excluded – whether he did this for a prank or with the purpose of debauching Caesar's wife.

Not only morals, but the cult of the gods disintegrated. Temples were, many of them, in collapse. Precious ceremonial was forgotten or disregarded. It was possible to mock the Haruspices. Omens and portents were observed, even fabricated, chiefly for the opportunity which they gave to the slick politician for some political sleight of hand. Under the impact of cynicism and scepticism Roman religious faith (except, often, in the home) disintegrated.

*See further, pp. 219–22.

The long disaster of the civil wars ensued – Rome's punishment, as, when Augustus had restored peace, the writers who were closest to his thoughts emphasized, Horace above all.

Religion was to be revived, and so were moral standards. For the reform of morals there was legislation, some in Augustus' own name, to reduce adultery and to increase the birth rate. It was unpopular legislation, largely unrealistic and, in its outcome, unsuccessful. The restoration of religion on the material and ceremonial side was easy enough, though expensive. The decaying and collapsing temples were restored and rebuilt. Once the office was vacant, Augustus became Pontifex Maximus and later Emperors followed his example. The Emperor, then, was head of the religion of the State, as of all else. There was august ceremonial, graced by the Princeps and his family, to mark the restoration of dignity and importance to the worship of the gods – the celebration of the Secular Games in 17 B.C. (the birthday of a new age, something which by traditional belief happened every hundred or hundred and ten years), and the dedication of the altar of Pax Augusta (the Peace which Augustus had restored).

In the eastern provinces it was possible to redress the slightly ambiguous position which had prevailed since the fall of the Hellenistic Kings, and cult and homage in one could be paid now to the world's ruler, Rome's first citizen or Princeps. Where there was a cult of Rome, it easily became a cult of Rome and Augustus, and Augustus' birthday and the day of his accession became great annual occasions for sacrifice and celebration. The cult of Rome and Augustus, with temples, altars and priests (provincials whom it was politic to honour) spread through the eastern provinces and into the western provinces of the Empire. In Italy and Rome cult (in which freedmen were given prominence) was paid to the Emperor's 'genius'. This was not offensive man-worship, but followed easily in the tradition of the cult of the 'genius' of the master of the house within the family.

This for Augustus – and, by intention, for his successors, when alive. Death in due course would make a god of him as, by one of the most extraordinary coincidences in history, it had made a god of Julius Caesar. There was happily the firm republican tradition of Rome's founder Romulus becoming the god Quirinus after his death. In July 44 B.C., four months after Caesar's murder, during the very celebration of the games in honour of his victory, an unexpected comet appeared in the sky. It was a prodigy, accepted by the populace as evidence – even before the expertise of the priests had been consulted – that Julius Caesar was now in heaven, a god, Divus Iulius. The constitutional formalities were observed, a vote of the Senate and a resolution of the people establishing this new god. So in a studiously indeterminate way the first Princeps who, with the awful name Augustus which he had received in 27 B.C., was recognized as having an almost superhuman prestige in his lifetime, could anticipate (and others with him) that after his death he too would become a god.

The Emperor's person was the focus of the Empire's loyalty, gladly and satisfactorily expressed in one form or another of the imperial cult, with the various formalities on which authority insisted and in a great many other ways on which authority wisely turned a blind eye.

If the restoration of temples was a simple matter, the restoration of earlier religious belief was not easy at all; it was not even possible. Nobody could cross off the slate two hundred years of progressive thinking. The notion of divination by birds and entrails was unacceptable to any thinking man, as Cicero had made clear in his *De divinatione*.

If the future was to be foretold, there was now a modern and 'scientific' method, for with all the forceful impact of a newly discovered scientific truth came the doctrine that the course of a man's life was determined from the moment of his birth or even of his conception by the conjunction of the stars. Astrologers, also called Chaldaeans from their Babylonian origin, had already made their first appearance in Rome, and had been expelled, in the second century B.C., and thereafter Rome was never free, any more than the modern world is completely free, of the sinister allure of their craft. Their knowledge of astronomy and the complicated nature of their calculations won awed respect and the temptation to know what the future held was irresistible. The woman with a lover, whose way would be easier if her husband died, the conspirator who planned an attack on the Emperor's life, among myriads of others, were impatient for assurance that their wishes would be fulfilled. There were honest astrologers; but there were also charlatans, ready for a fee to give a vain assurance of success to dishonest enterprise. Emperors employed them for themselves, in particular Tiberius and Septimius Severus, but made it a criminal offence for a commoner to have an Emperor's horoscope cast.

Confronted by the pretentiously scientific apparatus of astrological calculation, primitive devices for foretelling the future – divination and oracles – sank into inevitable decline. As for astrology, the fraudulence of many of its practitioners was common knowledge. Thinking men of intelligence – Lucretius, Cicero, the Elder Pliny and Juvenal – recognized that, even at its best, its claims were fallacious. But that did not prevent the universality of its appeal.

Still more sinister was magic. This could be a matter of pronouncing or writing the correct formula and burning, burying or devoting the appropriate object, sometimes for the pathetic purpose of winning back a lover, more often with the sinister intention of encompassing an enemy's death. Such practices were not restricted to the lowest levels of society; for a well-bred young politician under Tiberius was found in possession of a list of names of senators and members of the imperial family, against which there were mysterious marks; and when Tiberius' adopted son Germanicus died mysteriously in Syria in A.D. 19, incantations on lead tablets, on which his name was scratched, were among the sinister objects discovered under the floor of his house.

More properly religious was the individual's desire for salvation or redemption and his concern with survival after death. Here were deeply human instincts with which the religion of the Roman State was not concerned and to which innumerable foreign religions administered, 'superstitions', in contrast to 'religion', a word which was reserved for the traditional religion of Rome itself. They were eastern in origin, for the whole religious current in the Roman Empire flowed from east to west. The most prominent of such foreign cults were those of Cybele (the Great Mother), Dionysus (Bacchus), Isis, Osiris, and Serapis ('Egyptian rites'), Mithras, Judaism and Christianity. They mostly involved an initiation ceremony, which brought redemption and the beginning of a new life, a shared experience with the god, communion with whom might extend beyond death into a future life.

The Roman government viewed them with suspicion because of the orgiastic character of certain of their ceremonies and because of the discovery from time to time that they served as a cloak for criminal practices. Yet this inscription of the first century B.C. from Lydia in Asia Minor is significant. It concerns a shrine of Dionysus – in which were altars of numerous divinities, some Olympian, some Hellenistic – which was under the protection of the oriental goddess Agdistis. Admission to the cult was afforded to men and women, free and slave alike, and the inscription sets out the instruction of Zeus, revealed in a dream:

Worshippers must swear by all the gods that they harbour no evil intention towards any one, man or woman; that they do not indulge in poisoning or evil magic; that they do not practise or abet love charms, abortion, the use of contraceptives, rape or murder, that they do not steal, but are well-minded to this House, and if any one practise or plot such misdoing, they will not suffer it or keep silent, but will give information and punish it. A man will lie only with his wife and with no other free woman or married slave woman, and he will not corrupt any boy or young girl. . . . No man or woman who offends against any of these commandments may be admitted to the House.

When Cybele, the Great Mother, was received in Rome shortly before the end of the Second Punic War and a temple built on the Palatine, annual games, the Megalensia, were established, and once a year the stone was carried outside the walls and given a washing. So soberly did Roman officialdom mute the strident ecstasies of drum and cymbal which, in her native domain, accompanied her procession as she rode in a chariot drawn by lions. She was a vegetation goddess and her ceremonial celebrated the death and rebirth of her lover Attis. In wildest frenzy her initiates emasculated themselves and in Lucretius and Catullus we can read the horror which this roused in the minds of deeply sensitive Romans. How much of this wild ecstasy was countenanced in the Western world is hard to know; in a wall painting at Pompeii the procession of the goddess is certainly attended by great decorum. Claudius sought to make it a religion fit for Romans when he ordained that the chief priest, the Archigallus, should in the future be a Roman citizen, not a castrated man. And the ceremonies which Antoninus Pius and his wife, the elder Faustina, attended are unlikely to have been anything but, like themselves, respectable.

The cult of Dionysus, as has been seen, had caused the Roman government concern as early as 186 B.C. It had spread in the Hellenistic world, and offered its initiates, after various ordeals, the promise of an after-life, which was not devoid of sensuous pleasures. It appealed to rich people, and in the remarkable frescoes of the Villa of the Mysteries at Pompeii, an initiation ceremony involving flagellation is certainly depicted, although its full significance is still imperfectly understood.

The cult of Isis was the most widespread of all the mystery religions, brought by sailors and travellers to every Mediterranean port and to such important road-junctions as Benevento (Beneventum), where remarkable relics of the cult are still to be seen. Isis was worshipped with Serapis and with Osiris, god of the underworld, who had been killed and his limbs scattered, and whose resurrection was celebrated at the ceremony of the Finding of Osiris in November. Initiates were held to pass during the initiation ceremony through the underworld and before the presence of the gods. There was a transcendent calm and beauty in the expression of the goddess, if Apuleius, a convert, is to be believed. Isis was primarily a woman's goddess, demanding and receiving, even from courtesans, periods of abstinence, at which their lovers protested. Yet in her temple at Rome all was not innocence and, after the seduction of a guileless woman with the priests' connivance, Tiberius crucified the priests, destroyed the image of Isis and expelled numbers of her worshippers. The cult, indeed, had a chequered career from the start and it was after

Tiberius, when Gaius Caligula was Emperor, that it first received official recognition.

For men, in particular for soldiers the whole Empire over, Mithraism, which the Romans first encountered when, under Pompey, they defeated the eastern Mediterranean pirates, was the mystery cult which held the greatest appeal. There were no priests or temples; services were held in underground chapels, representing the cave in which Mithras was born. These have been discovered in all parts of the Empire, forty-five in Rome alone, fifteen in Ostia, one recently in London, many on Hadrian's wall and on other frontiers. Mithraism embodied a creed which derived from ancient Persia, from Zoroastrianism, a belief that two superhuman powers were in perpetual conflict, Good against Evil, Ahuramazda against Ahriman, Light against Darkness. Mithras, depicted in art wearing a Phrygian cap, was man's ally in the struggle for good, unconquered and unconquerable. The religion had its own creation myth. In the beginning was Mithras' fight to kill the bull (of which there are innumerable representations in art); from the blood of the slain bull came life and vegetation, and the first human couple whom Ahriman was unable to destroy. In the end Mithras was taken in the chariot of the sun to heaven, where he remained, caring for his believers. The initiation ceremonies (of which there were seven grades, corresponding to the seven planets) were a formidable test of endurance, and the exalted ideals of the religion were resolute courage and asceticism and chastity. A religion, it seems, which had no place at all for women.

A ceremony – the *taurobolium* or *criobolium* – which was associated most commonly with Cybele worship was one where a worshipper stood below a grill above which a bull's or a ram's throat was cut. The blood poured over every part of him. Blood in all sacrifice is the power of life and the worshipper, once he had been blooded, had the consciousness of redemption, crying out that he was redeemed for eternity.

The Jewish religion offered none of the blatant attractions which advertised many of the foreign mystery cults. Jews were exclusive, worshipping among themselves in their synagogues, and this very exclusiveness was perhaps an attraction to the curious. The peculiar marks of the cult invited ridicule. Circumcision seemed an unattractive practice, abstention from pork a laughable eccentricity, and observance of the Sabbath a mark of sloth – the devotion of a seventh part of a man's life to idleness. Jewish services, however, for any one who was admitted to a synagogue, were interesting in that, instead of the mere observance of a regular liturgy, there were readings and expositions of the scripture, something more like the proceedings in a philosopher's lecture room than those of a religious cult.

Their rigid monotheism distinguished the Jews from the devotees of other religions. This exclusiveness, marked all the world over by their absence from public religious ceremonies, made for unpopularity and gave Jews the reputation of misanthropes. They would not appear in court on the Sabbath or, if they were soldiers, on parade. They were in frequent conflict with their fellow townsmen who were gentiles. So, to authority, they were a nuisance. With the advent of the Empire they caused more trouble still, for celebrations of Emperor worship were now official occasions, and the Jews were informed against on account of their absence, and represented as disloyal. From time to time they were expelled from Rome; and when, after the sack of Jerusalem, Vespasian ordered that the contributions, which had previously been sent by members of the Dispersion to Jerusalem, should be paid to the Roman exchequer, they suffered as the followers of no other religion suffered. They were taxed for being Jews. Yet their religion was never proscribed, presumably because it had, unlike Christianity, a respectable antiquity.

Jesus was crucified within a year or two of A.D. 29. In 64 the first Christian persecution in Rome took place, Nero making scapegoats of Christians for the fire at Rome; St Peter and St Paul may have been among the victims. So quickly did the new religion spread.

Its attractions were infinite. The single and final redemption of man by God, himself made man, was a concept far more powerful than notions of redemption held by the popular mystery cults. Compelling, too, in a world in which notions of a Saviour had long been current, was the demonstration of redemption so recently achieved after centuries of Hebrew prophecy, of which it was the striking fulfilment. Christianity preached love of man for man, the union of Christian communities everywhere, and it made its direct appeal to men, women and children, bond and free. Its notion of the after-life was not expressed in vague metaphysical terms; it seemed to give an absolute promise of the physical resurrection of the body. And, strongest attraction of all, perhaps, in the early days, especially to the poor and underprivileged, who constituted the bulk of the early converts, was the belief that the Second Coming and the establishment of Christ's kingdom on earth were shortly to take place, even in the lifetime of these early believers themselves. Men and women faced martyrdom, not as Marcus Aurelius, in his only mention of Christianity, thought, 'from sheer opposition', but in absolute certainty – as strong as the certainty of the Arab warriors who welcomed death in the great conquests of the seventh century – of the reward which awaited them in a future life.

Like the Jews, the Christians were intolerant of Emperor worship. More serious still, their enemies misunderstood or misrepresented the nature of the Christian sacrament. Christians were represented as indulging in cannibal practice. There is no evidence that the Roman government at any level tried to get to the root of this particular question. The authorities proceeded on the rough and ready method of inviting any one denounced as a Christian to renounce his belief in Christ and, in evidence, to perform an act, however formal, in conformity with Emperor worship. If he refused, he was executed – as a Christian would say, martyred. Good Emperors did not at first regard this persecution with any satisfaction, and Trajan gave firm instruction to Pliny, when he governed Bithynia early in the second century A.D. that Christians were not to be hunted down. There was persecution of Christians under Domitian in the first century and under Marcus Aurelius in the second; but it was later, under Decius and Diocletian, that persecution was pursued on imperial instruction with grim intensity. In 311 the edicts authorizing the persecution were revoked, and there was an act of Toleration. Before the battle of the Milvian bridge in 312 Constantine saw the sign in heaven and gave his support to the Christian Church and on his death-bed in 337, having delayed for whatever prudent reason, he was baptized. Now the first Christian churches were erected in Rome, some on the sites of the catacombs, on the outskirts and out of sight of the pagan temples which monopolized the centre of the city.

Christianity, so long on the defensive, now moved to the attack and it was the turn of pagan temples to be forcibly closed and their sacrifice forbidden. Then in the middle of the fourth century the wind veered once more and Julian restored paganism. Pagan shrines, the last ever, were erected in Rome; the *taurobolium* was practised; there were processions of the Great Mother; Haruspices were revived; and there was even a literature of the reaction. Paganism, discouraged by Constantine, revived by Julian, flourished under Valentinian and the early years of Gratian. Then in 382 public approval and public financing of pagan cults was withdrawn. Gratian's murder in 383 and the hideous famine which afflicted the western Empire were, it seemed, the consequence. So in 384, through Symmachus, the Senate petitioned the new Emperor, Valentinian II for the restoration of pagan cult; but Ambrose, the Bishop of Milan, arguing against them, was successful. So long had the priesthoods and priestly Colleges of the Republic survived, but no longer. A few years later, in the presence of the Emperor Theodosius, the subservient Senate capitulated and voted that Christianity should be the religion of the State. The Emperor appointed special commissioners to the east and to the west of the Empire, in Gibbon's words

to shut the temples, to seize or destroy the instruments of idolatry, to abolish the privileges of the priests and to confiscate the consecrated property for the benefit of the emperor, of the church or of the army.

But paganism did not perish overnight. Much went underground, where it remains still. Much that seemed unexceptionable, too good to throw away, was kept and dyed Christian. The Megalensia, for instance, dropped their name, but, as games, survived. At the ancient Roman festival of Robigalia on 25 April worshippers had gone five miles out of Rome on the via Cassia to sacrifice and ask blessings on the crops; on the same day and over the same route the greater litany of St Mark was to be celebrated. 25 December the birthday of the Sun (Sol Invictus), was observed by the Christian church from the fourth century as the birthday of the Creator of the Sun; and when on Christmas Day you give presents and wear a paper cap, you are in fact an ancient Roman celebrating the Saturnalia.

BIBLIOGRAPHY

The great standard works on Roman state religion are in German, by Georg Wissowa and Kurt Latte. Best in English are H. J. Rose, *Ancient Roman Religion* (Hutchinson, 1949) and W. Warde Fowler's books, especially *The Religious Experience of the Roman People* (Macmillan, 1922). On pagan cults, F. Cumont, *After Life in Roman Paganism* (Dover, 1957), *Oriental Religions in Roman Paganism* (Dover, 1956) and *The Mysteries of Mithra* (Dover, 1956) and Jean Seznec, *The Survival of the Pagan Gods* (Princeton University Press) are all available as paperbacks. On Christianity and Paganism, *see* C. N. Cochrane *Christianity and Classic Culture* (Oxford University Press, 1944), A. D. Nock, *Conversion* (Oxford University Press, 1933) and *Early Gentile Christianity and its Hellenistic Background* (Harper Paperback, 1964), and *The Conflict between Paganism and Christianity in the Fourth Century* (ed. A. Momogliano, Oxford University Press, 1963), A. N. Sherwin-White, *Roman Society and Roman Law in the New Testament* (Oxford University Press, 1963); on Emperor worship, L. R. Taylor, *The Divinity of the Roman Emperor* (1931).

II

EDUCATION AND ORATORY

M. L. Clarke

IN a sense there is no such thing as Roman education. The educational system as we know it in the later Republic and the Imperial period was in all essentials a close copy of the contemporary Greek system, to which Rome contributed little except the language in which it was conducted. The Roman authorities did not make it their business to devise or direct a state system of education, and when under the Empire the State did take some interest in education all it did was to encourage and subsidize a system which had become established as a result of private enterprise. Yet the very fact that the Romans adopted the Greek system is of undeniable historical importance, and however close their borrowing was they gave a certain Roman character to what they borrowed. It is hard to imagine a Greek writing anything quite like Quintilian's *Institutio Oratoria*.

The adoption of Greek methods of education was part of that process described by Horace in the well-known words *Graecia capta ferum victorem cepit et artes intulit agresti Latio* ('Captive Greece took her fierce conqueror captive, and introduced the arts to rustic Latium'). Rustic Latium in early days had trained her sons in the home and, so far as concerned the conduct of public affairs, by a kind of apprenticeship in the camp and the forum. As the Younger Pliny puts it :

In old times the practice was for Romans to learn from their elders not by listening only but also by seeing what they should themselves eventually do and in turn hand down to the younger generation. In early youth they were initiated into service in the camp so that they might learn to command by obeying, to act as leaders by following; then as candidates for office they would stand at the doors of the senate house and watch the counsels of state before taking part in them. Each had his father as teacher, or if he had none, the oldest and most distinguished friend served in the place of father.

Then in the second century B.C. Rome's rapid expansion to the east brought her into close contact with the old-established and sophisticated civilization of the Greek-speaking world, where knowledge had been systematized, embodied in textbooks and made the object of instruction by recognized experts. Greek teachers came to Rome and the Romans willingly sat at their feet.

The contrast between the old and the new methods can be clearly seen in the accounts which Plutarch gives of the education provided for their respective sons by two eminent Romans in the second century B.C., Cato and Aemilius Paullus. Cato's son was taught reading, law and Roman history, throwing the javelin, fighting in armour, riding, boxing and swimming, his instructor in all these accomplishments being his father. Aemilius Paullus on the other hand engaged a whole army of Greek tutors to instruct his son, grammarians, philosophers, rhetoricians, teachers of sculpture and drawing and experts on hunting. The son who had the advantage of this elaborate Greek education is known to history, thanks to his adoption into the family of the Scipios, as Scipio Aemilianus, and it was to him that Cicero looked back as the model of the man who combined Roman traditions with Greek culture, one of those who 'to the traditional Roman way of life added the foreign learning originating in Socrates'.

The Greeks, secure in the consciousness of their own cultural superiority, made no attempt to adapt their education to the new rulers of the world and taught in Rome as they taught elsewhere, in their own language. In due course the Romans followed in their footsteps and developed a Latin version of two at any rate of the Greek disciplines, grammar and rhetoric. Grammar, the *grammatice* of the ancients, included the study of literature as well as that of language, and in the former aspect its Roman beginnings date back to the third century B.C., before Rome's expansion to the east, when Greeks and Hellenized Italians from southern Italy found their way to Rome and began to teach there; indeed Latin literature may be said to have owed its origin in part to 'grammar', for the earliest Latin epic, Andronicus' version of the *Odyssey*, appears to have been written in order to provide a textbook for literary study in Latin. By the end of the Republic the Latin grammar school was well established, though it can hardly have had the prestige of the Greek grammar school; there were a number of Latin schools in the capital and the subject had already spread to the provinces.

Rhetoric had a natural appeal for the Romans. They were accustomed to debate and public speaking, and though for generations they had managed to express themselves in the Senate, at public meetings and in the law courts without any formal training in speaking, and though old-fashioned Romans like the elder Cato thought it enough to keep hold of the matter and let the words follow (*rem tene verba sequentur*), the Greek professors found the Romans very ready to learn from them. It was not until early in the first century B.C. that rhetoric began to be taught in Latin, and even then this new form of teaching aroused opposition. When a school of Latin rhetoric was opened the young Cicero was advised against attending it on the ground that a better training could be obtained in Greek, and the censors issued an edict expressing their disapproval of the innovation. A generation later it was still thought right to train in Greek for speaking in Latin; Cicero's nephew at the age of twelve was declaiming under the Greek rhetorician Paeonius.

How the leading orator of the late Republic was trained for public life we know from the autobiographical passages in the *Brutus*. Cicero does not include his schooldays proper, but begins with himself at the age of fifteen, by which time he would already have been grounded in Greek and Latin literature and in rhetoric. He now attended the Forum daily and listened to the leading orators of the day, and at the same time engaged in writing and reading and in oratorical and other exercises. He also studied law and philosophy (for Greek philosophers as well as rhetoricians were to be found in Rome), the latter under masters of both the Academic and the Stoic schools. While pursuing the study of philosophy he did not neglect rhetoric, and daily engaged in declamation, often in Latin but more often in Greek, partly because there were more of the graces of style in the latter language, partly because the best teachers were Greek and could not correct him except in their own language. It was not until he was twenty-five years old that Cicero began to practise at the bar, and shortly afterwards, believing his health to be in danger as a result of his violent method of delivery, he resumed his studies; he travelled in the Greek-speaking lands of the eastern Mediterranean and continued his education in rhetoric and philosophy in Athens, Asia Minor and Rhodes. In reading Cicero's account of his education we are struck by its variety and by its combination of the theoretical and the practical; a thorough study of philosophy supplemented his literary and rhetorical education, and his constant attendance in the Forum and observation of the leading practitioners of the day ensured that his training was directed to practical ends.

Roman oratory for us means primarily Cicero. Only fragments of the speeches of his predecessors survive, but Cicero, who was well acquainted with the history of Roman oratory and wrote an interesting account of it in the *Brutus*, knew of nearly two hundred earlier orators. The first Roman to publish his speeches and so to make oratory a branch of Latin literature was the elder Cato. For all his affectation of a blunt and rugged conservatism his oratory was far from being the plain and unadorned statement of a simple peasant farmer; Cicero observed his mastery of the figures of speech and of thought and Aulus Gellius quoting a vivid passage from one of his speeches remarked that he had not been content with the eloquence of his own age but had wanted to do something that Cicero afterwards brought to perfection. He lacked, however, the smoothness and the rhythmical qualities which came from study under Greek masters. These were added with time; by the end of the second century Greek teaching was having its effect on Roman practice. Two orators of the mid century, according to Cicero, were in their different ways pioneers. Servius Galba was the first Roman to adopt the methods peculiar to the orator, digressions, exaggeration, pathos and commonplace, while M. Aemilius Lepidus Porcina was the first to display the smoothness, the periodic structure and the artistry of style that belonged to the Greeks. In the generation before Cicero the leading orators were L. Crassus (consul 95 B.C.) and M. Antonius (consul 99 B.C., grandfather of the Triumvir), whom Cicero made the chief speakers in his dialogue *De Oratore*, the former a man of wide learning, cultured and urbane, the latter less well educated, but with a vigorous delivery and a command of pathos. But all Cicero's predecessors, in his view, fell short of the ideal :

> I will say nothing of myself, [he writes in the *Brutus*] I will speak only of the other orators, none of whom gave the impression of having studied literature more deeply than the common run of men, literature which is the fountain head of perfect eloquence; no one who had embraced philosophy, the mother of all good deeds and good words; no one who had learnt civil law, a subject most necessary for private cases and essential to the orator's good judgement; no one who had at his command the traditions of Rome, from which if occasion demanded he could call up most trustworthy witnesses from the dead; no one who by rapid and neat mockery of his opponent could unbend the minds of the jurymen and turn them awhile from solemnity to smiling and laughter; no one could widen an issue and bring his speech from a limited dispute referring to a particular person or time to a general question of universal application; no one who could delight by a temporary digression from the issue or could move the judge to violent anger or tears, or in fact – and this is the special quality of the orator – could turn his feelings whithersoever the occasion demanded.

Though Cicero here declines to say anything about himself it is obvious that he is by implication giving an account of the characteristic features of his own oratory. There were other features, and important ones, such as rhythm and periodic structure, which he does not mention here, but the passage quoted gives sufficient indication of the character of his oratory. There is not much that can be attributed to the formal study of rhetoric. Ancient rhetoric as it was set forth in the school textbooks gave elaborate rules regarding the divisions of a speech, the arguments appropriate to different types of case and the adornments of style known as figures of speech and of thought. These rules, in Cicero's opinion, had their value, but were not enough; an orator should have a wider culture, should be thoroughly educated in literature and philosophy and should be acquainted with Roman law and Roman history, neither of which would come within the scope of the schools of rhetoric. Cicero himself was, he liked to claim, an orator sprung not from the rhetoricians' workshops but from the groves of the Academy. At the same time he was far from being a purely intellectual orator; he was well aware of the factors which made for success in pleading, in particular the use of wit and emotional appeal. He prided himself on his ability to play on the feelings of his audience. There was no method, he said, by which the emotions of the listener could be either aroused or calmed that he had not tried.

Cicero delivered and published a great number of speeches, many of which survive. It would be idle to pretend that the philosophy on which he prided himself inspires them throughout, that he constantly remained on that high level of wisdom and morality on which he moved when he thought and wrote as a philosopher. He can be unscrupulous, he is sometimes outrageously irrelevant and those whom he defended did not always deserve to be acquitted. But, as he himself said, it was the business of the judges to discover the truth; for an advocate occasionally to defend a guilty man was allowed by public opinion, by the principles of humanity and by the authority of the Stoic Panaetius. An advocate had to do his best for his client, and who his client was was often determined by the personal alliances in which a practising politician was inevitably involved. Today Cicero's speeches are read mainly as part of the material of history. In the ancient world they were read mainly as models of oratory. They were admired for their author's mastery of argument and of style and his vigorous use of all the arts of persuasion. Yet it was more than a purely professional competence that caused Cicero to be accepted by posterity as the great orator of Rome. His wide culture and lively intellect and his generally admirable qualities of character make him something more than a highly skilled advocate.

From the Ciceronian age we turn to the Augustan, from the education of an orator to the education of a poet. Horace's reminiscences tell us something of his schooling. His father, an Italian business man of humble origin, a former slave, had ambitions for his son, and like a modern parent choosing Eton in preference to the local grammar school, sent him to Rome to mix with the sons of senators and Equites in the best schools of the capital. There he was to be seen with his attendant slaves like any boy of noble family and, what one might think would have been a little embarrassing to the young Horace, with his father accompanying him to school in place of the usual *paedagogus* or slave-tutor. He studied Homer and, under the famous Orbilius, the earlier Latin literature, including Livius Andronicus, whose *Odyssey* must have seemed poor stuff after the genuine Homer; and from the Roman schools be proceeded to Athens for further study, as did other young Romans of the day, such as Cicero's son. Horace's friend and older contemporary, Virgil, began his education in northern Italy, but he too moved to Rome. He studied rhetoric there, but evidently with little enthusiasm, and turned from it with relief to philosophy. His philosophy was learned not, as was Horace's, at Athens, where the various schools had their headquarters, but in Italy under the Epicurean Siro. Horace no doubt had the better education of the two, but both grew up well acquainted with the literatures of Greece and Rome, with some knowledge of philosophy and perhaps with little taste for rhetoric. A generation later Ovid, though he preferred the pursuit of poetry to pleading in the courts, enjoyed declaiming in the schools of rhetoric, as we learn from the elder Seneca, and carried into poetry the facility and ingenuity which these schools encouraged.

Seneca's collection of extracts from the declamations of the Augustan rhetoricians shows us how rhetorical education not only survived the end of the Republic but flourished even more perhaps than before. Though with the end of free political life the scope for oratory had greatly diminished and the main opportunities for the exercise of talent were now to be found in imperial administration rather than in senatorial debate, the oratorical ideal still dominated education and continued to do so till the end of ancient civilization. It is a curious paradox that the great Roman work on oratorical education, Quintilian's *Institutio Oratoria*, was written under the repressive rule of Domitian, whose reign to Tacitus meant fifteen years of enforced silence.

Under the Empire education flourished as never before and there were numerous schools both in Rome and in the provinces. An ancient school, it should be remembered, was not like the school of today, an organization with a large staff teaching a number of different subjects. It consisted of a master, sometimes with an assistant, teaching a single subject, and there were as many different schools as there were subjects. In addition to the *ludi magister*, the primary school master who taught reading and writing and the elements of arithmetic, there was the Greek *grammaticus* and the Latin *grammaticus* the Greek *rhetor* and the Latin *rhetor*; there were schools of geometry and music and, lower in status, there was the *calculator* or teacher of commercial arithmetic and the *notarius* or shorthand teacher, whose school was so popular in the late Empire. It was possible to go to a number of different schools whether in succession or concurrently; Quintilian's educated orator would have attended not only a grammar school, both Greek and Latin, but also teachers of geometry and music, not to mention a teacher of elocution and a physical instructor, before going to the school of rhetoric. Nor should we forget the philosophers, the teachers of wisdom and morality, who corresponded in some ways more to the clergy than to the schoolmasters of the modern world.* But the most important schools, and those of which we know most, were those of grammar and rhetoric, and it was through these that well-born Romans destined for a public career passed.

The *grammaticus* had come down in the world somewhat since the days of the great Alexandrians like Aristarchus and Aristophanes of Byzantium. He was now a kind of preparatory schoolmaster taking boys of about twelve to fifteen before they went

* *See* pp. 187f.

on to the rhetoric school. He taught grammar in the modern sense, and taught it in some detail, but much of his time was taken up with the reading of poets, in particular Homer in the Greek school and Virgil in the Latin, and the schoolboy at least left the grammar school with a thorough knowledge of the classics of two literatures. The *grammaticus* did not, in theory at any rate, teach composition; that was supposed to be the function of the rhetorician. Under the Empire, however, there was a tendency for the *grammatici* to take over from the rhetoricians the series of graded exercises known as progymnasmata which provided the Roman with his early training in composition. In these, originality of ideas, which is now generally regarded as a virtue in essay writing, was not encouraged. The pupil was expected to develop the set theme on recognized lines; he would vary, expand and amplify, and display his command of the resources of language rather than his powers of thought.

In the school of rhetoric, which the Roman boy attended from the age of about fifteen to when he was eighteen or older there would be lectures on rhetorical theory. This had long ago been reduced to a system, but was still, or was still thought to be, capable of further refinement. But the average student probably did not share the experts' enthusiasm for minute classification and definition and was content with simplified handbooks. Nor did many of the professional rhetoricians have the scholarly interests of a Quintilian in their subject; their main concern was to win renown as declaimers. A declamation was a practice speech on a set theme of a type that might arise in the law courts or in deliberative assemblies, but such speeches had now become something more than preparation for speaking in public. Declamation was an end in itself, a form of oratory in its own right, and rhetoricians would declaim in public before appreciative audiences. The themes set tended to be unrealistic and melodramatic, and the treatment was as remote from the real world as the themes; the declaimers aimed at immediate applause, and they won applause by tawdry purple patches, highflown emotional outbursts and ingenious epigrams. Yet though we hear much of the triviality and bad taste of the popular declamatory style, we must remember that a sensible teacher like Quintilian considered declamation a valuable exercise and made full use of it; and a certain amount of showing off at least had the merit of enlivening what must have been a somewhat dreary routine. There survives in an incomplete state a collection known as the *Lesser Declamations*, attributed to Quintilian, which apparently consists of notes taken in class of specimen declamations, with explanation, given by a teacher who may or may not have been Quintilian. In its original form it included as many as three hundred and eighty-eight different declamations, all on themes of the type known as *controversiae*, that is cases resembling, though often remotely, those that might arise in the law courts. Our impression is of a curriculum of wearisome monotony.

The Roman schools (leaving out of account the philosophers) did not profess to do anything more than inculcate a particular branch of learning. They did not claim to build character, to teach religion or patriotism or morality, and some ancient teachers were notoriously ill equipped for such teaching, for example Remmius Palaemon, of whom it was said that (on moral grounds) no one was less fitted to be put in charge of the young. Yet there was certainly a feeling abroad that a schoolmaster should be something more than a mere instructor, that he should take the place of a parent, perhaps even supply that moral guidance that some Roman homes conspicuously failed to provide. The Younger Pliny, asked to advise a friend on the choice of a rhetoric master for his son, is primarily concerned to find one of good moral character; Quintilian shows a prudishness worthy of a Victorian schoolmaster in regard to the choice of reading in the grammar school. We find too some interest in the technique of teaching. We hear of book prizes, of organization into classes and of a form order based on merit; Quintilian stresses the value of emulation and of sympathy and encouragement on the part of the teacher and expresses strong disapproval of corporal punishment. Thought was given to such problems as the advantages and disadvantages of school as opposed to education at home under a private tutor. There was indeed a fair amount of intelligent interest in education problems combined with a strong conservatism as regards the content of education which made even minor changes hard to put into effect.

School to the Roman boy can have meant little but the daily task in the schoolroom, especially as he was strictly guarded in his walks to and from school by his *paedagogus*. Yet though the routine would seem intolerably dull to a boy used to the numerous and varied activities of the modern English school, we find Romans looking back to their schooldays with the kind of sentimental feelings which we associate with the late-Victorian public school. According to Cicero everyone looks back with gratitude to the scenes of his education and the masters from whom he has learnt, and to Pliny schooldays are the happiest time of one's life; Quintilian mentions as one of the advantages of school over education at home that the friendships one makes there last for life.

Moreover their education left the Romans with a lifelong interest in literature. The supposedly practical and hard-headed Romans were in fact keen students who kept up their literary and scholarly interests long after they had put the grammar school behind them. Cicero at the age of sixty writes to Atticus urging him to send a book on Greek accents by the *grammaticus* Tyrannio and expressing his regret that his friend has not waited until the two could read the book together. At a later period Silius Italicus, after a public career ending with a provincial governorship, spent the years of his retirement cultivating the memory of Virgil and writing an epic after the Virgilian model, much as a retired politician or Indian Civil Servant of the Victorian era might spend his leisure writing Latin verse or translating Homer.

The rhetoric school was perhaps more open to criticism than the grammar school. Certainly it was criticized in antiquity. So far from preparing young men for practice in the courts, it was pointed out, the schools accustomed them to a thoroughly unreal atmosphere and sent them into the world with much to unlearn. Teachers like Quintilian were aware of these weaknesses and did their best to make declamation a serious intellectual exercise, but even with a Quintilian as teacher it is doubtful whether it was a good thing to spend three or four years learning nothing but the art of speech. To learn how to speak is of little use if one has nothing to say.

To judge the imperial schools of rhetoric by their products is not easy for us when so little of the oratory of the period has survived. But contemporaries who applied this criterion found them wanting. There was a widespread feeling that oratory had declined since the great days of Cicero and his contemporaries. There were those who willingly and deliberately abandoned the republican tradition and condemned Cicero as long-winded and boring. Seneca, so it is said, refused to let his pupil Nero read the older orators because he wished to have no rival as a stylistic model, and his manner of writing, with its short sentences and epigrammatic sparkle, proved for a time irresistibly attractive to the young. Quintilian tried to counteract its influence and to recall the youth of Rome to sounder standards. He was optimistic about the results of his efforts. Future writers on oratory, he says, would find plenty of material for praise among the orators flourishing at the time of writing; consummate advocates who rivalled the ancients (that is, Cicero and his contemporaries) were practising in the courts and there were young men ready to follow in their footsteps. One naturally thinks of Quintilian's pupil, the Younger Pliny. His one surviving speech does not, however, make us long for more. Indeed when we compare Pliny's admirable letters with his *Panegyricus*, we are tempted to conclude that the more men tried to write well the less they succeeded.

The educational ideas and methods of the ancient world did not die with the fall of the Roman Empire. They survived to some extent in the Middle Ages and they were consciously revived by the humanists of the fifteenth and sixteenth centuries. In England the term grammar school survives to remind us of the continuity of our system with that of the past, and though there have been many changes in the institution in the last hundred years or so, at the beginning of the nineteenth century the English grammar school was not so very different from that of the Roman Empire. The rhetorical side of ancient education shrank, but the literary side survived, and schoolboys continued to read the classics of Greek and Latin poetry as their counterparts had done in the time of Quintilian. They still read them today, though they read other literatures as well. Today we have our English *grammatici*, not to mention the teachers of other modern literatures, in addition to the Latin and Greek *grammatici*, but all descend from the *grammatici* of the ancient world, as our annotated school editions descend from the commentaries of men like Servius. So far as our education is based on literature this is part of the legacy of Rome; that is to say, to reiterate the point made at the beginning of this chapter, it is due to the fact that Rome adopted and made her own this part of the learning of Greece.

If the content of education since the Renaissance owes much to the Romans, its spirit owes something too. It was a Roman writer, Quintilian, who presented the modern world with the ideal of the humane and sympathetic schoolmaster keenly interested in his pupils' welfare and progress in place of the irritable pedant terrifying his victims with the rod. The modern world has not been able to add much to Quintilian's picture of the good schoolmaster:

Let him above all adopt the attitude of a parent towards his pupils and think of himself as taking the place of those who have committed their children to his charge. He should neither be vicious himself nor tolerate vice in others. He should be strict without being gloomy, genial without being slack; otherwise the first quality will make him disliked, the second will bring him into contempt. He should have much to say on what is good and honourable; for the more he advises the less he will punish. He must not be prone to anger, though at the same time he should not ignore faults that need correction; he should be straightforward in his teaching, ready to take trouble, assiduous but not excessively so. He should willingly reply to questions, and should himself question those who do not ask. In praising the compositions of his pupils he should be neither grudging nor effusive; the former causes a distaste for work, the latter complacency. In correcting faults he must not be harsh and certainly not insulting; there are some teachers whose rebukes give the impression of dislike, and this has the effect of discouraging many from study. . . . Pupils rightly instructed regard their teacher with affection and respect.

And it is scarcely possible to say how much more willingly we imitate those whom we like.

BIBLIOGRAPHY

Bonner, S. F., *Roman Declamation in the late Republic and Early Empire*, University of California Press, 1949.

Clark, D. L., *Rhetoric in Greco–Roman Education*, Oxford University Press, 1957.

Clarke, M. L.,*Rhetoric at Rome*, New York, 1953.

Gwynn, A., *Roman Education from Cicero to Quintilian*, New York, 1926.

Marrou, H. I., *History of Education in Antiquity*, English translation, Sheed & Ward, 1956.

Smail, W. M., *Quintilian on Education*, Selections in Translation, Oxford University Press, 1938.

12

THREE ROMAN POETS

Colin Hardie

THIS chapter can take only one short but critical period in the history of Latin literature, selecting the three great poets in it, Catullus, Lucretius and Virgil, for a closer look (and of Virgil chiefly the *Eclogues*), and looking at them largely from one point of view, that of the unique philhellenism of the Romans and how they made out of their dependence on Greek models the starting point for a new personal poetry of their own. Roman originality is the more extraordinary in that it is so rooted in imitation and adaptation. The Romans felt the need of a Greek precedent for whatever they attempted and an ambition to produce in Latin the counterpart to the Greek achievement in each branch of literature. Yet they also liked to break the bonds of the 'kinds' and fuse them into new hybrids.

At the beginning of the first century B.C. in Rome a new literary ingredient can be detected, the amatory elegiac epigram, which a few Roman aristocrats try to turn in Latin. Meleager's (140–70 B.C.) anthology of elegiac epigrams, the core of our *Palatine Anthology*, was probably diffused at Rome, and also all his own poems, some of which he had included in his *Garland*. They are polished variations on themes of love, poems of sentiment rather than passion; and his loves, Heliodora, Zenophila and the rest have little reality. It is the contrast with Catullus, rather than Catullus' debt, that is striking. About 70 B.C. a Greek poet, Parthenius of Nicaea, was brought to Rome as a captive, like Andronicus, Terence and Polybius earlier, and became the literary mentor of a circle of young poets, introducing them to the poetry of the Alexandrians.

The group of 'new poets' were living in a society that was politically dangerous and disintegrating, but artistically exciting.

Grandiose Hellenistic architecture, for instance, was appearing in Rome, and portrait sculpture, testifying to a new interest in individuality. Oratory, enthusiastically studied and disputed between rival theories, offered great opportunities of fame and advancement. Literary theory too was discussed. The new poets were not professionals, producing for festivals, but gifted and highly educated amateurs, such as Cicero had been in his youth when he translated Aratus' *Phaenomena*. But they had professional standards of technique, and regarded poetry not as a mere pastime and side-line. They specially disliked the hybrid historical epics decked out with mythological gods, that were turned out in the stale manner of Ennius on any political event, like Cicero's poem on his consulship. In this they felt supported by the example of the Greek poets Callimachus and Theocritus who scorned the post-Homeric epic tradition. The poetry and society of Lesbos in the sixth century B.C. alone provides any parallel to Catullus and his circle, since there, quite exceptionally, personal poetry had been written by leisured aristocrats in the vernacular.

But Lesbian poetry is an isolated phenomenon without imitators, until it appealed to Catullus and Horace. The normal poet in Greece was a professional who produced epics or hymns, choral lyrics, tragedies or comedies, for public performance and competition. He was a teacher of his people, and his subject-matter was essentially their history, or rather their prehistory, myth. Lesbian poetry and the Hellenistic poetry of Callimachus, Philetas and others, provided pegs for the new generation in Rome; but social and literary influences are much less important than the genius of Catullus.

He was the son of the leading citizen of Verona, highly educated and sent to Rome, no doubt to begin a political career by a brilliant prosecution of some highly placed malefactor. Catullus describes how his friend Licinius Calvus, the scion of a great Roman family, admired by him as the centre of the group, made his name by prosecuting Vatinius, a supporter of Julius Caesar. The circle of like-minded friends could defy popular and traditional standards of taste. Catullus joined Calvus in pasquinades against Caesar, but poetry as a way of life, and not merely a pastime on the side, claimed Catullus as later it claimed Virgil.

This seems to have been due to what distinguished his love for his Lesbia from the short-lived affairs of his friends with courtesans. Those girls might be educated like the 'second Sappho with more taste than the Muse herself' but Lesbia was almost certainly the great lady of one leading family, wife of a consul from another, full of wit, charm and piquancy, but amoral, irresponsible and promiscuous. She came to Catullus, in his friend Allius' house, 'like a goddess', his 'mistress'. This is developed by Propertius (the *servitium* of one *domina*) and becomes a commonplace in later poetry, but begins with Catullus who in fact has reversed the usual relations in Hellenistic love poetry. The Greek poets describe the uncontrolled passion of women in love, not of men. But Catullus transfers to himself what Sappho said of herself (the pseudonym Lesbia is an allusion to Sappho of Lesbos); he compares himself to Juno putting up with Jupiter's infidelities. Further he wanted his and Lesbia's love to last and to be much more than passion. When she offers an 'enduring' passion, he clutched at her promises and stifled his misgivings with an accumulation of stronger words and the climax 'a life-long bond of inviolable *friendship*' – and poem 30 shows how seriously he took friendship. In another poem he tries to convey his conception of love by a 'comparison unique in ancient literature': his love for Lesbia is like a father's affection (he uses the very different word *diligere*) for his sons and daughters and his sons-in-law. In another poem he draws the same distinction between love and 'good will' (*bene velle*). Presumably Catullus wanted to marry Lesbia when her husband died; but passionate love as celebrated by poets had nothing to do with marriage. Poem 70 may serve to illustrate how Catullus gives a personal meaning to a theme from Callimachus: Callimachus reports the oath of a man, Callignotus, to a woman, Ionis, and its betrayal: the oaths of lovers are not registered by the gods; Catullus substitutes Lesbia (*mulier mea*) for the man and himself for Ionis, and adds a hyperbole to the oath, 'not if Juppiter himself were to woo her'. This is referred to in 72, and thus what might seem impersonal is taken up into a personal history of desperate intensity from the first ecstasy of his love for Lesbia* to her betrayal of it and to his false friends turned rivals; from reconciliation to her renewed falsity.

In his final repudiation, he returns to the Sapphic metre, and ends the poem with a simile, himself 'cut down like a flower by a plough-share', that Virgil was to remember when he described one who dies even younger than Catullus, Euryalus. Poem 76 is a powerful and solemn prayer in twenty-six elegiacs for help to shake off his love, 'that hideous disease'. Poem 8 handles the same theme in a lighter and ruefully humorous way. Catullus turns the heavy bludgeon of the scazon (halting iambic with spondee in the last foot) against himself and exhibits himself as a 'melancholy clown', torn between repudiating his love and looking back on it with longing. Very characteristic is his mode of addressing himself as Catullus or referring to himself in the third person as Catullus. The playfulness and humour of the Alexandrians is paradoxically combined with intense passion and despairing sincerity. If poetry is 'the clear expression of mixed feelings' (Auden), Catullus is one of the first to strike this modern note. He can feel intensely and analyse sharply, as in poems 83 and 92, where he infers Lesbia's love of him from her obsessed abuse of him, and from his identical feelings:

* Come, my Celia, let us prove,
  While we can, the sports of love;
  Time will not be ours for ever,
  He at length our good will sever.
  Spend not then his gifts in vain,
  Suns that set may rise again.
  But if once we lose this light,
  'Tis with us perpetual night.
  Why should we defer our joys?
  Fame and rumour are but toys.
  (from BEN JONSON, *Volpone* III, vii, 166ff.)

> Lesbia for ever on me rails;
> To talk of me, she never fails.
> Now, hang me, but for all her art
> I find that I have gained her heart.
> My proof is this : I plainly see
> The case is just the same with me;
> I curse her every hour sincerely,
> Yet, hang me, but I love her dearly.
>
> (JONATHAN SWIFT)

In poem 85 in a single couplet, the famous 'Odi et amo', he expresses the clash of feelings with consummate simplicity. It is a Hellenistic conceit, often ingeniously turned, but Catullus gives it a poignant sincerity, and behind it lies all his passion for Lesbia :

I hate and I love. You ask why? I do not know, but this is what I feel and it is torment.

The sheer directness and naturalness, apparently without artifice, of this, as of many among Catullus' shorter poems, their exquisite clarity, has caused him to seem to be two irreconcilable poets, the spontaneous child of nature who wrote good poetry when he was not trying, and bad when he was trying, to be the scholarly Alexandrian. But this is to mistake the supreme art of the occasional poems, which seem so artless : Catullus knows exactly when to use the simplest colloquialism and when the pompous traditional poeticisms, within the same poem, as in poem 11, where the first fourteen lines in their geographical elaboration contrast with the directness of the last ten.

It is also easy to misunderstand the long poems 61–9, especially the longest of all, the *Marriage of Peleus and Thetis*. Lesbia made of Catullus more than the occasional poet, though many of his best poems about her are just those occasional poems in various metres (not elegiacs) which make up the first part of our collection of Catullus' poetry, poems 1–60. Catullus (and his contemporaries) probably regarded them as trifles, *nugae*, – and many are – and aspired to prove himself to the world as an accomplished professional poet. Poem 76, already mentioned, and 101 on his brother's death, are already more elegies than epigrams. Poem 65 to Cicero's rival, Hortensius Hortalus, explains that though crushed by his brother's death (which expands in grief to five couplets) Catullus has roused himself to translate Callimachus' *Lock of Berenice* (a poem full of arch sentimentality and witty affectation). Poem 68 is a more ambitious elegy, if it is not two, somehow fused, on the same themes, his friend Allius and his services to Catullus, his brother and Lesbia, who is compared to Laodamia; this leads to Troy where his brother is buried. Catullus moves to and fro amid his intricately connected themes. It is an experiment in elegy, almost an autobiography, not wholly unified, but all full of intense personal feeling. The theme of marriage inspired Catullus to two very different epithalamia: the lyrical dance of 61, maintained over 200 lines in at least twenty-five stanzas, in contrast to the festal solemnity of 62 in weighty hexameters, divided between answering choruses of young men and girls. Poem 63, the Attis, which one would rather not relate symbolically to Catullus' own experience, is an astonishing achievement in making the Latin language quiver in a quick flicker of movement, physical and mental. In one poem Catullus speaks of the excitement of trying now this metre, now that (as Parthenius too is said to have done), in Calvus' company.

Peleus and Thetis is Catullus' most ambitious poem, in hexameters, on two contrasted themes of love, taken from mythology and told in the traditional poetic language of epic and tragedy. It begins in fact with a reminiscence of Ennius and Apollonius, but it is not a palinode or conversion to epic. It is an example of the kind of narrative 'short epic' that Calvus' school practised, elegiac and lyrical rather than narrative, and Catullus puts the poetic language to a new use. It is true that there are no personal references in it, but it is inconceivable except as the work of a man who had been through his (poetic) experiences with Lesbia. It has the labyrinthine structure and interweaving of 68, but is more fused; it rehandles myth boldly, and rises to an epithalamium in the form of a prophecy by the Fates, and to a final sombre, almost Lucretian note, where he looks for a moment seriously at the Rome of the civil wars, not as in his epigrams on Caesar and his minions. Without this poem we should not see what range and variety Catullus was capable of; the lament of Ariadne when abandoned by Theseus, an elegy within the 'epyllion', is what seems to have made the deepest impression on Virgil. The arrival of Bacchus, with its evocative alliteration, inspired Titian.

This essay has space only to mention the variety and charm of Catullus' other occasional poems that have nothing to do with Lesbia, the yacht, Sirmio, the literary squibs, the bridge at Cologna, and also the numerous poems of uninhibited obscenity and ferocious attack. One subject, however, is wholly untouched by Catullus, namely philosophy.

There could be no greater contrast than with Lucretius. Instead of 116 poems running to only over 2,000 lines, we have one massive poem, *On the Nature of the World*, in six books, of nearly 7,500, expounding the materialist philosophy of Epicurus. Instead of a group of like-minded friends, unconventional and defiant of popular taste, we have a solitary figure, without predecessors or followers, of whom we know nothing except what his poem tells us. There is one point of contact: Lucretius addresses his poem to Memmius, almost certainly the Memmius who figures twice in Catullus' poems, praetor in 58 B.C. Cicero describes Memmius as versed in Greek, but despising Latin literature, too lazy to speak well or even to take the trouble to think. Lucretius would seem to have chosen him as the man most unlikely to respond and yet most in need of enlightenment, but whether it was as an equal or as a client in need of a patron, as a Roman or as a provincial, that Lucretius addressed Memmius, we do not know. It is difficult to imagine Lucretius living in a harmonious and cheerful household of friends, which was Epicurus' ideal and practice. Epicureanism, proscribed a century earlier, was free to spread in the new climate of opinion.* Cicero, who disliked it as dogmatic and superficial, unpolitical and uncultured, testifies that it 'had occupied the whole of Italy'. It was

* *See also p. 187.*

a protest against the anarchy and bloodshed that emanated from the centre, Rome. Its exponents in Latin seem to have been too naïve and inelegant to appeal to educated Romans. Here was an opportunity for a Roman to annex another province of Greek literature to the growing Latin empire, and to show how poetic technique could master the most unpromising and prosaic subject-matter, as the Alexandrian didactic poets had done. Aratus had versified the astronomy of Eudoxus in the old epic convention, and in Rome Cicero translated the *Phaenomena*, with less knowledge and inner relation to the subject than Aratus, and Cicero mentions how Nicander, a 'man wholly remote from the countryside', had written a poem on agriculture, *Georgics*. This is only a minor aspect of Lucretius' attitude to his didactic epic. The artist is swallowed up in the convert and the apostle, and it is not to the Alexandrians that he looks, but to Empedocles, the great classical poet of the fifth century B.C. when poetry was still the natural medium of philosophical reflection. Empedocles was a prophet as well as a philosopher, and it is his exalted tone that Lucretius assumes (and gossip transferred to him Empedocles' madness and suicide). Under Empedocles' influence Lucretius chose the physical and cosmological side of Epicurus' philosophy, though for Epicurus it was only the indispensable basis for his positive ethical views. In Latin Ennius was Lucretius' model. Lucretius was thus opposed in every way to Calvus and Catullus, including his attitude to 'love' as they understood it.

But how could Lucretius conceive an Epicurean poem at all when the Master had so scorned poetry and indeed all 'culture'? Epicurus hated mythology, the staple of Greek poetry, and wished to appeal to the uncultivated and to induce serenity. But poetry excites disturbing emotions, and so Epicurus followed Plato in banning Homer from his ideal society. Lucretius must have been already a poet when he was converted to Epicureanism and felt that the pleasure of poetry could fitly be put at the service of the philosophy of pleasure, and it is true that without Lucretius Epicureanism would have excited much less interest. It is just Lucretius' imaginative grasp of the materialist atomic

universe that is lacking in what we have of Epicurus. But if
Epicurus had read Lucretius, he might well have felt that he was
right to suspect poetry. Certainly Lucretius is faithful to
Epicurus' doctrine, and there is nothing in the *de Rerum Natura*
that cannot be proved to be Epicurus' where our evidence is
sufficient. But the great difference is in what Lucretius omits
altogether or alters by infusing his own emotion.

Lucretius gives the impression that *all* religion is disturbing
error and mere supersition. But this was far from Epicurus' view;
he was known for his piety, and he conformed to the religion of
Athens, and enjoyed the gaiety of festivals whereby man could
share in the serenity of the gods. He was no atheist, but accepted
much of Plato's view of what gods must be, free from anger and
envy and any fussy concern with thunderbolts or human behaviour. But Lucretius has hardly anything to say about the gods
in the serene spaces of the aether. He seems indeed to be rather a
Euhemerist (like Ennius in his sceptical prose) and to believe
in the divinity of only Epicurus.

Similarly, Lucretius exhibits the restlessness and fear which he
purports to cure much more vividly than the achievement of
calm, though the great opening of Book II must not be forgotten. The closely knit argument of the first three books culminates
in the proof of the mortality of the soul; the great obstacle to
calm of mind is removed, namely the fear of death and of the other
world of Hades. Lucretius breaks out into a song of triumph over
death, but it is more like the triumph of death and is not followed,
as in Petrarch's *Trionfi*, by the triumph of fame or of divinity.
Lucretius' emotions are deeply stirred as his great phrases show:
'when once immortal death has swept away mortal life':

Now it is all over. Now the happy home and the best of wives will
welcome you no more, nor winsome children rush to snatch the
first kiss at your coming and touch your heart with speechless joy.
No chance now to further your fortune or safeguard your family.
'Unhappy man,' they cry 'unhappily cheated by one treacherous day
of all the uncounted blessings of life.' But they do not go on to say:
'and now no repining for these lost joys will oppress you any more.'
If they perceived this clearly and acted according to their words,

they would free their breasts from a great load of grief and dread. 'Ah yes. *You* are at peace now in the sleep of death, and so you will stay to the end of time. Pain and sorrow will never touch you again. But to *us*, who stood weeping inconsolably while you were consumed to ashes on the dreadful pyre – to us no day will come that will lift the undying sorrow from our hearts.' Ask the speaker, then, what is so heart-rending about this. (III, 894–910.)
(R. E. LATHAM, Penguin Classics, 1951.)

In this moving dialogue Lucretius invests more pathos in his opponent's case, and more irony in his own. Poetically his tragic sense wins. Translation cannot give the tremendous effect of the three-word line and spondaic ending :

insatiabiliter deflevimus aeternumque.

Instead of soothing Lucretius shatters us, and dramatizes and intensifies where in theory he should relax.

So too the 'army of unalterable law' that daunts Meredith's Lucifer, the spectacle of nature's seamless garment with no crack for divine interference to get through, should calm the mind, but Lucretius is obsessed with the idea of imminent destruction of our universe :

all these (sea, land, sky) a single day will blot out. The whole substance and structure of the world, upheld through many years, will crash ... may reason rather than the event itself convince you that the whole world can collapse with one ear-splitting crack ! (V. 95–109, cf. VI, 596–607.)

When Lucretius contrasts 'the youth of the world' with its present feebleness and exhaustion like a mother beyond childbearing, he is thinking in Empedoclean terms rather than Epicurean of the present era as one in which Love is on the way out and Strife takes charge, in contrast to the earlier in which Love was coming in. In theory he is committed to a belief in technical (and philosophical) progress, but towards the end of Book V in describing the intemperate use of technical advances, he adds :

it is this discontent that has driven life steadily onward, out to the high seas, and has stirred up from the depths the surging tumultuous tides of war. (1,434–5, cf. V, 999–1,010.)

Discoveries only make war more destructive.

Lucretius has a way of opening his books with confident splendour in set pieces, but of ending them in gloom as in II, III, V and VI, the last book but perhaps unfinished. Book VI opens with praise of Athens as the inventor of crops and law, and mother of Epicurus, but culminates in the ghastly plague at Athens in 430 B.C. Book I opens with the great invocation to Venus, Mother of Aeneas and the Romans, who is creative nature dressed in mythical form. Lucretius celebrates her fecundity but in Book IV where he discusses sex he takes a gloomy view of it as 'madness', 'no uncertain pain'. Lines 1,133–4 are famous:

to no purpose. From the very heart of the fountain of delight there rises a jet of bitterness that poisons the fragrance of the flowers.

Sexual love, Venus, is seen sometimes as weakening men, sometimes as preparing them for social life.

It may seem unfair to stress these incoherences, but it is they that add depth and mystery to the poem, and we can see it as a vital struggle to achieve a solution, not its triumphant but flat presentation, as it would have been if Lucretius had been merely a Nicander or a Cicero. But he is so deeply engaged with his subject that the whole man and his problems come to the surface in deeply felt passages and weighty lines that only Latin could compass. 'Surge and thunder' seem to belong to him more than to the *Odyssey*, and a long piece of argument in Lucretius can be like an Atlantic breaker sweeping up a western bay. Like his language, his vivid illustrations and similes are his own, and not Epicurus'. He had no need to complain of the poverty of the Latin language. Epicureanism was superficial and denied all mystery. Lucretius is un-Epicurean because he is truer to life and has a more tragic sense of it.

Virgil is said to have assumed the adult gown (at about sixteen or seventeen) on the very day that Lucretius died, and Catullus was dead too by the time that Virgil came up to Rome very much in his footsteps, from the same background with the same sort of ambitions. Virgil was no impecunious rustic without education; his father was a landowner rich enough to aspire to a senatorial career for his son and to give him the best education available in Mantua, Milan and Rome, and perhaps Naples. Virgil was even more deeply and widely read in Greek literature than Catullus. Nothing in Greek or Latin was lost on him, including philosophy and history. When he came to Rome to learn rhetoric, he became a member of what had been Catullus' circle, with Calvus, Pollio and Cinna to maintain it. One appearance in the law-courts seems to have convinced him that a political career was not for him, and probably when the civil war broke out in 49 B.C., he renounced rhetoric and politics, and retired to Naples to embrace Epicureanism under the Greek Siro. Four years later, in 45 B.C., Pollio returned from the wars to Rome, and it was he who suggested to Virgil to follow Catullus' example and attempt something more ambitious and new to Rome, the imitation of Theocritus' pastorals. A Roman had already written Greek pastorals, and Lucretius has a charming pastoral scene in Book V, 1,379–1,411 (which characteristically, however, ends in a sombre contrast with contemporary luxury). Virgil was thus twenty-five when he wrote the first in time of his occasional poems, *Eclogue* II. It at once shows his style and personality, for all that it is closely modelled on Theocritus. Virgil's Corydon is introduced without preface, and it is clear that the poet is in full sympathy with him and on the side of the country against the town. Greek culture was essentially urban, but Romans lived much more in the countryside. Corydon, like Catullus' Ariadne, is alone and only imagining himself in speech with Alexis, where as in Theocritus Polyphemus knows that he is overheard by Galatea. Hence Corydon addresses himself as Corydon, and calls himself Corydon in the third person, in Catullus' manner, and his monologue becomes a dramatic development, in this unlike the static lament of Ariadne. Seen from inside by the poet as Corydon is, he develops, and emerges different in the end from what he was at the beginning, because he has recognized his mistake in leaving the countryside and his work there (these are notes that the *Georgics* take up). The lines in which he blames himself were put by Milton on the title-page of *Comus*:

Poor fool that I was, to have such day dreams. Now in my folly
I've let the wind get at my flowers, the boars muddy my spring.
(C. DAY LEWIS, *The Eclogues of Virgil*, Cape, London, 1963).

There is perhaps a hint of allegory in the *Eclogue*, of Virgil as
pastoral poet courting the favour of Rome. In a much later
Eclogue, VIII, Virgil refines on this 'empathetic' dramatic handling, again using Meleager to give epigrammatic point to Theocritus, and the lover drives himself to suicide. Dido's death in the
Aeneid with its many reminiscences of *Eclogue* VIII shows how
Virgil eventually made from this germ a tragic and epic theme,
and throughout the *Aeneid* Virgil seems always urgently inside
his heroes, seeing their inner drama – something quite unlike the
leisurely objectivity of Homeric narrative.

In his next experiment, VII, Virgil took from Theocritus his
his favourite theme of the competition between shepherd-poets.
He makes it into a tightly organized garland of varied epigrams
and vignettes. The setting is removed from Sicily to an already
half-ideal Arcadia, which is also Italy, since the Mincius, the river
of Mantua, runs through it. This is the beginning of a process
in which we can see Roman themes gradually taking charge. We
can also see the first stirrings of ambition to be a great poet, not
merely a humble pastoral poet; to equal Codrus who stands next
in merit to Apollo himself, to be already *crescens poeta* (Greek)
and (Latin) *vates futurus* –

> 'You shepherds, crown me your budding singer –
>   let Codrus burst with jealousy :
> Or if he flatter me, wreathe him with foxgloves
>   lest sugary words harm your bard to be'
> (C. DAY LEWIS, ibid.)

The last words were put by Milton on the title-page of the
volume that contained *L' Allegro* and *Il Penseroso*, and no one
had a stronger sense of mission to be England's epic poet than
Milton.

Eclogue III carries Virgil further on the same lines, but he pre-
faces his next poetic contest (which is faster, being in couplets,

not quatrains) with a mime-like scene of quarrelling shepherds. Theocritus had ennobled the mime, and it was as a writer of dramatic sketches that Virgil made his name in Rome, when the *Eclogues* were acted on the stage, notably by his friend Gallus' mistress, Cytheris. When on Virgil's entrance into the theatre the populace rose to greet him, as they did Augustus, it was the poet of the *Eclogues* that they saluted; and an apocryphal story had it that Cicero saw an *Eclogue* performed and on being told the name of its author remarked 'magnae spes altera Romae' 'great Rome's *second* hope', Cicero himself being the first!

Eclogue V celebrates the death and apotheosis in glory of the founder of pastoral song, Daphnis. It has been taken to allude to the death and deification of Julius Caesar, but this is far-fetched, and in fact the poem refers to something much more poetic and nearer Virgil's heart, the idea of the 'sympathy' of all nature and of the enchanting power of music and poetry over mountains, trees and animals, the myth of Orpheus in fact. Virgil may have thought of closing his Theocritean phase with this poem, but events suggested a new extension of the pastoral; rather, his deep emotion, as much for all Italy as for himself, when Antony's and Octavian's veterans 'turned all Italy upside down' by evicting thousands of landowners from their estates, compelled him to poetic expression in the instrument that lay to hand. *Georgics* II, 198–9 make it quite clear that Virgil was not spared the confiscation nor ever had the family estate restored. Eventually Augustus gave him two estates, but he probably never returned to Mantua. *Eclogues* IX and I (in that chronological order) are an extraordinarily skilful and indirect protest against the Triumvirs' assault on the rural foundations of Italy. The 'star of Caesar', that is the comet which appeared at the posthumous games in honour of Julius Caesar's victory in July, 44 B.C., appears to be praised, but the context shows that such hopes as it had excited had proved delusory. Moreover, which Caesar is meant? The dead Julius to whose deification Octavian in public attributed the comet as a sign, or Octavian himself, as Octavian privately (and not so privately) believed? The *Eclogue* is in form based on Theocritus' most charming *Idyll* VII, the country walk to the harvest-home, in which Theocritus teases us with his half-masking, half-revealing of himself and his friends as shepherds. *Eclogue* I introduces the name of *Rome* for the first time in Virgil's work. An old slave working on the land, Tityrus, goes there and somehow obtains his freedom and the grant of his 'peculium', the marginal land that he had been working in his spare time. But that the 'young man' who makes this grant of freedom and land is the terrible Triumvir himself, Octavian, though ancient authorities and modern (except one) assume it, is, to me too, incredible. Octavian had ordered that all confiscated estates must be handed over complete with slaves and equipment. Did he make an exception in favour of an old slave? and if so, why does Meliboeus, the free citizen, whose devil the Triumvir has been, without question accept the same man as Tityrus' god? Anyhow, two years after this Virgil was still under the Antonian Pollio's patronage, and Pollio in this very year twice approached Perusia to attack Octavian in open war. The evidence seems rather to show that Virgil was captivated, or captured, by Octavian only after the publication of the *Eclogues* (37 B.C.?) as a whole under his own name. *Eclogue* I has the further interest that Virgil in it quotes Horace's *Epode* XVI, that fierce and despairing protest against the condition of Rome, exposed to foreign enemies by her own civil strife. This was the beginning of their friendship.

In October 40 B.C. the threat of open war between Octavian and Antony was averted by the Peace of Brundisium, negotiated on Antony's side by Pollio. The reconciliation was sealed by Antony's marriage to Octavia, Octavian's sister. This was the occasion of the famous *Fourth Eclogue*. There was evidently a Sibylline oracle in circulation (in Greek hexameters, as always) which in some way 'prophesied' the peace and its importance as a turning point, and start of a new age. Virgil more than shared the general relief and joy; he expressed it in a slightly pastoral setting, openly adapting the prophetic epithalamium sung by the Fates in Catullus' *Peleus and Thetis*. The question of the child's identity would distract from something even more important, the personal climax which Virgil adds to the prophecy: he

himself will perhaps be the Roman Homer to the second Roman
Achilles :

> To sing thy praise, would heaven my breath prolong,
> Infusing spirits worthy such a song,
> Not Thracian Orpheus should transcend my lays,
> Nor Linus crowned with never-fading bays;
> Though each his heavenly parent should inspire;
> The Muse instruct the voice, and Phoebus tune the lyre.
> Should Pan contend in verse, and thou my theme,
> Arcadian judges should their god condemn.
>
> (DRYDEN)

In this inspired moment of exultation Virgil felt as Ennius did
when Homer told him he was being reborn in him. The expected
boy was never born, and the peace soon disintegrated, but Virgil
was somehow committed to what, in an adherent of Callimachus'
ideals and in a 'new poet', was a perverse and crazy ambition,
worthy of a Bavius, to write a historical epic on a contemporary
theme. No wonder that in the next *Eclogue*, VI, he makes Apollo
himself rebuke the ambition and tell him, in an adaptation of
Callimachus, to stick to pastoral. But what follows is much more
ambitious than a pastoral; it is a revelation as enchanting to all
nature as Orpheus himself, and a cosmology in miniature in the
language of Lucretius. It makes a quite new use of mythology,
and inserts into it as its climax another personal reference, not
indeed to Virgil himself, but modestly to his friend and contemporary, Cornelius Gallus. Gallus, like Virgil, is a poet of love,
and love whether in the form of pastoral or elegy is the humblest
genre. Gallus is told by Apollo's son, Linus, to aspire to a higher
genre, the Callimachean, the didactic poem on 'origins' (αἴτια,)
and presented with the pipes of Hesiod, the founder of the personal didactic kind :

> With which of old he charmed the savage train,
> And called the mountain ashes to the plain.
>
> (DRYDEN)

Eclogue VIII, in its curiously inserted address to Pollio, contemplates an epic on Pollio's recent exploits in Dalmatia, which had won him a triumph; but the body of the poem is purely pastoral without a Roman name in it, working out the theme of tragic and destructive love, with only a passing glance at Virgil's problem, when as an example of absurdity the shepherd Damon mentions the idea of Tityrus turning into Orpheus. Now again an external event pushed Virgil to take the next step. His friend Gallus who had celebrated the actress Cytheris under the name of Lycoris in four books, was abandoned by her. An elegy was to be expected, but the Muses too deserted Gallus, and he turned to a political and military career. So Virgil stepped in and in *Eclogue* X himself plays the part of Gallus-Daphnis, the pastoral elegist of Arcadia. Under this mask he laments Lycoris' departure with exquisite sympathy:

> Ye frosts and snows, her tender body spare!
> Those are not limbs for icicles to tear.
> (DRYDEN)

He says farewell to the ideal pastoral golden age, Arcadia, but has to bow to the power of love; he cannot rise above love:

> Love conquers all; and we must yield to Love.

Disguised as Gallus, Virgil has now got hold of the pipes of Hesiod, and himself goes on to the *Georgics*, his Ascraean or Hesiodic poem, but bearing with him the theme of love into the *Georgics* (Orpheus and Eurydice) and beyond into the *Aeneid* (Dido), as Catullus carried Lesbia into his more ambitious poems.

The *Georgics* are Virgil's *Auseinandersetzung* with Lucretius, as the *Eclogues* with Catullus (and others). How this is so would take too long even to indicate, and has anyhow been done by Perret, Klingner and Brooks Otis. The latter, however, has completely ignored the evidence in the *Georgics* for Virgil's struggle with himself to envisage the forthcoming epic. Ostensibly and officially it is to be an epic on Augustus, and he puts it in terms which in palmary fashion express our general thesis:

I, first of Romans, shall in triumph come
From conquered Greece, and bring her trophies home,
With foreign spoils adorn my native place,
And with Idume's palms my Mantua grace.
Of Parian stone a temple will I raise,
Where the slow Mincius through the Valley strays ...
Full in the midst shall mighty Caesar stand ...
All Greece shall flock from far my games to see ...
A time will come when my maturer Muse,
In Caesar's wars, a nobler theme shall choose.

All this is put under the sign of Ennius whose epitaph on himself is quoted:

> New ways I too must try, my humble name
> To raise aloft in triumph and in fame
> Live on the lips of men.
> (DRYDEN adapted)

The philosophical or cosmogonical epic in the manner of Lucretius is given a glance in *Georgics* II, 475–82, and in *Georgics* III, 3–8, mythological themes are rejected as trite. Yet the poem culminates in the myth of Aristaeus, which like Catullus' *Peleus and Thetis* contains its counterpart within itself, Orpheus and Eurydice, and is set in the Homeric framework of the capture and prophecy of Proteus. These myths had never before been conjoined. The 'Bugonia' is a Callimachean 'origin', the production of a new transformed life out of death, of bees from the carcase of a sacrificed ox, and bees have 'something divine about them' according to Aristotle who describes the 'Bugonia'. Their product, honey, is a symbol of poetic inspiration. It may, therefore, be suggested that Virgil makes Aristaeus the vehicle of his own problem. He has all the makings of an epic poet except the subject. Augustus as hero could not admit, still less hold together, Virgil's cherished themes of poetry, love, Arcadia, the underworld, as Aeneas could. Virgil needed mythology to formulate even, rather than explain, the cause of that tragic element in human life that so constantly forced itself up into Lucretius' Epicureanism; the theft of Prometheus, the fraud of Laomedon, the fratricide of Romulus. For Virgil mythology was not a kind of early history as it was to the Greeks, but a psychological symbolism. He ended by seeing truth in all three of Varro's kinds of religion, poetic, civic and philosophical, and his philosophy, though showing much influence of Stoicism, was essentially the new comprehensive Platonism, not the sceptical Academy to which Cicero adhered. The Trojan origin of the Caesars is mentioned in the poem of *Georgics* III, but curiously not Aeneas; and when Aeneas appears in Italy, the omen of his arrival is precisely the prodigy with which *Georgics* IV ends, the new swarm of bees settling on a tree. Aeneas was at first sight too hackneyed a hero, in Naevius and Ennius and all the historians, to be mentioned in *Georgics* III. But in fact he could serve where Augustus was useless, to reconcile myth and history, Greece and Rome, Homer and Ennius, and his story gave Virgil the freedom to put much more of himself into Aeneas than he could put of Augustus.

Donatus' *Life of Virgil* says that Virgil took eleven years to write the Aeneid (29–19 B.C.), but at once itself provides proof that Virgil in fact began it only in 26 B.C. when Augustus was in Spain. When Augustus left Rome the previous year, Virgil had not drafted the famous 'outline' of the poem, nor written a single passage. So he must have spent four or five years more, after finishing the *Georgics*, in hesitations; and when he began, he nearly stopped again at once, saying that he needed 'even more profound studies', and when he was dying he wanted to burn the poem. His problem was a double one, how to extend his meticulous artistry on so vast a canvas of narrative, and how to make a modern, personal poem in a manner that belonged to seven hundred years before, when the tradition in which Homer worked was living. The language and style of Homeric epic had gone dead shortly after, as Callimachus and Theocritus had seen. A Roman epic committed Virgil to the tradition of Ennius. To write a poem like Cicero's on his consulship would be to repudiate everything that he had learnt from Catullus and his circle. Virgil had somehow to insinuate his modern consciousness into his Aeneas without anachronism and to create a style that could blend the traditional with the fresh and even colloquial. Augustus' right-hand man, Agrippa, derided Virgil's manner as affectation, but Horace admired it as the subtle linking of words so as to give them a fresh turn. Virgil's art conceals itself.

We have concentrated on the *Eclogues* because in them a development can be seen, and the unity and continuity of Virgil's life work exhibited, and because the personal element, though indirect, is not so masked by the classical restraint which Virgil felt epic to require, and Horace felt even lyric and satire to impose. Classicism means too a renewed sense of public responsibility to the nation, outweighing the pleasure of self-expression, and an apparent return to the poet as teacher.

No space is left to consider other aspects of Augustan poetry, how Propertius worked out the elegiac vein that Catullus had prospected, the 'enslavement' to a single 'mistress', or how Horace developed what Catullus had scarcely indicated, the naturalization of the short lyric in Latin. With the achievement of Virgil and Horace Latin had been put on a level with Greek, and its development becomes more independent, especially as after Meleager nothing new was produced by Greek poets. The influence of Virgil, 'the divine flame that has fired more than a thousand poets' (Dante), might be traced. Aspects of it are often surprising: the early hostility, and the maladroit tributes of the *Gnat* and the *Ciris*; above all the Christian interpretation of the Fourth *Eclogue*, from the Emperor Constantine and St Augustine to the unknown French poet of the twelfth century who wrote the two stanzas on St Paul at Virgil's tomb, and Dante. In Dante's works three stages in the understanding of Virgil can be traced: the traditional and allegorical; the imperial; and the last and most profound, the spiritual, in the *Comedy*, where Virgil is Dante's guide in self-exploration for sixty-four cantos out of the hundred. There is too the rediscovery of Arcadia as a 'spiritual landscape' by poets in the sixteenth and painters in the seventeenth centuries.

BIBLIOGRAPHY

Perret, Jacques, *Virgile, l'homme et l'oeuvre*, Paris, 1952.

Klingner, Friedrich, *Römische Geisteswelt*, Munich, 1956.

Otis, Brooks, *Virgil, a Study in Civilized Poetry*, Oxford University Press, 1963.

The poets discussed in this chapter have been translated into English by the following:

Catullus: by Jack Lindsay (London, 1948); Hugh Macnaghten (London, 1899); Sir William Marris (Oxford, 1924).

Lucretius: in verse by Charles Foxley (Select Passages, Cambridge, 1933); W. H. Mallock (Select Passages, London, 1900); R. C. Trevelyan (Cambridge, 1937): prose by C. Bailey (Oxford, 1910); H. A. J. Munro (Cambridge, 1864); R. E. Latham (Penguin Classics, 1951).

Virgil: C. Day Lewis (*Eclogues*, London, 1963; *Georgics*, London, 1940; *Aeneid*, London, 1952); John Dryden (1697, World's Classics, 1961); W. F. Jackson Knight (*Aeneid*, Penguin, 1956, in prose); Samuel Palmer (*Eclogues*, illustrated with engravings, London, 1883).

13

HUMOUR AND SATIRE

J. P. V. D. Balsdon

IN the sense of broad fun, Rome's earliest humour is its best – the comedies of the Umbrian Plautus, who died in 184 B.C. Terence, his direct successor in the theatre, an African by birth and not a native Roman at all, had Plautus' other gifts, but not his sense of humour.

Plays are written to be acted rather than read; but in default of the opportunity of seeing and understanding the Plautine comedies on the stage, we must read them; and very good reading they are. Their plots were not original; they were in fact Latin adaptations of that New Comedy which had held the Athenian stage in the late fourth century B.C., with Menander as its most renowned playwright. Unless the Greek original of one of Plautus' twenty-one surviving plays, written on papyrus, is some day discovered, we shall never be able to assess the full extent of Plautus' own originality. (The two Menander plays which have been recovered on papyrus are poor, anaemic things, contrasted with Plautus' full-blooded vigour.) The language of Plautus is, naturally, Plautus' own. He exploited all the fascination of alliteration and punning; he enjoyed military metaphor and simile (for the free men in his audience had done military service, many of them on the battlefield); he frequently employed Greek words, many of them words which the soldiers had brought back from the wars; he invented wonderful new compounds, conceits ('The day is half dead already, dead down to the navel') and superlatives such as the modern Italian enjoys using (Ego sum exclusissimus – 'I could not be more locked out than I am'). The divinities are Greek in character: Mercury speaking the prologue of the *Amphitryon*:

You all know, I think, what kind of a man my father Juppiter is

... ; he is indoors, in bed with Alcmena at this moment, which is why this night has been made extra long;

the star Arcturus speaking his unexceptionable prologue to the *Rudens*:

Juppiter, lord of heaven and earth, appoints us to our various observation posts, and we report the names of malefactors to him in writing;

even the Lar, the household god (a Roman, not a Greek conception at all), who speaks the prologue of the *Aulularia*:

After the father died, I began to see whether his son perhaps would show me greater devotion. Instead he grew more and more careless about my cult. So I repaid him in kind, and he is dead.

The characters were what Plautus found in his Greek originals, and so were the plots. In general the women have too little individuality, and the men almost too much. There is the expensive courtesan; there is the innocent girl who, through kidnapping or some other disaster, has fallen into bad hands, often those of a pimp; and there is the insufferable bully of a rich wife, exploiting the power which her dowry gives her. Among men, there is the noble lover, the young spendthrift, the villain (sometimes a sheer buffoon, like the soldier in *The Conceit of a Soldier* (*Miles Gloriosus*)), the avaricious, pitiful or genial old man, and, best of all, the resourceful slave. The last is a man who, except in loyalty to his master or to the person whom he regards as his true master, has no moral sense at all. He possesses boundless ingenuity, and no audience could fail to love him: Tranio in the *Mostellaria*, who as one foundation after another of his deceit collapses, continues undaunted to build higher still, and Palaestrio in the *Miles Gloriosus*, the plotter whom fortune never deserts. The horror of a slave's punishment is good for a laugh:

I know the cross will be my tomb; it was my father's and *his* father's and *his* father's and *his* father's before that.

But in fact the ingenious slave will generally have been freed as a reward for his ingenuity before the play is over.

The *Menaechmi* is the foundation of Shakespeare's *Comedy of Errors*, and that could be given as a title to a great many of Plautus' plays. Nobody could distinguish one Menaechmus from his brother, not even the married one's wife. In the *Miles Gloriosus*, on the other hand, one woman, the heroine Philocomasium, is turned into two; the soldier's spying slave who caught her in her lover's arms is persuaded that it was not Philocomasium that he saw, but her (imaginary) sister. In the *Amphitryon*, Amphitryon's slave Sosia is persuaded by Mercury (who has assumed Sosia's image, just as Juppiter has assumed Amphitryon's) that he is not himself at all. And there are artfully comic misunderstandings, as when in the *Aulularia* Lyconides makes his confession to old Euclio. He is in fact confessing that he has got Euclio's daughter with child. Euclio thinks that he is confessing the theft of his precious pot of gold.

There is always a happy ending. Virtue will triumph, or venial weakness will be forgiven. And from time to time there are interesting gently satirical accounts, in long speeches or in dialogue, of features of social life which, even if in their origin they were Greek, had already taken on a Roman colour. In the *Miles Gloriosus*, for instance, a play of 1,400 lines, more than a hundred are taken up in the portrayal of the character of a genial old man (he is fifty-four years old), who is befriending the lover and who explains his philosophy of life in answer to the lover's and the slave's questioning:

I can crack a good joke; I take my fair share in talking – and in listening too; I never quarrel at dinner – if any one annoys me, I simply leave and go home; I like spending money on entertaining guests, because I like making friends, and money spent on religion is always a good investment, but take a wife and impoverish myself in paying her bills, no, sir – that is why I have never married. Admittedly I lose something by not having children – but then I have been spared a parent's anxieties, and I have plenty of relations who fall over one another in generosity to me. After all, I shall die sometime, and they will come into my money. I control my servants and do not let them control me. In fact, if I dislike anybody, it is guests who complain all the time that you are entertaining them too lavishly; such people never refuse a dish, but wolf down their food more greedily than anybody else.

Without Plautus and Terence we should not have so great a knowledge of Greek New Comedy. Having Plautus, we have that and much beside. Molière is only one of the playwrights whom he has powerfully influenced. Indeed Giraudoux's *Amphitryon 38* was the thirty-eighth known adaptation of the *Amphitryon*. The play in one dramatist's hands and another's has been given varying moral overtones and psychological interpretations, but all that is ever funny in it goes back to Plautus himself.

Satura was a mixed dish, the equivalent in literature of what on the stage we know as Revue, a series of 'take-offs' of people and things, satirical pictures (whether mildly quizzical or savagely venomous) of the foibles of individuals, of features of contemporary society or of humanity itself.

Outstanding figures in public life had been lampooned with unrivalled savagery in Greek Old Comedy, as we know from the surviving plays of Aristophanes; and in fourth-century Greece Theophrastus had analysed the various peculiarities of individuals with skill and, in his *Characters*, reproduced them with delicious wit. Nonetheless, the Romans, slightly abashed by the fact that in other literary forms (in epic, lyric, drama, historical writing, rhetoric and philosophy) the Greeks had been there before them, and they were themselves in greater or smaller degree imitators, claimed with pride and with justice that satire (written generally in hexameter verse) was their own original creation. Lucilius, living in the second century B.C. and a friend of Scipio Africanus the younger, was the originator of the genre, covering a wide field of subjects and attacking the political enemies of the Scipios with some savagery. We hear much of his reputation, but nothing more than fragments of his work survive. Persius' rather stuffy compositions apart (he wrote at the time of Nero), we are left with two master-satirists, with the gentle penetrating irony of Horace, the savage indignation of Juvenal. Dryden wrote well, 'Horace is always on the amble, Juvenal on the gallop.' Horace is often amusing; Juvenal is not amusing at all.

They were different kinds of men, living in different times, and their private circumstances were different. Horace had secured in Maecenas what every writer sought, who had to make a living by his wits – a powerful, generous supporter; he was the poet with a patron.

As for humour, which is not a necessary element of satire, the Romans would have claimed that it was a quality which, as a people, they possessed and esteemed. The humour of the mimes and farces which they witnessed was broad and scurrilous. When a Roman general rode in triumph through the streets of Rome in the Republic, he was assailed by scurrility and bawdy of the crudest kind; we know what Julius Caesar's soldiers shouted in his triumph. And in the law courts humour was a valuable weapon in the barrister's armoury; it was useful to be able on occasion to make the jury and the spectators laugh, either by broad ridicule or by a sudden, sharp and unexpected witticism. Cicero made the point strongly in his oratorical works, and so did Quintilian. Such humour and wit was regarded as an important element of Cicero's own talent; Quintilian, indeed, contrasted Demosthenes and Cicero in this respect, declaring that, if Demosthenes was never amusing, that was not because he disdained humour, but because he lacked the gift. Cicero's ostensibly polite ridiculing of Cato (the opposing Counsel) as a Stoic prig when he defended Murena in 63 B.C. – which provoked Cato's, 'gentlemen, *what* an amusing consul we have' – and his travesty of the prosecution's case – hidden witnesses, and the handing over of a phial of poison in a chamber of the public baths – in his defence of Caelius are both wonderfully funny, and must amuse anyone who reads them today.

The extempore witticism, on the other hand, is an ephemeral thing; when it is repeated, its sting is lost. So Quintilian sensibly claimed that Cicero's reputation as a wit was damaged, not enhanced, by the collection of his public witticisms which his freedman Tiro published after his death. Similarly the witticisms of great orators of the past quoted by Cicero in his books on oratory are as frigid as ice.

Yet the Romans had a great gift of quick wit. There is a story, for instance, of a Roman from the provinces visiting Rome, whose likeness to Augustus was striking, the talk of the town. Augustus summoned him and rudely asked, 'Was your mother once in Rome?' The man answered, 'No, but my father was.' When a delegation from Spain announced as a happy prodigy to Augustus that a palm tree had sown itself in his altar at Tarraco, he answered, 'Then the altar is evidently not in frequent use.' Macrobius listed Augustus' witticisms and those of his daughter Julia, and the *Lives* of Suetonius are punctuated by imperial epigrams. The epigram, indeed, was a striking feature of the speech and writing of the early Empire. Tacitus was its master.

Varro and Horace were contemporaries. Of Varro's *Satires* we know little more than the titles – fascinating titles sometimes, like 'Nobody knows what the late evening has in store'.

The satires of Horace, his earliest writings, belong to the years of Octavian's gradual estrangement from Antony, the decade which ended in the battle of Actium. They are called not *Saturae* but *Sermones*, Literary Conversations, and indeed those in the second book are cast in the form of dialogue. They are free of intemperate extravagance and, though their subjects differ, they have a little of the spirit of sermons; they are like the advice of an extremely well-balanced and sensible godfather, as unsympathetic with puritanical Stoicism on the one hand as he is with profligacy and libertinism on the other. You must take the world as it is, and realize that human beings, as they exist, are none of them perfect: 'Nam vitiis sine nemo nascitur.' Where serious human weaknesses and vices are concerned, ridicule is more effective than the whip. Obsession with money-making, for instance, is not life but a substitute for living. The avaricious man talks always of retirement but, however great his wealth, he always wants a little more; the ant is more sensible, collecting in a good season food which it devours in a bad. In avoiding one extreme, fools rush to the other ('Dum vitant stulti vitia in contraria ruunt'); good sense should lead a man always to choose the mean. If you are highly sexed, you need not squander your money on a cheap prostitute at one extreme or cultivate the seduction of a married woman at the other. Snobbery – believe the freedman's son, favoured client of a rich patron – is silly.

It is all good, sensible, charitable, man-of-the-world advice. And sometimes Horace is extremely amusing. There is the vivid picture of the seducer of a married woman surprised at the very moment of his triumph by the husband's return (i, 2, 127): a banging at the front door, the barking of the dogs, the wife in hysteria, her thoughts on her imperilled dowry, the seducer's panic. How much money is this going to cost him? Will he have the skin thrashed off his back? Will the story be all around the town? The famous account of the bore who cannot be shaken off (i, 9) is frighteningly funny, an experience which only the most fortunate of readers has never suffered. Best of all is the satire – a 'satire' in the true sense – on legacy-hunting (ii, 5), that chronic disease of Roman social life, a disease which Martial and Juvenal were to savage and which Petronius, like Plautus and Horace, mocked. Horace's mockery is a brilliant invention, cast in the form of advice on how to be a successful legacy-hunter, put into the mouth of the seer Tiresias, as if it was a continuation of his conversation with Ulysses in Hades in the eleventh book of the *Odyssey*. There Tiresias had prophesied Ulysses' ultimate return in safety to his home in Ithaca. Now, in Horace, Ulysses asks how, once he gets home, he is to find money to live. The answer: acquire a rich man's legacy. Choose your man; his record may be criminal, but that does not matter as long as he is rich. Call him by his first name; they like that. Insist on defending him if he is brought to court; the justice of his case is immaterial. A victim with a delicate son is as good as a bachelor. If he offers you the sight of his will, refuse to read it – but take in its content quickly, to make sure that what you want is there. If there are scheming women or freedmen in his house, befriend them; they will speak well of you. If the man is a lecher, go out of your way to be accommodating; no nonsense about Penelope's virtue. Listen to him patiently, however insufferable you find his conversation; never interrupt. Take ostentatious care of his health. Praise him extravagantly to his face. And when the long servitude reaches its successful conclusion and the will is read, express amazement at your legacy. Why you? Weep, if you can.

Spare no expense on the funeral; the neighbours will praise you.
And if one of your elderly fellow legatees has a nasty cough –
then the game can start all over again.

Seneca's pantomime, the *Apocolocyntosis*, is the epitome of
crude vulgarity. Written to be performed before the court of
Nero, it ridiculed Nero's adoptive father, his imperial predecessor Claudius, who had just died. Claudius was the first Emperor
after Augustus to be officially consecrated after his death; the
pantomime suggested that, on the contrary, he had not become a
god at all. The name of the piece, *The pumpkinification*, recalled
a Greek comedy in which there had been a debate of philosophers
to decide whether the *colocynta* (pumpkin) was a beast, a tree
or a potherb. *Nor Fish nor Fowl nor Good Red Herring* would be
a fair English version of the title of this burlesque of imperial
consecration.

The ascent of a mortal to heaven after death was a prodigy, a
supernatural event in need of evidence. The comet (*sidus Iulium*)
had been the evidence for Julius Caesar; when Augustus' corpse
was burnt, an eagle flew out of the funeral pyre. And there had
been, in the case of Augustus and of Drusilla, consecrated sister
of Gaius Caligula, a senator who, as he assured the Senate, had
witnessed the ascension: good evidence which, reasonably
enough, called for good pay.

So now :

You demand evidence? Right. Ask the man who saw Drusilla *en
route* for heaven. He will tell you that he saw Claudius going up too,
cloppety-cloppety in his usual fashion. That man just can't help
seeing what goes on in the sky. He is keeper of the Appian way....
Ask him. He will tell you, provided there is nobody about. In
company he will be silent as a clam. Because when he gave evidence
on oath in the Senate of seeing Drusilla mounting to heaven, nobody
believed him and his splendid news. As a result he has sworn
solemnly that he will never give evidence again, not even if he
witnesses a murder in a public square.

Claudius died in a vulgarity (this is the theme of the pantomime), Clotho having been persuaded by Mercury to take her

shears and snip off his life before he did further mischief. In heaven Juppiter was informed of the arrival of an extraordinary character whose speech was unintelligible; it was not recognizable Latin or recognizable Greek. Hercules, as a god of the world, was sent out to see. He looked and quailed. Was this a thirteenth labour? He reported, and a committee meeting of the gods was summoned, its procedure being that of the Roman Senate. Janus proposed that an end should be made forthwith to the consecration of human beings:

and should anyone henceforth be made, called or portrayed a god, he should be given over to the hob-goblins and take his place at the next gladiatorial show, to be thrashed publicly among the gladiatorial recruits.

Diespiter proposed that:

Since it is in the public interest that Romulus should have an associate to join him in devouring boiled turnips, Claudius as deriving from a family with a strong recent tradition of consecration, should be made a god and a note of his transformation should be added to Ovid's *Metamorphoses*.

Then Augustus moved an amendment:

Since divine Claudius is guilty of the murder of his father-in-law, his two sons-in-law, his daughter's father-in-law and mother-in-law and his own wife Messalina, and others too numerous to mention, that he should be deported from heaven as a *persona non grata* and ordered to leave within thirty days.

The amendment was carried. Claudius, therefore, descended from heaven by way of Rome (where he was intrigued by the sight of his own funeral) to the underworld. There, accosted by all the distinguished people whom he had put to death in his lifetime, he greeted them with typical *gaucherie*:

Ah, friends everywhere. How did you all get here?

He was then summoned before Aeacus ('a perfect judge; he refused the defence leave to plead'), charged with 256 murders, condemned to dice for eternity with a bottomless dice box –

then claimed by his nephew Gaius Caligula as a slave. Adjudged to him, he was then given as a present to a freedman, who employed him as his law clerk.

Nothing in this rollicking piece is left unmocked – no physical or mental peculiarity of Claudius, no part of his government and administration; and there is room, too, for satire on other features of the age, the bombast of poets, the wiles of the astrologer.

The *Satyricon* of Petronius was a comic, satirical and bawdy account of the adventures of three young, gay, penniless, resourceful, mischievous and utterly immoral youths (the youngest, Giton, was sixteen years old), told by one of them, Encolpius, who was Giton's lover. Their counterparts are easily discernible in the back streets of Naples today. 'God in heaven,' Encolpius once reflected, 'an outlaw's life is a hard one – always waiting for punishment.'

The book in its entirety is lost; so we do not know the number and variety of their adventures. In the surviving fragments the *ragazzi* play truant from the tedium of lectures in rhetoric and asking their way, find themselves directed to a brothel; try their hand at thieving in the market; are involved in a salacious episode with a priest of Priapus and then, by invitation, attend a fantastic dinner party which lasts until dawn, in the house of a millionaire vulgarian of a freedman, Trimalchio. This episode, which happened probably at Puteoli, is happily preserved almost intact. Next the young heroes join Eumolpus, a dissolute philosopher from Asia Minor who tells a story as comic as it is revolting, to show that his morals are no better than theirs. With him they board a ship bound for Tarentum. Once on board they find the captain is a man from whom they are running away, and they are in danger of detection; so their hair is shaved and their foreheads given an imitation of branding, so that they may be passed off as runaway slaves. They are detected, nonetheless, thanks to a sailor who was being sea-sick on deck and who witnessed the transformation. However, after they have received a good beating a general reconciliation follows, in which Eumolpus tells the story of the Widow of Ephesus. The ship is wrecked, but our heroes are saved, and move to Croton, which is a city utterly devoted to legacy-hunting. Here is rich entertainment to be had free for the asking. Eumolpus presents himself as a childless millionaire. One fortune has gone down in the ship which was wrecked, but he has an estate worth millions in Africa; his health is anything but good, be is always to be seen totting up his accounts, and every thirty days he revises his will. Given the gullibility of legacy-hunters of Croton, the imposture is an inevitable success. At Croton Eumolpus recites a long and brilliant pastiche of Lucan's poem on the Civil War. Encolpius, seduced by the attractive lady Circe –

As for your admission that you are merely a humble slave, that only makes my mistress want you more –

is suddenly impotent, and must submit to the revolting attention of witches and to Priapic cult before his virility is restored. It is all a splendid game, as long as it lasts, but soon even the Crotoniates begin to ask questions :

The legacy-hunters are getting tired and are not as generous as they were. If I am not mistaken, it is the old story again – bad luck, and misfortune ahead.

The rest of the book is lost.

What kind of a book is it ? Is it a pastiche of the *Odyssey*, names from which – Circe and Cyclops, for instance – occur, with Encolpius a mock Odysseus and Priapus his tormentor, as Poseidon was of Odysseus ? Certainly for Encolpius, life, which should ideally have been one uninterrupted phallic carnival, was instead a series of distressing frustrations.

Nothing is more remarkable about the book than its speed. Episode follows episode, and the story never drags. This is partly because the author concentrates the whole of his satire on one object at a time. In the long account of Trimalchio's dinner, it is the tasteless and amiable vulgarity of the *nouveau riche* and his companions, women as well as men, which is travestied at every single point where it is vulnerable. The legacy-hunters are reserved for treatment elsewhere. Yet as Trimalchio made much of his childlessness and the fact that at his death his line would die out, and as he was obsessed by the thought of death and of the importance of a funeral which would be in keeping with his style of living, it would have been easy to complicate the story by the presence at dinner of the legacy-hunter:

'Stichus,' he called to a slave, 'go and fetch out the clothes I'm going to be buried in. And while you're at it, bring along some perfume, and a sample of that wine I'm having poured on my bones.'

Stichus hurried off and promptly returned with a white grave-garment and a very splendid robe with a broad purple stripe. Trimalchio told us to inspect them and see if we approved of the material. Then he added with a smile. 'See to it, Stichus, that no mice or moths get into them or I'll have you burned alive. Yes, sir, I'm going to be buried in such splendour that everybody in town will go out and pray for me.' He then unstoppered a jar of fabulously expensive spikenard and had us all anointed with it. 'I hope,' he chuckled, 'I like this perfume as much after I'm dead as I do now.' Finally he ordered the slave to pour the wine into a bowl and said, 'Imagine that you're all present at my funeral feast.'

The whole business had by now become absolutely revolting. Trimalchio was obviously completely drunk, but suddenly he had a hankering for funeral music too and ordered a brass band sent into the dining room. Then he propped himself on piles of cushions and stretched out full length along the couch. 'Pretend I'm dead,' he said; 'say something nice about me.' The band blared a dead march, but one of the slaves ... blew so loudly that he woke up the entire neighbourhood. Immediately the firemen ..., thinking that Trimalchio's house was on fire, smashed down the door and rushed in with buckets and axes to do their job. Utter confusion followed, of course, and we took advantage of the heaven-sent opportunity ... and rushed out as though the place was really in flames.

(*Satyricon* 78, tr. WILLIAM ARROWSMITH.)*

Here – even allowing for the differences in Roman and modern social convention and moral standards – is the same rollicking, comic, full-blooded, coarse bawdy which we meet in the eighteenth century in Rowlandson and Hogarth and in Gay's *Beggar's Opera*. It shares the uninhibited frankness of *Fanny*

*University of Michigan Press, 1959.

Hill, and has none of the licentious prudery of D. H. Lawrence. It is a portrait of a low-class and middle-class life which is at the same time a cartoon. And there is much else, in particular a brilliant variety of vulgar dialect and of high-flown language, which no translation into a modern language can hope to reproduce; there is, too, the mockery of philosophers and rhetoricians – that is to say, of contemporary education.

It was written, probably for recital aloud, at about the same time as Seneca's *Apocolocyntosis.* Its author was almost certainly the C. Petronius whom Nero made his 'Master of Good Taste' and subsequently in A.D. 66 drove to suicide:

He slept all day and devoted his nights to the business and pleasures of living. Some people work to win a reputation; he won his reputation by turning his back on work and was accounted not (like most of those who squander their resources) a debauchee, but a person of refined taste. There was a licence and off-handedness about what he did and said which appealed to people; it was so unaffected.

And at the end:

He did not die in too much of a hurry. He slit his veins, then bound them up, then opened them again, and talked to his friends, not seriously or with any idea of dying a heroic death. They recited and he listened – nothing about the immortality of the soul or the beliefs of philosophy, but flippant poems and light verse. He gave presents to some of his slaves and had others of them beaten. He dined and dozed off, so that his death, though forced on him, might appear a natural one. Instead of adding a codicil to his will, as most people did in his position, flattering the emperor or one of his powerful minions, he wrote out a list of the emperor's debaucheries, named the pathic or woman involved, described each case in detail, sealed the document and posted it to Nero.
(TACITUS, *Annals* xvi, 18f.)

From Petronius, who is all love of human weakness, one moves to Martial, who is all scorn and to Juvenal, who is all hate; but while Petronius could smile at the world from a position of affluence – he could not even be serious over the business of his own suicide – Martial and Juvenal had both experienced poverty, and had been made to feel their social inferiority. Juvenal, indeed, was probably in banishment in Egypt (which he hated), expecting, like Ovid before him, to end his days in exile – until, after three years, the good news came that Domitian was dead and that he could return to Rome.

The writings of Martial (a Spaniard) and of Juvenal (who came from southern Latium) were often directed at the same objects, but Martial's was a smaller world, a smaller mind, a smaller talent.

His imperial patron Domitian accepted his sycophantic poems and even rewarded him. Pliny admired his wit; but Trajan, confronted by Martial's attempt to speak the manly language of Trajan's new age, is not likely to have been impressed by such tomfoolery and Martial returned to Spain. Some few of Martial's epigrams are pretty, in praise of a happy marriage or of the countryman's simple life; most of them are barbed, shot at the social horrors of the circle in Rome in which he moved : literary plagiarists, bad poets who gave recitations of their own poems; bad doctors; unattractive and unfaithful wives; hideous and revolting women; legacy-hunters; the sordid sufferings of the cadging client and the tasteless meanness of rich patrons; gross aspects of bathing (including mixed bathing) in the public baths; and, in a wealth of crudity, every known vice, natural and unnatural. Nobody could read these virulent witticisms for long on end without sharing Byron's judgement :

> But then what proper person could be partial
> To all those nauseous epigrams of Martial?

They are slick, of course, and often the stab is sharp; for instance :

> No friend of Lycoris ever had long life
> I could have wished her friendship – for my wife.
> (iv, 24)

And he has found imitators. Oxford after 300 years repeats the epigram of Thomas Brown at the expense of Dean Fell of Christ Church

> I do not love you, Dr Fell,
> But why I cannot tell;
> But this I know full well,
> I do not love you, Dr Fell,

which is simply Martial's

> Non amo te, Sabidi, nec possum dicere quare;
>   hoc tantum possum dicere, non amo te. (i, 32)

The grim rule of Domitian, whose horrors the Younger Pliny could shake off as easily as a thin film of dust, warped, to literature's great advantage, the more sensitive characters of the historian Tacitus and of Juvenal. They lived into happier days, writing under the not unsympathetic rule of Trajan (when Tacitus held high office) and – Juvenal certainly and probably Tacitus – under Hadrian, who was a friend of literature. Yet the dark gloom of Domitian's rule was something which neither could forget. The only lesson of the Empire for them was one of despair: the tyranny of rulers, the servility of subjects. And for Juvenal the life of contemporary society in Rome, the culmination of the whole imperial process, was in every one of its features vile and contemptible. Though untrained, as Tacitus was trained, in rhetoric, he was, like Tacitus, master of the brilliant merciless epigram. Both writers dipped their pens in contempt and hatred when they wrote. Each was born a genius.

Chiefly Juvenal hated avarice, the more bitterly because at the start of his life he was so poor, and the dissolute and distorted objects on which, by those who were not avaricious, wealth was squandered. He hated foreigners (Greeks, Syrians and Egyptians above all) and, had he had a chance, would have put an end to immigration. Two satires (ii and ix) pillory homosexuality in its grossest forms; one (vii) deplores the fact that there is no money to be made from writing. And he does not forget the familiar butts of every Roman satirist, the legacy-hunter and the arrogant patron who humiliates his clients. Life in Rome was, in his eyes, a profusion of horrors: aliens, bad housing conditions, burglary, murder, noise, fire and intolerable traffic conditions (Satire iii). Was marriage ever a success? (We do not know if

Juvenal himself was married.) He lists the categories of disastrous marriage in Satire vi. You married, and your wife ran off with a gladiator or, like Messalina, wife of the Emperor Claudius, turned harlot. You might marry a wealthy wife, a beautiful wife, a woman of culture, a wife who would wear the trousers, your mother-in-law's daughter, an athlete; you might marry with an agreement that you should each go your own way; you might marry a religious woman, an extravagant wife, a musician, a would-be politician; you might marry only to become *le mari de madame*; you could marry a forceful personality or a bluestocking; you might be a complaisant husband, you might marry a woman who was cruel to the servants, a superstitious woman, devoted to astrology, a woman who did not want children, a woman who would not condone your own peccadilloes: in no case at all was there the smallest chance of happiness in your married life:

> What! and is none of all this numerous herd
> Worthy your choice? not one, to be preferr'd?
> Suppose her nobly born, young, rich, and fair,
> And (though a coal-black swan be far less rare)
> Chaste as the Sabine wives, who rush'd between
> The kindred-hosts, and closed the unnatural scene;
> Yet who could bear to lead an humbled life
> Cursed with that veriest plague, a faultless wife!
> (vi, 161–6, tr. WILLIAM GIFFORD, 1802.)

Juvenal was middle-aged when he published his earliest satires, though he may well have given recitals of them earlier, even from the years soon after Domitian's death. As he grew older there was occasionally the suspicion of a charitable and generous chink in the black clouds of his anger and scorn. The tenth satire is sheer cynicism, in which every achievement for which people pray in life, for themselves or for their children, is shown to be profitless or pernicious. Grow rich, and be poisoned; achieve power, and be overthrown, like Sejanus; win a reputation, and die as miserably as Demosthenes or Cicero; seek military distinction, and taste failure, as Hannibal and Xerxes tasted it; pray for a long life, and endure the misery of Priam; pray for glory, and

die as ingloriously as Marius or Pompey; pray for good looks, and
die for them, like C. Silius, with whom Messalina fell in love.

Then comes the unexpected conclusion:

> But, (for 'tis good our humble hope to prove,)
> That thou mayst, still, ask something, from above;
> Thy pious offering to the temple bear,
> And, while the altars blaze, be this thy prayer.
> O THOU, who know'st the wants of human kind,
> Vouchsafe me health of body, health of mind;*
> A soul prepared to meet the frowns of fate,
> And look undaunted on a future state;
> That reckons death a blessing, yet can bear
> Existence nobly, with its weight of care;
> That anger and desire alike restrains.
>
> (x, 346ff., tr. W. GIFFORD.)

In this gentler, more constructive, mood he makes a plea
in Satire viii) for integrity in provincial administration and (in
Satire xiii) commends a friend for accepting philosophically the
loss of a small sum of money which he had deposited with a dishonest acquaintance. 'Guilt is its own punishment' is the theme
of the satire – which, alas, does not gain from its conclusion, that
crime inevitably becomes a habit, so that in this case the self-
restraint of his friend will one day be rewarded by the spectacle
of the criminal's punishment for some other and graver crime.

There is nobility as well as excellent good sense in his attack
in Satire xiv and elsewhere on the blindness of parents who are
surprised when their children are influenced by the example of
their own corrupt lives.

Your son marries a rich heiress, and strangles her to death; it
is quite easy:

> But you will say hereafter, 'I am free:
> He never learn'd those practices of me.'
> Yes, all of you: for he who, madly blind,
> Imbues with avarice his children's mind,
> Fires with the thirst of riches, and applauds

---

* Mens sana in corpore sano.

> The attempt to double their estate by frauds,
> Unconscious, flings the headlong wheels the rein,
> Which he may wish to stop, but wish in vain.
> (xiv, 220–32, tr. W. GIFFORD.)

One would have expected Juvenal to make a tremendous impact on his contemporaries; the evidence – of silence – suggests that he made no impact at all. But in due course Christian scholars noticed him, for the gross evils of pagan Rome which he abused were the evils which they abused also. By the end of the fourth century Romans were reading him. After which, where there have been scholars and writers, he has never lacked notice. In late seventeenth- and eighteenth-century England he came in to his own, for the abuses which he satirized were, many of them, in evidence once more : the evils of the big city, bad writers, ungenerous patrons. Dryden and Gifford translated him better than anyone has done since. Dr Johnson made the tenth satire his model in his *Vanity of Human Wishes*.

So much for satire. As for Roman humour, this owed its start in Latin literature to the New Comedy of Greece which Plautus adapted; and, in the second century A.D., it is in the Greek-speaking East that it makes its last appearance. For, though the *Golden Ass* of Apuleius, himself an African, was written in Latin, it is wholly Greek, set in Thessaly and largely based on the lost collection of amusing stories known as the *Milesian Tales*, which Petronius also used. And Lucian, who wrote in Greek, came from Sarmosata in eastern Asia Minor. The *Golden Ass* is rightly set beside the Decameron; the subtle and witty irony of Lucian in his most amusing sketches of gods and men was something which was to be inherited, as if by some metempsychosis, by Anatole France.

BIBLIOGRAPHY

Texts and translations of Plautus, Terence, Horace, Petronius' *Satyricon* (with, in the same volume, Seneca's *Apocolocyntosis*), Martial, Juvenal, Apuleius and Lucian are to be found in the Loeb classical library, the translation of Apuleius being a revision of that of W. Adlington, done in the sixteenth century. There are paperback translations of a selection of Plautus' plays and of Martial, Juvenal, Apuleius and Lucian. William Arrowsmith's translation of Petronius into 'a contemporary version, and an American one' is outstandingly good (University of Michigan Press, also available as a paperback). Gilbert Highet, *Juvenal the Satirist* (Oxford University Press paperback 1962) is warmly recommended. On Roman satire generally J. W. Duff, *Roman Satire* (Hamden, Conn., 1937) and *Critical Essays on Roman Literature* (ed. J. R Sullivan, Routledge, 1962–3) : *Satire*.

14

LIFE AND LEISURE

J. P. V. D. Balsdon

A ROMAN was – once in practice, later in theory – liable to military service, in the class of 'Iuniores', between the ages of seventeen and forty-six, and in that period, the prime of his life, he might be called a young man (*iuvenis* or *adolescens*) until he was well advanced in his thirties. He had ceased to be a boy (*puer*) and had become a *iuvenis* when he adopted the *toga virilis* at the age of fourteen. From forty-six to sixty came 'the decline into old age' and at sixty, when liability to jury service ceased and a senator was excused attendance at the Senate, old age itself. Age clamped down on women earlier than on men; at the age of thirty-eight Julia, the wayward daughter of Augustus, could be said to be face to face with old age already. There was general agreement that life spent itself far too quickly. Trimalchio, 'who kept a clock and a uniformed trumpeter in his dining room to remind him of time passing beyond recall', sentimentalized morbidly over a bottle of vintage wine: 'it has a longer life than man.' Preaching as a philosopher, Seneca urged men to realize before it was too late that life, as most people led it, was not life at all (in the sense of philosophical preoccupation with the problems of truth and reality) but a mere waste of time.

By upper-class standards public service was the noblest activity of man – the life of the barrister, the soldier, the administrator and the politician; for normally the senator's life embraced all those four activities. Rhetoric was a main constituent of his education and at an early age he put his learning into practice by pleading at the Bar. He climbed the ladder of a senatorial career, absent from Rome sometimes for considerable periods in which he served as an army officer or governed a province. If he committed no indiscretion, he was a life-member of the Senate –

if he held the consulship, an important elder statesman from then onwards. In the Empire he might be one of the Emperor's privy counsellors.

This was not a career in which, except in the last centuries of the Republic, great fortunes were to be made. The senator therefore needed to be a wealthy man, in particular to own considerable landed property. To this he escaped when he could, particularly if he came of a good family, for the Roman aristocrat was a countryman at heart, interested in farming well, happy in the saddle, fond of hunting. He would have been shocked by the parvenu Sallust's description of farming and hunting as 'occupations fit for a slave'; and other Romans no doubt were shocked too, for in the case of the farmer (and perhaps only of the farmer) the notion of work had a wide romantic fascination. Everyone like to be reminded of Cincinnatus in the fifth century B.C., of how, when they sent for him to be dictator, they found him ploughing and how, once the business of saving Rome as dictator was accomplished, he returned happily to his farm. When Scipio Africanus found himself driven from public life, he worked on the land with his own hands.

If an artistocrat's means were not sufficient to support him in a life of public service, he might turn to business, banking, trading, tax-farming, the activities of the 'equestrian order'. In this way distinguished families sometimes disappeared from politics for a generation or more and then, their wealth restored, they returned. There was nothing disgraceful about being a business man, as long as you were rich and successful enough, in which case you were likely to invest largely in land and to become one of the land-owning gentry. Equestrians, whether business men or rich country residents were fathers of senators often and sometimes sons, frequently close personal friends, Atticus of Cicero for instance.

A man who avoided or deserted 'the sweat and toil' of a public career in favour of industrious seclusion – 'a shady life' (*vita umbratilis*) – could excuse himself and indeed (like Cicero and Sallust when, elbowed out of an influential position in public life, they became writers) found it desirable to excuse himself.

If he became a writer, then he made it clear that he wrote as an educationalist, employing his seclusion to teach valuable lessons to his readers, particularly his young readers, a purpose which nobody disparaged. But if his retirement was the retirement of self-indulgence (*desidia*), like the later life of L. Lucullus, an obsession with fantastically expensive landscape gardening and extravagant fish ponds, he was a traitor to serious and responsible standards of living (*gravitas*) and won the contempt – however envious – of all but his like-minded friends. There was no secure happiness in such a life, as serious men like Lucretius, Horace and Seneca knew. One form of self-indulgence palled; so despair pursued another:

The Senate is often in session all day long, at the time when the good-for-nothings are idling their time away taking exercise in the parks, out of sight in restaurants or wasting time gossiping with their friends.

Worse still:

People set out on journeys with no particular objective in view. They wander down the coast. In a purposeless way they go by sea, they go by land, always wishing they were doing something else. 'Let us go to Campania.' 'No, smart resorts are a bore. Rough country is the thing to see.' 'Let us go to Bruttium and see the ranches in Lucania.' Once in the bush, they must find a nice resort; after the extensive tedium of these uncultivated districts, something civilized is needed for their cultured gaze to feed on. 'Let us go to Taranto. People are always talking about its harbour and its splendid winter climate' ... 'No, let us go back to Rome.' It seems a lifetime since they last heard the applause and din of the games. 'It might be rather nice, too, to see somebody killed.'
(SENECA, *De Tranquillitate Animi*, 2, 13.)

Romans in public life, particularly if they wrote in their spare time, worked hard. Meetings of the Senate started very early in the day and might continue until dark. The same was true of the law courts. Emperors (at least, the good ones) perhaps worked hardest of all, up before daybreak and poring over their papers late at night. Such was Vespasian's life. Marcus Aurelius even took official papers to study at the games, as Julius Caesar once had done. And business men did not make their fortunes in idleness; when Trimalchio was establishing his wealth, his life was not the fantasy of vulgar enjoyment which the *Satyricon* depicts.

Literature, alas, does not introduce us to the daily life of the shopkeeper or the artisan, whether in the city of Rome or in other towns, men who took sufficient pride in their pursuits for them to be recorded (often with illustrations) on their tomb-stones. And, worst of all, we know little of the manner in which the proletariat earned its bread and butter. These men were the dregs of Rome (*faex Romana*) for Cicero – unless someone else had used the expression, and cheap credit was to be won by de-nouncing him in public. They cannot have supported themselves on 'free corn and the games' (*panem et circenses*), in Juvenal's contemptuous phrase. Nor can they have lived by daily atten-dance at the morning levees (*salutationes*) of the affluent, as Martial might be thought to indicate. Like the slaves and the freedmen, a large number of them must have done an honest day's work.

There was no such thing as a 'retiring age', except for non-commissioned soldiers, who would have been below their mid-dle forties when they were discharged and, with their gratuities, started a new life as farmers or shopkeepers or turned their hand in civilian life to the exercise of what had been their army trade. The freedman Trimalchio – with an astrologer's assurance of thirty years four months and two days life ahead – was evidently not far advanced into middle age when he realized that he was indecently rich, and retired from commerce and speculation to a life of colourful self-indulgence. Most business men were not so wise, if the satirists, epigrammatists and moralists are to be believed. Pursuit of wealth became an ingrained habit, impossible to arrest. The money-lender sighed enviously at the thought of a countryman's retirement – and continued with his money-lending. Men talked of retiring, but never retired – like the Em-peror Augustus. Diocletian was in fact the only Emperor to retire (and enjoy growing cabbages), just as Celestine V was the only Pope. Yet a respected retirement – *cum dignitate otium* – was thought proper for a man who by his public service had earned it. But even in the retirement of old age he should not be self-indulgent like Lucullus, but respectably occupied, like Scipio Africanus, or like the elder Cato, who thought that the time had come to improve his Greek. Though we know more under the late Republic and Empire of politicans who found retirement of an unwanted kind in exile (or, in the Empire, through the withdrawal of imperial favour), we have descriptions of others who retired voluntarily and wore retirement well – Vestricius Spurinna, for instance, at the end of the first century A.D., with perhaps three consulships to his credit, whose active daily life at seventy-seven won the Younger Pliny's admiration. It started with a three-mile walk and included exercise with the medicine ball when he went to the baths.

The Roman day was a daylight day, its twelve hours being twelve hours of daylight; so that an hour at midsummer was, by our reckoning, thirty minutes longer than at midwinter. Water clocks must have required almost daily readjustment. Daylight marked the beginning of the first hour of day, darkness the conclusion of the twelfth. Midday was the conclusion of the sixth hour, the time at which people knocked off work. The first six hours of the day constituted a 'good day's work' (*solidus dies*).

The first two hours of the day were the time of the *salutatio* when in Rome clients jockeyed in discomfort, for the exiguous reward of a small sum of money or a ration of food, to call on their patrons, in a ceremony which was as undignified for the caller as it was tedious for the host. Once the client had received real benefits (good legal advice, perhaps, if he was in a difficulty), but in the Empire the ceremony had lost its usefulness, and the prevalence of this daily round by the hangers-on of society may be greatly exaggerated by the modern historian from the fact that it was evidently such an important part of the poet Martial's daily life and also of Juvenal's.

Breakfast (*ientaculum*), except for a glutton like the Emperor

Vitellius, was an exiguous meal, as it is on the continent of Europe today. Lunch (*prandium*) at midday was not a large meal either. After lunch in summer, but not for most people in winter, came the siesta, to be followed by exercise, mostly of a kind which the Romans adopted, under the general influence of Hellenism, from the Greeks in the second century B.C. – running, wrestling, discus and javelin throwing, boxing, gladiatorial-type exercises and strenuous ball games for the young, gentler ball games for the old. For youths under seventeen, especially if they belonged to the Youth Movement (*Iuventus*) which Augustus had started, exercise was very strenuous indeed. This was taken, in cities, in the open spaces (*palaestrae*) often attached to the public baths. After his exercise the young man might plunge into an open air pool (*piscina*) just as in earlier and simpler days the young Roman, who had taken his exercise in the Campus Martius, plunged into the Tiber. But generally a man repaired to the baths (with a slave, if he was rich enough, to carry the bag containing his oil flask, his strigil and his towel, and to attend to his oiling, scraping and towelling in the baths themselves). He stripped and proceeded through the temperate room (the *tepidarium*) to the hot bath (*caldarium*) or sweat chamber (*laconicum*), where oiling and strigilling did for him what soap does in a bath today, and then he went to the cold bath (*frigidarium*), returning thence to the *tepidarium* and the changing room, and might receive a second light oiling, to prevent him from catching a cold when he went out.

The great imperial baths in Rome contained art galleries of statuary, recreation and reading rooms, and had all the social adjuncts found by the eighteenth and early nineteenth centuries at Bath. These buildings – splendid even in their ruins – apart, baths varied in comfort and elegance, down to the lowest in the scale, which were thinly disguised brothels. There were one hundred and seventy baths (most of them charging for admission and run by private enterprise) in the city of Rome at the time of Augustus, more than nine hundred in the late period of the Empire; and a man had his favourite baths, just as today the Frenchman and Italian have their favourite cafés. Snacks were to be had in baths, and also drinks. We can well believe Seneca, who lodged over one, that they were often extremely noisy.

Women bathed in separate baths, often contiguous to the men's baths, so that the same hypocaust might be used to supply the heat; and sometimes they bathed in the men's baths at different hours. Mixed bathing, which probably flourished only in the lowest baths, was twice forbidden by Emperors, by Hadrian and by Alexander Severus.

The time was shouted aloud by slaves; and at the conclusion of the ninth hour (in the middle of the afternoon) it was time for dinner (*cena*), the one substantial meal of the day.

In Rome, unlike earlier Greece, women and men dined together. Though in rich households of a certain kind the meal was often the gross orgy which modern imagination, stimulated by ancient satirists, likes to imagine, most families dined alone or with a few guests, and the meal was a three-course meal. The use of emetics, approved by doctors, was not always a mark of gluttony; for Julius Caesar, who ate and drank very little, had recourse to emetics. Reading aloud by a slave with a good voice (*comoedus*) often supplemented conversation. At parties there was sometimes prolonged drinking after dinner – or you went to another house for drinks; your head was wreathed with flowers, and entertainment was often provided by professionals (acrobats, perhaps, or dancing girls from Cadiz).

Life in early Rome was a countryman's life and the year was divided into eight-day periods, the eighth day (*nundinae*) being market day. On this day the farmer spruced himself up. He cut his nails and, in those primitive times, had a bath. He went to market, consulted his lawyer if necessary (for it was a day on which lawyers were available for consultation), and schoolchildren had a holiday from school. In the public calendars the division of the year into eight-day periods was marked; they were not an exact division of the year either before or after Julius Caesar, because the year – before on 1 January, 45 B.C. Julius Caesar gave the Romans a 365-day year and the calendar which, with minor adjustments, we use today – was a year, with alternate insertions of an intercalary month, of 355, 377, 355, 378 days in a four-year cycle. The first day of each month was the Kalends, the 13th (in certain months the 15th) the Ides and the 5th (or 7th) the Nones.

Somewhere and at some time in the Hellenistic world the seven-day week (itself in the East a far earlier thing) came into existence in the form in which Latin Europe knows it today, with its successive planetary rulers, Saturn, the Sun, the Moon, Mars, Mercury, Jupiter and Venus. This seven-day week was known in Rome at the time of Augustus and its days were often called by their planetary names by the middle of the first century A.D. A graffito from Pompeii gives a date (6 February, A.D. 60) as:

In the consulship of Nero Caesar Augustus and Cossus Lentulus, eight days before the Ides of February, on Sunday, on the sixteenth day of the moon, market-day (*nundinae*) at Cumae, five days before market-day at Pompeii.

Saturn's day was the first day of the seven until in the third century Aurelian's exaltation of Sun-worship made Sunday the first day. Sunday was not a day of rest until the Empire's official conversion to Christianity.

The market day, then, had the regularity and importance which, outside great cities, it everywhere retains, but Roman life had no regular relaxation comparable with the modern weekend. Every day of the year had its individual public and private significance. A mark on the calendar showed whether it was a *dies fastus* (on which the law could take its full course) or *comitialis* (a day on which public meetings could be held) or whether it was neither. In private life there was unlucky days (*dies religiosi*) on which it was imprudent to start a journey, for instance to announce an engagement or to get married. And nearly every day of the year was sacred to some divinity or other, many of them of limited significance – the primitive festivals, for instance, which being concerned with one critical moment or other in the farmer's year, had little meaning for the city-dweller. Others were colourful and important, like the Lupercalia on 15

March, when the half-naked priests ran about the streets of Rome striking women with leather thongs which were believed to engender fertility, and the Saturnalia, the seven days starting on 17 December, when the slaves enjoyed a short pretence of freedom. The Empire brought new festival days, small and great, some local (a benefactor's birthday, perhaps, remembered by the terms of his benefaction, with cakes and wine) others common to the whole Empire, like the Emperor's birthday or accession day. And, outside the fixed festivals (many of which were individual to particular cities) there were irregular festivities (triumphs and celebrations for imperial victories), and also the games. The most important games were held in April and early May (the Ludi Megalenses, Cereales and Florales, twenty-two days in all), in July (the Ludi Apollinares and, after 44 B.C., the games in honour of Caesar's Victory, nineteen days in all), in September (the fifteen, later sixteen, days of the Ludi Romani) and in November (the fourteen days of the Ludi Plebeii). The first days of the games were the occasion of theatrical performances, the last days were devoted to chariot racing. All these games and festivals, whether in Rome or the municipalities, were a responsibility of magistrates and a charge on their pockets. In the late Republic they were often given with reckless extravagance by the aediles at Rome, in the hope of a popularity which would be reflected in the voting when they proceeded to stand for higher office.

Gladiatorial exhibitions were at first no part of the regular games. Of Etruscan – perhaps in the circumstances of their first introduction to Rome, of Samnite and Campanian origin, they were first celebrated in Rome in 264 B.C. as funeral games, and throughout the Republic the pretence was observed that they were given for this purpose. Julius Caesar's extravagant gladiatorial exhibition during his aedileship in 65 B.C. was ostensibly in memory of his father, who had died twenty years earlier and his exhibition in 46 B.C. was in part given in memory of his daughter, who had been dead for eight years. The scale of these immensely popular exhibitions increased inside and outside Rome during the Empire. Ten thousand men fought in eight different games given by Augustus. After the Dacian war, Trajan exhibited ten thousand fighters in a display lasting a hundred and twenty-three days.

Neither comedy (after Plautus and Terence) nor tragedy had any important history at Rome. Audiences only enjoyed mime and pantomime, and tolerated tragedy only if it was a spectacular riot. Chariot racing and gladiatorial fighting, on the other hand, appealed to all ranks of society, in Rome and in Italian and provincial towns; also the sight of rare wild beasts on display, performing animals and, more commonly, animals fighting one another (bulls fighting elephants, for example) or wild beast hunts (*venationes*), the hunters as well as the beasts having been brought from overseas. The immense interest taken in wild animals, and in the vast business of their hunting, trapping and transport is illustrated by sculptured reliefs and by mosaics from all over the Roman world, notably from Antioch, North Africa and Piazza Armerina in Sicily. This, like the training (mainly at Capua in Campania) and exhibition of gladiators, was a business in which there was a lot of money to be made. As for the chariot racing, great numbers of people in all ranks of society from Emperors like Commodus and Caracalla downwards, were circus-mad, passionate supporters of one or other of the Colours (White, Green, Red, Blue), idolizing charioteers (some of whom made great fortunes), and betting heavily on the races.

Whoever condemns the Romans for the coarse brutality of their spectacles must condemn large sections of society in modern civilized countries too, for tastes which are hardly more refined. It is a bold hazard that gladiatorial games, with the frequent sight of death, would not attract spectators today. Only in their tolerance of the spectacle of condemned prisoners mauled to death by animals (something which was even depicted in rich people's houses in North Africa) are the Romans an utterly unsympathetic people. Even public executions, which survived until not so long ago in Europe, were not so horrible. The throwing of men to the beasts was deplored even in Rome, as gladiatorial fighting and mania for horse-racing was deplored, by sensitive persons like Cicero and Seneca, and of course by the Christian writers. Yet even Tertullian, when he instructed Christians to avoid the games and spectacles, offered them, for consolation, the ultimate prospect of a far more terrible carnage, on the day when the world came to its glorious end.

All over the Empire in theatres and amphitheatres people flocked to see the sort of innocent spectacle which survives in the modern circus: jesters, buffoons, gymnasts, conjurers, acrobats, tricksters, tight-rope walkers and trapeze artists, clowns, jugglers, performing monkeys, elephants walking the tight-rope.

Apart from the *nundinae*, school-children had a five-day holiday at the Quinquatrus in March, a seven-day holiday at the Saturnalia in December and a summer holiday almost exactly as long as school-children enjoy in Rome today, from 1 July to 15 October. The Senate adjourned for about a month in April (a good time to escape to Campania and the spring sunshine) and in the Empire most senators were free to visit their estates in the autumn. In the autumn too work normally slackened off in the courts, and lawyers could usually get away from Rome in the last four months of the year. Travelling in itself was not a thing of ease or pleasure; it was expensive, and holidays in the country (and escape from the intolerable midsummer heat of Rome) were an enjoyment of few beyond the rich. The rich Roman had, beside his house in Rome, at least two villas in the country, a 'suburban villa' in the neighbouring hills, perhaps at Tivoli, or on the coast, from which he could slip easily in and out of Rome, and one or more at a greater distance, perhaps in Campania, perhaps in the district of Italy from which his family originally came. Here he shed the townsman and enjoyed the life which his ancestors had led, entertaining guests, hunting, meeting his tenants, going round the estate with his bailiff, enjoying every moment of it and complaining, like the Younger Pliny, that his days were so full that it would be a relief to return to his work in Rome.

BIBLIOGRAPHY

Balsdon, J. P. V. D., *Life and Leisure in Ancient Rome*, Bodley Head –
McGraw Hill, 1969.
Carcopino, J. *Daily Life in Ancient Rome*, Peregrine Books, 1941.
Cowell, F. R., *Everyday Life in Ancient Rome*, Batsford, 1964.
Friedländer, L., *Roman Life and Manners under the early Empire*,
4 volumes, London, 1913.
Paoli, U. E., *Rome, its People, Life and Customs*, Longmans, 1963.

INDEX

Index

Index

Index